ACADEMIC FREEDOM AT THE
DAWN OF A NEW CENTURY

Academic Freedom at the Dawn of a New Century

How Terrorism, Governments, and Culture Wars Impact Free Speech

---

Edited by EVAN GERSTMANN
and MATTHEW J. STREB

Foreword by DAVID M. RABBAN

STANFORD UNIVERSITY PRESS

STANFORD, CALIFORNIA

2006

Stanford University Press
Stanford, California

Printed in the United States of America on acid-free, archival-quality paper

Library of Congress Cataloging-in-Publication Data

Academic freedom at the dawn of a new century : how terrorism, governments,
and culture wars impact free speech at universities at home and abroad / edited
by Evan Gerstmann and Matthew J. Streb ; preface by David M. Rabban.
    p. cm.
    Includes bibliographical references and index.
    ISBN-13: 978-0-8047-5444-6 (cloth : alk. paper)
    1. Academic freedom.   2. Academic freedom—United States.   3. Education,
Higher—Political aspects.   I. Gerstmann, Evan.   II. Streb, Matthew J.
(Matthew Justin), 1974–
    LC72.A435   2006
    378.1'213—dc22

                                                                2006017971

Original Printing 2006

To my father, Kurt Eli Gerstmann, who always taught me to stand up for my beliefs, and for my children, Isaac and Sam— may I do the same for them.
E. G.

In memory of my grandfather, Justin Streb, a World War II veteran who fought for freedom, and to my parents, Ed and Linda Streb, who have always inspired me to pursue knowledge.
M. S.

Contents

Foreword

David M. Rabban

THE 1915 DECLARATION OF PRINCIPLES, approved by the American Association of University Professors (AAUP) at its initial annual meeting, was the first comprehensive statement on academic freedom in the United States. Almost a century later, the Declaration remains the intellectual foundation for the defense of academic freedom and the primary guide for determining whether it has been violated. Composed by a committee of fifteen eminent professors, the 1915 Declaration made bold claims about academic freedom. These claims asserted substantially more protection for the speech of professors than provided by existing law. Employment law allowed employers to fire employees "at will," for almost any reason at all. The First Amendment, which courts overwhelmingly construed to permit the regulation or punishment of speech for its alleged "bad tendency" on the public welfare, provided little security to political dissent by citizens and virtually none to speech by public employees. Yet the 1915 Declaration declared that academic freedom should be understood to safeguard professors against discipline or dismissal. It identified three elements of academic freedom: "freedom of inquiry and research; freedom of teaching within the university or college; and freedom of extra-mural utterance and action."

How could such extraordinary protection of professors be justified? The answer, according to the 1915 Declaration, lies in professors' distinctive social function: to use their expertise, developed through long years of training, to advance knowledge, and to impart their findings both to students and to the general public. That function cannot be per-

formed if professors are subject to discipline or dismissal for the expression of views that upset trustees, politicians, or the public at large.
The Declaration states: "To the degree that professional scholars, in the
formation and promulgation of their opinions, are, or by the character
of their tenure appear to be, subject to any motive other than their own
scientific conscience and a desire for the respect of their fellow-experts,
to that degree the university teaching profession is corrupted; its proper
influence upon public opinion is diminished and vitiated; and society
at large fails to get from its scholars, in an unadulterated form, the pe-
culiar and necessary service which it is the office of the professional
scholar to furnish." Treating professors as employees, subject to the
general law of employment, the Declaration concluded, manifests "a
radical failure to apprehend the social function discharged by the professional scholar." Rather, professors, like federal judges, should be
treated as appointees who, once appointed, cannot be fired for per-
forming their professional functions. Just as the president is not able fire
the judges he appoints when he disagrees with their legal decisions, the
appointing authorities at universities should not be able to fire professors with whom they disagree. Correspondingly, just as the president is
not assumed to approve the legal views of the judges he appoints, university authorities should not be held responsible for the opinions of
professors.

Reflecting the actual controversies of the period, the 1915 Declaration focused on the threat to academic freedom posed by university
trustees. But it recognized as well that the state could violate academic
freedom. State universities, it pointed out, depend on state legislatures
for funding, and some universities had succumbed to legislative pressure. After observing that trustees tend to be more conservative than
professors, the 1915 Declaration speculated that legislators are often to
the political left of professors. Although clearly an attempt to appear
even-handed in opposing restrictions on academic freedom from all
points on the political spectrum, this speculation might also have been
an accurate perception of the actual dangers from legislators during the
progressive era. Consistent with its general defense of academic freedom and as part of its effort to be politically neutral, the 1915 Declaration emphasized that the university should be both "an intellectual experiment station, where new ideas may germinate," even if they are
"distasteful to the community as a whole," and "the conservator of all
genuine elements of value in the past thought and life of mankind

which are not in the fashion of the moment." The 1915 Declaration also warned professors that the right of academic freedom entails "certain correlative obligations," including their own duty not to violate academic freedom.

Remarkably, the 1915 Declaration achieved widespread acceptance within the university community, among trustees and administrators as well as among professors themselves. A generation later, the Association of American Colleges joined the AAUP in formulating and approving the 1940 Statement of Principles on Academic Freedom and Tenure, which concisely summarized the understanding of academic freedom that the 1915 Declaration had initially proposed and defended. In subsequent decades, numerous learned societies and other educational organizations endorsed the 1940 Statement, and its protections for academic freedom have been incorporated into the governing regulations of most U.S. colleges and universities.

Yet the widespread acceptance of basic principles of academic freedom within the academic community afforded little protection to professors during the McCarthy era of the late 1940s and 1950s, when concerns about the Communist threat to national security prompted widespread investigations by the federal and many state governments into the loyalty of professors. Although they rarely initiated similar investigations, U.S. colleges and universities dismissed and blacklisted professors who had affiliations with the Communist Party and other allegedly subversive organizations, who refused to answer questions about their academic and political views and associations, or who were unwilling to reveal information about their colleagues. Even organizations previously committed to the protection of academic freedom and civil liberties, including the AAUP and the American Civil Liberties Union (ACLU), acquiesced in these dismissals for much of the McCarthy period, to their subsequent embarrassment. These investigations and dismissals intimidated numerous other professors and often inhibited their academic and political speech.

After the height of the McCarthy era and especially after its end, many Americans, both within and outside the academy, resolved to be more vigilant in resisting violations of academic freedom and civil liberties in the name of national security. The United States Supreme Court contributed to this response by transforming U.S. constitutional law. Among these transformations, the Court in 1957 for the first time included academic freedom within the protection of the First Amendment, and, especially in the 1960s, it departed from prior decisions by holding that the Constitution does not permit the state to condition employment on the waiver of First Amendment rights.

The attacks of September 11, 2001, produced new concerns about national security, but they also raised the specter of the McCarthy era more prominently than at any time since its demise. In contrast to its belated response during the McCarthy era, the AAUP established the Special Committee on Academic Freedom and National Security in a Time of Crisis on the first anniversary of September 11. At the end of 2003, the Special Committee published a comprehensive report, on whose findings many of the essays in this volume rely. The report reveals a dramatically less restrictive environment than during the McCarthy era, perhaps in large part because many people both within and outside the academy remembered the McCarthy era and wanted to avoid its repetition. Most strikingly, in substantial contrast to the McCarthy era, few professors have lost their jobs as a result of their academic or political expressions or associations, perhaps only one or two. Even lesser sanctions have been quite rare. The report concludes that "policies already in place seem to have served the interests of academic freedom surprisingly well." In addition, there is no contemporary political counterpart to Senator Joseph McCarthy, university administrators and trustees have been much more vigilant in protecting controversial professors, and many organizations have defended faculty rights of academic freedom and free speech. By recognizing First Amendment rights of academic freedom and political expression that did not exist during the McCarthy era, the Supreme Court has contributed legal bulwarks against repression.

The much more fragile condition of academic freedom and political expression elsewhere in the world, as reported in several informative essays in this volume, underlines their relative protection in the United States, even in the context of the atmosphere of crisis produced by September 11. Around the world, faculty members have not just been dismissed but have been imprisoned, beaten, and even killed in retaliation for their academic and political views. Repression has come from public officials, high and low, authorized and rogue, as well as from private actors, including terrorists, sometimes acting with the tacit approval of the state. Even the substantial repression during the McCarthy era pales in comparison to these reports from abroad. In contrast to the United States, moreover, many foreign countries have much weaker legal safeguards for speech, lack even the most rudimentary definitions of academic freedom, and have no organizations devoted to its protection. Many foreign governments are much more directly involved in university life than either federal or state governments in the United States, making it easier for them to restrict the expression of professors.

The relative protection of academic freedom and free speech in the aftermath of September 11 compared to the McCarthy era and conditions abroad should not, however, induce complacency. As the AAUP Special Committee and several essays in this volume report, substantial pressures on controversial views by professors, in support of as well as in opposition to the official positions of the government, have occurred since September 11. Although these pressures have overwhelmingly been resisted within the academy, their existence itself is troubling. Members of the U.S. House of Representatives, state legislators, university trustees, alumni, administrators, students, members of the general public, and sometimes faculty members themselves have called for restrictions on controversial speech by professors and visiting speakers on campus. Some universities took actions against faculty and student speakers that they later withdrew or modified. And, in some instances, universities did suspend or reprimand faculty and student speakers and withdrew invitations to controversial outsiders. Provisions of the Patriot Act have been invoked to demand the records of patrons of libraries, bookstores, and Internet service providers; under the Patriot Act, foreign scholars have had difficulty obtaining visas to attend academic conferences, and government contracting officers have attempted to include provisions allowing them to review research results before publication and to prevent the disclosure of "sensitive" but unclassified information. Another terrorist attack on the United States, as many commentators have observed, could easily increase pressures on academic and political expression that have mostly been resisted to date.

The judicial extension of First Amendment protections after the McCarthy era, moreover, may be fragile and reversible. It is important to remember that at the height of the McCarthy era, after years of construing the phrase "clear and present danger" to limit government restrictions on speech, the Supreme Court redefined that phrase in ways that made it much easier to obtain convictions. Similar restrictive transformations of current First Amendment analysis could easily occur in another period of perceived dangers to national security. Even before September 11, the Supreme Court had not developed an elaborated definition of the constitutional meaning of academic freedom and its relationship to general rights of free speech. Some cases both before and after September 11, particularly in the lower courts, have construed academic freedom narrowly and have limited the protected speech of public employees by defining much of it as unrelated to "matters of public concern" and therefore outside the scope of the First Amendment.

The definition and defense of academic freedom set forth in the AAUP's 1915 Declaration of Principles remain valid today. Measured by the standards of the 1915 Declaration, academic freedom has been largely protected in U.S. colleges and universities since September 11, 2001, particularly in comparison to the McCarthy era, although understandably heightened concerns about national security have produced additional, and occasionally successful, pressures to restrict it. Even in periods when threats to national security have not been at the forefront of national consciousness, attacks on academic freedom persist, from both traditional and novel sources, within and outside the academy. The protection of academic freedom and free speech require constant vigilance, the kind of vigilance that has contributed thus far to the relatively fortunate experience since September 11, 2001.

Acknowledgments

IN FEBRUARY 2004, Loyola Marymount University and the Institute for Leadership Studies hosted a conference titled "Academic Freedom after September 11th." This was the third conference in a series revolving around the theme "Dilemmas of Democracy." Some of the leading scholars in the United States attended the conference, and their papers form the heart of this book, along with additional papers submitted by Enrique Desmond Arias, Antonio Brown, and Tim Shiell.

Our first thanks go to those who provided the financial and institutional support for the conference. These include Father Robert Lawton, President of Loyola Marymount University; Joseph Jabbra, Academic Vice President; Michael Engh, Dean of the Liberal Arts College; and Michael Genovese, Director of the Institute of Leadership Studies. With their help and support, the conference went smoothly and was a great success. With the help of Melissa Abraham, Loyola Marymount's media relations manager, the conference received substantial media coverage.

Of course, we wish to thank the distinguished group of panelists who participated in the conference and this book. All the panelists were major contributors to the project, but we would like to especially thank our keynote speaker, Paul Sniderman, and Robert O'Neil, who, because of a potential scheduling conflict, joined the conference at the last minute and found his own funding to do so. These are two men whose accomplishments are matched by their humility. We also wish to acknowledge Alan Charles Kors, founder of the Foundation for Individual Rights in Education and a fiery defender of free speech on campus. Kors participated in the conference and submitted a chapter for this book. At the strong recommendation of two outside reviewers, we decided not to include the chapter, although it was a difficult decision.

As always, thanks go to Michael Gauger, a first-rate editor who worked on the book prospectus, and to Donald Downs, who, in addition to participating in the conference, was an important source of advice from the inception of this project.

We also had outstanding help from several Loyola Marymount students, including Katie Jones, Abby Onderdonk, Marjorie Campbell, Michael Keane, Adrienne Tygenhoff, and Chris Zepeda. The entire Department of Political Science attended the conference and was supportive throughout, especially our chair, Seth Thompson. Professors Rebeca Acevedo, of the Department of Modern Languages, and Suzanne O'Brien, of the Department of History, ably chaired the conference panels.

And finally, thanks to Evan Gerstmann's wife, Lauren, who edited the last chapter and put up with him throughout the conference and all its anxieties.

All projects of this sort are a group effort, and we were lucky indeed to have the team that we did.

ACADEMIC FREEDOM AT THE

DAWN OF A NEW CENTURY

PART ONE

Introduction

CHAPTER 1

The Reemergence of the
Academic Freedom Debate

Matthew J. Streb

THE TERRORIST ATTACKS of September 11, 2001, changed the world in many ways, including rekindling the debate over academic freedom on college campuses. In the wake of September 11, many of us in academia and elsewhere worried that we were in danger of losing much of the freedom we have enjoyed since the demise of McCarthyism. Would universities suffer through a second McCarthy era? Would there be other more subtle yet powerful threats to free inquiry and expression? What would the impact be on universities outside the United States? How would the tragedy influence the ability of American professors to collaborate with scholars in other countries?

The federal government quickly responded to the attacks by enhancing its own powers of surveillance. Under the USA PATRIOT Act, government has access to a plethora of private information about U.S. citizens. The ability of law enforcement to obtain phone taps has expanded greatly, and Americans can also be subjected to secret government surveillance of medical, financial, and library records. Even banks require personal information, such as social security and driver's license numbers, "to help the government fight the funding of terrorism."[1] Further, as a number of the contributors to this book note, government officials and watchdog groups have become more aggressive about denouncing and calling for the punishment of professors who challenge the war against terrorism and the invasion of Iraq. Will the government's new powers and aggressive attitude threaten freedom of speech at American universities?

The debates surrounding academic freedom after the terrorist attacks also brought back to the forefront debates over "culture wars" on college campuses that had dominated discussion during the late 1980s and early 1990s. With the rise of what some perceived as a "political correctness" movement and with the widespread enactment of speech codes, many conservatives (and even some liberals) argued that academic freedom was threatened by "thought police" who were limiting what could be said in the classroom in order to create what supporters of speech codes thought was a more conducive environment to learning. Although the codes were designed to eliminate hostile, harassing learning environments, opponents of the codes argued that they often drastically overreached—for example, codes that punished students for laughing at sexist or racist jokes. Political conservatives also maintained that a double standard existed. Students were prohibited from making statements that offended women, African Americans, or gays and lesbians, but speech that offended religious fundamentalists, for example, was fair game.

Since September 11, the culture war has emerged again and new battles are being fought on campuses. This time it is conservatives who want to stifle speech, as they protest a few outrageous (and many not so outrageous) statements made by professors criticizing President Bush, U.S. foreign policy, and the war in Iraq; several of these cases are discussed in this book. Those on the right condemned several colleges and universities for course content that they found offensive, including criticizing the University of North Carolina for assigning a book on the Koran to all incoming first-year students. In almost every instance, the professors' comments or the content of the courses was defended by administrators as being protected under academic freedom (see Robert O'Neil's discussion of several of these cases in Chapter 3). Again, though, those on the right maintain that a double standard exists. In Chapter 4, Donald Downs discusses the case of Zewdalem Kebede. Kebede, a San Diego State University student, was admonished by a university judicial officer for confronting several Arabic students who were expressing delight about the September 11 terrorist attacks. The Arabic students received no admonishment or punishment from the university. Those on the left charge that free speech must be protected and that professors and students must have the ability to criticize government; those on the right assert that only speech criticizing government is protected and that many who support government policy after September 11 feel the need to censor their speech.

Academic freedom has long been seen as an essential aspect of learning in a free society; however, the previous discussion indicates that there is a great deal of debate over what academic freedom means and how much should exist. Still, although the United States has occasionally lost sight of the immense importance of academic freedom (e.g., the wide support of the McCarthyites' successful purging of academics because of their political beliefs—or alleged political beliefs—more than fifty years ago), the value of the ability to openly discuss controversial topics—both in the classroom and in research—seems firmly embedded in today's American culture. Or is it? The essays in this book set out to examine the state of academic freedom both in the United States and abroad. With new threats and fears, have Americans remembered the importance of academic freedom or have we entered a new era of censorship and self-censorship?

In this chapter, I provide an overview of the book. First, however, I discuss the recent controversy that has emerged once again over the indoctrination of students by professors. I then turn to the importance of protecting academic freedom and provide some recent examples that leave cause for concern.

The Debate over Education vs. Indoctrination

The terrorist attacks of September 11, 2001, appeared to unify Americans, but that unification did not necessarily hold true on college campuses. Almost immediately after September 11, conservative groups accused liberal professors of indoctrinating students by criticizing U.S. foreign policy and pushing their beliefs on people who were still developing opinions about the world. Others argued that professors' comments made students who backed the government feel intimidated to express their support. Conservatives claimed that the academic freedom of professors allowed these environments to exist. As William P. Murphy wrote more than forty years ago, "Too often . . . the claim of academic freedom is put forth in a guise which makes it appear to be a bid for special privilege."[2] To those who charge indoctrination, academic freedom certainly looks like a "special privilege."

If true, the indoctrination of students by professors should be cause for concern for anyone committed to education; after all, indoctrination is not education. Because of these charges of indoctrination, conservative activist David Horowitz created the organization Students for Academic Freedom to challenge professors who the organization believes are promoting their personal beliefs in the classroom. The organization has chartered chapters on more than 135 college campuses and continues to grow. Students for Academic Freedom is pushing an "Academic Bill of Rights" that encourages universities "to recognize and promote intellectual diversity on campus[es]" in state legislatures and in the U.S. Congress.[3] The group has had some success. The Georgia senate passed a resolution "encouraging public colleges and universities to refrain from discriminating against students because of their political or religious beliefs."[4] Another group, NoIndoctrination.org, provides students with the opportunity to post complaints about biased professors on a website.

The controversy over education versus indoctrination is at the center of the debate over academic freedom, and, as the previous examples illustrate, it is more contentious than ever. Certainly we should be concerned about indoctrination simply because it may create a classroom atmosphere in which open, honest discussion of issues is not encouraged. Professors' ability to speak their minds is protected; yet students may be censoring themselves. In the end, academic freedom is threatened. But organizations such as Students for Academic Freedom and NoIndoctrination.org also have been criticized because they pose a threat to academic freedom in their own right. Many university faculty members and administrators assert that these two groups are engaging in a witch hunt to stifle thought and limit speech. They maintain that professors should have the freedom to decide the content of classes. They also argue that sometimes these "academic freedom" movements themselves promote indoctrination and limit the free exchange of ideas. For instance, the American Council of Trustees and Alumni (ACTA) closely monitored what occurred in the classroom immediately after September 11. In November 2001, ACTA, an innocuous sounding group founded by Lynne Cheney, issued a report titled "Defending Civilization: How Our Universities Are Failing America and What Can Be Done About It." The report listed several "controversial" comments made by students and faculty after the 9/11 terrorist attacks. Some of the comments that made the list were simple claims of fact. For example, Todd Gitlin, professor of communications at New York University, was taken to task for saying, "There is a lot of skepticism about the [Bush] administration's policy of going to war."[5] Learning cannot be fostered in an environment where simple claims of fact, much less controversial comments that may be made for the sake of debate, are condemned by those outside the classroom. It is not difficult to understand why a professor might shy away from discussing extremely important—yet divisive—issues. Again, education suffers.

The recent controversy over education and indoctrination highlights the renewed importance of the academic freedom debate, especially since September 11. The growth of organizations such as Students for Academic Freedom, ACTA, and Campus Watch will continue to affect academic freedom, perhaps in some ways for the better, but in most ways for the worst. We should be concerned with the potential indoctrination of students—although actually defining indoctrination or knowing when it is occurring is difficult—but we also must be uneasy about groups that try to limit speech in the classroom and on college campuses. Murphy is correct: Academic freedom may appear to be a special privilege. In reality, however, it is an essential component of an open, engaged learning environment.

The Importance of Academic Freedom

To many academics, the importance of academic freedom is obvious. After all, it is the cornerstone of the university's mission to educate students and expand the boundaries of knowledge. For education to be most effective, professors and students must be in environments where they are free to learn about and debate complex and controversial issues. Also, as specialists in certain fields, professors should have the freedom to decide the content of their classes. Although concerns over indoctrination may be justified, academic freedom is a principle that must be protected for education to flourish.

Perhaps the best-known advocate of academic freedom is John Stuart Mill, who argued that the free exchange of ideas is needed in a society that values truth. Mill's views have long influenced the way Americans think about academic freedom.

Although speech codes were not in existence during Mill's time, he surely would have been opposed to them. Mill believed that only by allowing the expression of *all* ideas could we falsify what we thought to be previous truths or learn to defend more vigorously what we know to be true but is challenged. While supporting the concept of academic freedom, Mill no doubt would have been concerned about charges of indoctrination as well. Mill would have encouraged open debate in the classroom of all ideas, something that cannot happen if academic freedom does not exist.

The importance of academic freedom may have best been summarized by Justice Douglas in *Adler v. Board of Education of the City of New York* (1952).[6] In *Adler*, the Supreme Court upheld a New York civil service law that "provided for the disqualification and removal from the public school system of teachers and other employees who advocated the overthrow of the government by unlawful means or who belonged to organizations which had such a purpose."[7] In his dissenting opinion, Douglas forcefully argued that:

> The Constitution guarantees freedom of thought and expression to everyone in our society. All are entitled to it; and none needs it more than the teacher.
>
> The public school is in most respects the cradle of our democracy. . . . The impact of this kind of censorship in the public school system illustrates the high purpose of the First Amendment in freeing speech and thought from censorship. . . .
>
> The very threat of such a procedure is certain to raise havoc with academic freedom. . . . Fearing condemnation, [the teacher] will tend to shrink from any association that stirs controversy. In that manner freedom of expression will be stifled. . . .
>
> There can also be no real academic freedom in that environment. Where suspicion fills the air and holds scholars in line for fear of their jobs, there can be no exercise of the free intellect. . . .
>
> This system of spying and surveillance with its accompanying reports and trails cannot go hand in hand with academic freedom. It produces standardized thought, not the pursuit of truth. Yet it was the pursuit of truth which the First Amendment was designed to protect. . . . We need be bold and adventuresome in our thinking to survive. . . . The Framers knew the danger of dogmatism; they also knew the strength that comes when the mind is free, when ideas may be pursued wherever they lead. We forget these teachings of the First Amendment when we sustain this law.[8]

Although the Court disagreed with Douglas in *Adler*, five years later a majority first recognized academic freedom as a constitutional right in *Sweezy v. New Hampshire* (1957).[9]

Mill and Douglas were right: Academic freedom is an essential component to education. Without the ability to openly discuss controversial topics, students—and for that matter professors—cannot develop intellectually. As David Moshman wrote, "To encourage intellectual progress, we must promote reflection, coordination, and social interaction, the basic processes of development." Moshman continued, "There are many ways to do this, but the fundamental context for all of them . . . is one that encourages students to consider, propose, and discuss a variety of ideas—that is, an environment of academic freedom."[10]

However, there is great concern today over protecting that "environment of academic freedom." Just a quick glance at some recent events makes it easy to understand why. Largely in response to September 11, both the federal and state governments have taken steps—or tried to take steps—to limit academic freedom. At the federal level, the largest assault on academic freedom—as well as many other cherished civil liberties—is, of course, the USA PATRIOT Act that Congress hastily passed almost immediately after September 11 and reauthorized in 2006. As mentioned, the Patriot Act is not usually associated with the restriction of academic freedom but rather with the restriction of due process rights. Although the due process rights of individuals are certainly of immense importance, the Patriot Act's effects on academic freedom are also of great concern. The Act has led several academic groups, including the American Association of University Professors (AAUP), the American Library Association Council, and the National Council of American Studies Association, to name a few, to raise questions about academic freedom post-9/11.

Although there are several aspects of the Patriot Act that threaten academic freedom, one provision in particular stands out. The Act expands the federal government's authority to demand "business records," including lists of library records and recent book orders. In addition, librarians and bookstore employees are barred from disclosing any request from law enforcement for book records. As O'Neil writes elsewhere, "It will be difficult, if not impossible, to report with any accuracy the extent to which the 'business records' provisions of the Patriot Act have affected academic freedom—save for the unlikely prospect that the responsible agencies either volunteer such information, or a court compels its disclosure."[11] Initial evidence is troubling, however. "Surveys conducted in late 2001 and in October 2002 by researchers at the University of Illinois at Urbana–Champaign found that since the USA PATRIOT Act became law, some 550 libraries had received requests from federal and state law-enforcement agencies for the records of patrons."[12] The "business records" provision could possibly lead professors or students to think twice about checking certain materials out of the library or buying certain books, which, in turn, could keep important research from being conducted.

Many in Congress have tried to repeal the "business records" provision, but without any success. In July 2004, the Republican leadership extended the time available to vote on the Freedom to Read Protection Act by an additional twenty-three minutes in order to ensure enough votes to make certain that the act did not pass. A year later, the Senate voted to significantly change the library provision, but the House—through controversial rules limiting debate on proposed amendments—stifled any attempt to change the law.[13] Finally, in 2006, small changes were made to the so-called library provision (e.g., libraries can now challenge whether the government acted in bad faith in demanding the records), but critics were not appeased. "This deal does not prevent the government from obtaining the library, medical and other sensitive business records of people with no link to suspected terrorists," argued Wisconsin senator Russ Feingold, the only senator to vote against the original USA PATRIOT Act. "The records just have to be 'relevant' to a terrorist investigation, which is not adequate protection against a fishing expedition."[14]

Library records and book orders are not the only aspect of academic freedom threatened by laws such as the Patriot Act. The Patriot Act amended the Electronic Communications Privacy Act (ECPA), making it easier for law enforcement agencies to obtain wiretaps or to use search warrants to seize any voice-mail or e-mail messages. It also amended the Family Educational Rights and Privacy Act (FERPA), allowing law enforcement officials to circumvent students' rights to confidentiality of their academic records if the records are deemed relevant to an investigation of terrorism. University officials do not have to notify students that their educational information has been disclosed. All these aspects of the law seriously threaten academic freedom.

The Patriot Act is not the only instance in which the federal government has shown a lack of commitment to academic freedom. After one Columbia University professor, Nicholas De Genova, said at a campus event that he wished for "a million Mogadishus," more than 100 members of the House of Representatives called for his resignation.[15] De Genova's comments were certainly offensive to most Americans, but if academic freedom is to mean anything, we cannot simply censor speech that we do not like; a slippery slope would no doubt ensue.

The federal government has been relatively restrained regarding academic freedom compared to some state governments. State legislatures have castigated university officials for defending academic freedom. When a "teach-in" on U.S. foreign policy was held at the University of North Carolina, Chapel Hill, by four faculty members, several members of the North Carolina legislature chastised university officials for allowing the event to occur. As previously mentioned, UNC officials took more heat from the state legislature after the school assigned a book about the Koran to all its incoming students. The lower house of the state legislature "attached to the university's appropriations bill a requirement—clearly intended as a form of punishment—that if any religion were to be studied at Chapel Hill, equal time must be given to the study of 'all other religions.'" The state senate, however, rejected the amendment.[16]

After Ward Churchill's controversial essay, in which he compared the victims of the September 11 World Trade Center terrorist attacks to Nazi Adolf Eichmann, the governor of Colorado, Bill Owens, and many state legislators demanded that Churchill be fired. The university president at the time of Churchill's statements, Betsy Hoffman, refused to fire him because of the statements; however, the University of Colorado is—at the time of this writing—conducting an investigation of Churchill regarding a variety of other charges, including plagiarism, which should not be protected under academic freedom.

The Churchill case is likely the most documented case of a threat to academic freedom after September 11. Ironically, the controversy did not emerge until well after September 11 (and after several of the contributors to this book finished writing their chapters). Although Churchill's essay was written within hours of the terrorist attacks, it flew under the radar until Churchill was invited to speak at Hamilton College. A student, Ian Mandell, the editor-in-chief of the student newspaper, was doing some background research on Churchill and came across his essay. The essay quickly became media fodder after Mandell wrote an article about the essay, and after Hamilton's president, Joan Hinde Stewart, cancelled Churchill's appearance because of, according to Hinde Stewart, threats of violence.[17] Churchill's remarks were certainly incendiary, but if academic freedom is to mean anything, scholars must have the ability to criticize the United States government and its policies. The Churchill case also illustrates the power that the media has had in questioning the right of academic freedom after September 11.

State governments haven't just called for the dismissal of certain controversial professors and questioned the curriculum. As discussed earlier, state legislatures, including Colorado, Georgia, Indiana, and Ohio, have deliberated over the "Academic Bill of Rights" put forth by Students for Academic Freedom. The Ohio bill, introduced in January 2005, would "prohibit instructors at public or private universities from 'persistently' discussing controversial issues in class or from using their classes to push political, ideological, religious, or anti-religious views."[18] However, in September 2005, the bill was shelved in favor of an agreement made by the state's university presidents that "universities are committed to respecting diverse viewpoints and that neither students nor faculty will be evaluated based on political opinions." The bill was largely seen as an acceptable compromise.[19]

Although the governments' actions were primarily in response either directly or indirectly to September 11, one event that has severe implications for academic freedom was not related to the terrorist attacks. At a conference on gender imbalances in science, the president of Harvard at the time, Lawrence Summers, raised the possibility that the imbalances came from innate sex differences. Summers, who was not advocating the position but simply raising a point that has been made by many, was harshly criticized. The National Organization for Women called for his resignation, many prominent alumni threatened to withhold donations, and more than 100 Harvard faculty members signed a letter condemning Summers.[20] Those on the right argued that the response to Summers's statement was political correctness run amuck. Certainly the rebuke of Summers, ironically even from many who are committed to academic freedom, will make others think twice before discussing contentious issues. This issue of self-censorship is Paul Sniderman's focus in Chapter 9.

The preceding examples all illuminate the fact that debates over academic freedom are as heated as ever and are not likely to subside anytime soon. It is the goal of this book to examine some of those debates and to assess the state of academic freedom, both in the United States and abroad.

The Plan of the Book

The book is divided into four sections. In Chapter 2, Tim Shiell continues the introduction by providing a strong defense regarding the importance of academic freedom. According to Shiell, there are three conceptions of academic freedom and he believes that the civil libertarian conception is the most virtuous. However, he is also concerned that, today, the civil libertarian conception of academic freedom faces grave threats.

In Part Two, the contributors examine academic freedom in American universities today. Two of the chapters focus on the most blatant threat to academic freedom: Would faculty and students be explicitly punished by the government or by university administrators for unpopular or unpatriotic speech after September 11? Robert O'Neil (Chapter 3) and Donald Downs (Chapter 4) argue that, although in some cases it appeared that this was going to happen, calmer voices prevailed in the end. O'Neil and Downs both come to a cautious but positive conclusion regarding the effects of September 11 on academic freedom, although their reasons for why academic freedom survived are somewhat different. According to O'Neil, academic freedom was generally upheld because of the state of the law regarding academic freedom, which has much improved since the days of McCarthy. The Supreme Court, O'Neil argues, has consistently come to the defense of academic freedom over the last fifty or so years. In addition, the norm of free speech has become more institutionalized on college campuses. Downs also supports the norms of free speech argument that O'Neil puts forth, but he believes that, in cases where those norms have been challenged, First Amendment organizations, such as the Foundation for Individual Rights in Education (FIRE), or faculty organizations, such as the one at the University of Wisconsin, Madison, have been there to protect academic freedom. Still, according to both O'Neil and Downs, academic freedom in the classroom today might not be completely the same as academic freedom in the classroom on September 10, 2001, but it does not appear to be that different either.

However, Downs does express some concern that thought on the right could be open to attack. Yet, in the cases cited by Downs, academic freedom was upheld in the end. Again, Downs argues that this result was not necessarily because of a general commitment to academic freedom, as O'Neil argued, but more because of organizations such as FIRE. Even if the cases that Downs cites were resolved in ways consistent with upholding academic freedom, his argument about censorship from the left should be taken seriously by anyone who is committed to the concept. Academic freedom may have been upheld, but not without a strong fight.

O'Neil's and Downs's conclusions may be positive, but they are not blinded by optimism. Indeed, both O'Neil and Downs are well aware that not everyone is committed to protecting academic freedom. Every case that O'Neil or Downs mentions was met with some sort of response from the public, usually calling for the "offender's" dismissal.

Certainly academic freedom entails more than just speech in the classroom. Restrictions on academic freedom can exist in far less obvious ways, especially regarding research. In Chapter 5, Susan Lindee documents the significant scrutiny of scientists by the government since September 11. In fact, no group of scholars may be affected more by that day than scientists.[21] Government has been critical of many scientific studies since September 11 and is often the major source of academic research funding. In some cases, as Lindee notes, government scrutiny led to self-censorship.

The third part of the book examines academic freedom from a global perspective. The chapters are not designed to build a broad theoretical framework for looking at academic freedom overseas; rather, they serve as snapshots to provide a basis for comparison of threats to American academic freedom. Although the restriction of academic freedom in the United States—both explicitly and implicitly—is a serious concern, the contributors of Chapters 6–8 remind us how grave the problem of academic freedom remains around the world compared to the United States.

In Chapter 6, John Akker looks at academic freedom in the Middle East, Africa, and Asia, where, in many cases, academics have been imprisoned, beaten, and/or murdered because of their lectures or writings. In Chapter 7, Antonio Brown focuses on academic freedom in Western Europe, the birthplace of academic freedom, and finds that governments in these countries may not be as committed to the principle as one might expect. According to Brown, there has been a significant struggle between proponents of academic freedom and those who see the need for a degree of censorship to promote community and social cohesion. In Chapter 8, Enrique Desmond Arias examines the academic freedom landscape in Latin America. According to Arias, non-governmental groups, such as guerrilla organizations, can pose just as great a danger to academic freedom as do authoritarian governments.

One consistent theme that surfaces throughout Part Three is government's role in protecting academic freedom. Although a strong, powerful government can be a threat to academic freedom, a weak national government is not necessarily desirable either, as Arias shows in Chapter 8. And, as Akker's numerous examples make clear, many governments remain uncommitted to academic freedom entirely. Even in Western Europe, as Brown notes, commitment to academic freedom varies.

Understandably, September 11 affected issues of academic freedom in countries around the world less than in the United States, but the countries discussed in the chapters by Akker, Brown, and Arias were not immune from threats to academic freedom after 9/11. All three contributors are in agreement that, since September 11, foreign-born researchers studying in Western Europe and the United States face greater scrutiny and visas are more difficult to obtain, limiting noncitizens' participation in academic conferences and attendance at colleges and universities. As the AAUP notes, "Given the pace at which university recruitment of foreign visitors must often proceed, such delay and confusion threaten international scholarly collaboration."[22] Potential graduate students must postpone their studies because of problems implementing SEVIS, the federal government's system for monitoring foreign students and visiting scholars while they are studying in the United States. In fall 2002, the backlog of applicants was estimated to be 25,000. One survey found that 30 percent of participating institutions saw a decline in the enrollment of foreign students during the 2002–03 school year. The decline in foreign students is troubling because "over the past twenty years, noncitizens have accounted for more than 50 percent of the growth in the number of Ph.D.'s earned [in the United States]."[23] Pressures to either cancel or restructure Middle Eastern studies have emerged.[24] Federal regulations have limited editing and publishing papers by researchers in embargoed countries.[25] None of these facts present a positive outlook for American scholars' abilities to learn from and collaborate with researchers and students from other countries in the future. As a result, the writers of these chapters argue, the pursuit of knowledge is threatened.

In the final section, Paul Sniderman and Evan Gerstmann offer some concluding remarks and comment on some of the less explicit restrictions on academic freedom. In Chapter 9, Sniderman maintains that the most serious threat to academic freedom actually comes from self-censorship rather than from overt punishment for unpopular views, and he argues that certain university policies make self-censorship, even by tenured faculty, more likely. In Chapter 10, Gerstmann provides a broad overview of several less obvious threats to academic freedom, including mandatory loyalty oaths for faculty members, the expansion of institutional review boards, and ever-increasing numbers of faculty without the protection of tenure. If O'Neil is correct that the commitment to academic freedom in the classroom has indeed become institutionalized, then it is these subtle restrictions on academic freedom noted by Lindee, Sniderman, and Gerstmann that should be the greatest concern for academics post-9/11.

Balancing Safety and Academic Freedom

The terrorist attacks of September 11 were unlike anything the United States had encountered before. As a result of the attacks, Americans were scared—and rightly so. Preventing another terrorist attack should be the primary goal of government and law officials. Certainly new security measures are needed to prevent another 9/11; the question is, At what cost? September 11 presented the American people with a classic example of conflicting rights. How do we balance individual freedoms with the need to protect society from another terrorist attack?

The most obvious response, and perhaps most understandable given the tragedy of the event, is to err on the side of stopping terrorism. We give up some rights in order to be protected by government. This makes us feel safer, and it is important for citizens to feel safe (although it is difficult to determine how effective measures that force us to give up some of our rights have been at preventing terrorism). But reactions out of fear often lead to bad consequences, such as restricting academic freedom. As Benjamin Franklin wrote, "They who would give up an essential liberty for temporary security, deserve neither liberty or security."

The general conclusion of the contributors to this book is that academic freedom in the most obvious sense was upheld after September 11. A few problems emerged, but almost all were handled in a satisfactory manner. For that, academics (and in a broader sense, all Americans) should be happy; although we should remain vigilant. However, two other more troubling conclusions emerge. Less obvious threats to academic freedom exist, and these threats are increasing the risk that the United States will become isolated from the rest of the academic world. For education to be most effective, academic freedom must be protected. Colleges and universities must be places where open dialogue on divisive issues can occur and where scholars can feel free to research controversial questions whose answers will add to the body of knowledge (even if people do not like the results). Events as tragic as September 11 cannot make us lose sight of this central premise of education. If they do, education in the United States and, indeed, around the world will suffer immensely, and that is something that no one can afford.

CHAPTER 2

Three Conceptions of Academic Freedom

Timothy C. Shiell

IN 1894, UNIVERSITY OF WISCONSIN professor of economics Richard T. Ely faced the dire prospect of being fired for criticizing laissez-faire capitalism.[1] Fortunately for him, an enlightened UW Board of Regents concluded:

We could not for a moment think of recommending the dismissal or even the criticism of a teacher even if some of his opinions should, in some quarters, be regarded as visionary. Such a course would be equivalent to saying no professor should teach anything which is not accepted by everyone as true. This would cut our curriculum down to very small proportions. We cannot for a moment believe that knowledge has reached its final goal, or that the present condition of society is perfect. We must therefore welcome from our teachers such discussions as shall suggest the means and prepare the way by which knowledge may be extended, present evils be removed and others prevented. . . . In all lines of academic investigation it is of utmost importance that the investigator should be absolutely free to follow the indications of truth wherever they may lead. Whatever may be the limitations which trammel inquiry elsewhere we believe the great state University of Wisconsin should ever encourage the continual and fearless sifting and winnowing by which alone the truth can be found.[2]

Ely's case had both immediate and long-lasting national consequences and is one of the landmark incidents whereby academic freedom became an important value in American primary, secondary, and post-secondary public education.[3]

But consider the regents' claim that knowledge has not yet reached its final goal. To be sure, new discoveries and insights are continually expressed and none of us is omniscient. So, with former U.S. Supreme Court justice Oliver Wendell Holmes Jr., we might conclude that

when men have realized that time has upset many fighting faiths, they may come to believe even more than they believe the very foundations of their own conduct that the ultimate good desired is better reached by free trade in ideas—that the best test of truth is the power of the thought to get itself accepted in the competition of the market, and that truth is the only ground upon which their wishes can be carried out.[4]

On the other hand, how much room for doubt is there about the Nazi perpetration of the Holocaust? Do you doubt that *quid pro quo* sexual harassment or plagiarism ought to be penalized? To say that academics should be "absolutely free" to follow the truth wherever it may lead is hyperbole, for everyone believes academic freedom has limits.[5] The question really is, What types and scope of constraints ought to be placed on academic activities, especially academic speech, and why?

Second, consider the regents' neglect of public accountability and competing values. Public education is responsible for seeking the truth but also for preparing students for citizenship and careers.[6] Indeed, Ely himself said he should be fired if in fact he was guilty of the charges against him.[7] Why should taxpayers fund disrespectful or hateful or irresponsible or just plain immoral speech? Why should teaching or research that threatens national security be permitted? Why should the majority not have its way in restricting course content or teaching methods it objects to? After all, it is on moral grounds that democratic majorities regulate perjury, threats, bribes, unlicensed medical or legal advice, false advertising, child pornography, military secrets, classroom topics, disrespectful speech in the classroom, and the like.[8]

In fact, the nature and justification of academic freedom is so disputed that it has been characterized by some scholars as an "essentially contested concept,"[9] as "incoherent,"[10] and even as an "illusion" or "myth."[11] In empirical terms, consider this: The American Association of University Professors (AAUP), which receives only a percentage of the disputes, nevertheless handled 1,121 complaints and cases regarding academic freedom during the two-year period from May 31, 2002, to May 31, 2004.[12] Or this: In 1966, 20 percent of high school librarians indicated challenges to books and other instructional materials at their school, increasing to 28 percent in 1973, 30 percent in 1977, and 50 percent in 1982.[13] In this chapter, then, I hope to provide some insight into these disputes by describing three conceptions of academic freedom, defending the most robust conception, which I call the civil libertarian conception, and addressing three major threats to the civil libertarian conception.

I must sound two notes of warning before proceeding. First, the three "conceptions" of academic freedom are not mutually exclusive but exist on a spectrum so that one might be more or less civil libertarian or legal moralist or egalitarian.[14] I focus each discussion on what might be described as the paradigmatic civil libertarian or legal moralist or egalitarian conception. Second, addressing as broad a topic as this in a short essay necessarily requires simplifications and omissions. For example, I address academic freedom in grades K–12 and post-secondary public education without much distinction, even though there are differences in some cases.[15] Further, I address academic freedom primarily in the context of the teacher as opposed to the student or the institution,[16] and I address the rights rather than the responsibilities of academic freedom.[17] Information provided in the notes should help readers pursue their interests in these three further issues to greater depth.

The Civil Libertarian Conception

The typical defenders of "academic freedom"—including the contributors to this book, the 1894 UW Board of Regents, the AAUP, the National Education Association (NEA), the American Library Association (ALA), the American Civil Liberties Union (ACLU) and its state affiliates, the Foundation for Individual Rights in Education (FIRE), and the First Amendment Center (FAC)—use the civil libertarian conception of academic freedom.[18] This point of view also is reflected in numerous legal precedents, the most important of which are regularly cited.[19] It has been characterized as the view that teachers "should not be penalized on any non-professional basis,"[20] "the insulation of professors and their institutions from political interference,"[21] and "the right to pursue the truth unhindered."[22] Please note that I use the term *conception* rather loosely because I am focusing on the kinds of restrictions on academic speech that a point of view finds acceptable or not rather than postulating a full-blown conception through a set of necessary and sufficient conditions or a Platonic essence. I do so because these kinds of restrictions succeed in meeting the present purposes.

Consider five examples in which the spirit—if not also the law—of academic freedom as the civil libertarian understands it is violated.[23]

- Following school procedures, a high school political science teacher has guest speakers from different political parties speak to his class without incident, including a Democrat, a Republican, and a member of the John Birch Society. However, when a Communist is invited to speak in class, public pressure causes the school board to rescind the invitation.[24]

- A community college seeks to discipline a professor for his confrontational teaching style and controversial course content based on a student's complaint about an assignment requiring her to define "pornography."[25]

- In the wake of the widely publicized flag-burning cases *Texas v. Johnson*, 491 U.S. 397 (1989), and *United States v. Eichman*, 496 U.S. 310 (1990), a university political science instructor burns an American flag during class as a demonstration of his constitutional rights. A disapproving public airs their objections and his contract is not renewed by the administration.[26]

- A professor writes a letter to the editor rebutting a staff editorial in the student newspaper that had declared, among other things, the truth of Christianity and the United States as a Christian nation. A student's parent offended by the rebuttal seeks to have the professor fired on grounds of moral turpitude.[27]

- A high school English teacher assigns a popular magazine article containing the word "bastard." Although none of the students (who were seniors) complain, some parents protest to the administration and seek to have the teacher fired when he refuses to change the assignment.[28]

From the civil libertarian perspective, each of these cases involves a clear and wrongful "political" interference in an academic matter. In no case is an academic justification given by an academic authority for the intervention; rather, the intervention results from the feelings of offense or personal moral sensitivities of nonacademics.[29]

But let us take up the burden of argument. Why should academics be insulated from nonacademic interference? Following John Searle, I want to begin to answer these questions through five basic claims. First, knowledge is valuable and should be advanced and disseminated. Second, a public educational institution is designed for the advancement and dissemination of knowledge. Third, knowledge is best advanced and disseminated in an environment of free inquiry. Fourth, professional teachers by virtue of their knowledge of methods and content are qualified to advance knowledge in ways that amateurs are not. Finally, teachers retain the same constitutional rights to free expression and the like as general citizens.[30] Although all five of these claims deserve additional discussion, for the purposes of this essay I must focus my remarks primarily on the third claim (knowledge is best advanced and disseminated in an environment of free inquiry), and, to a much lesser extent, the fourth claim (professional teachers by virtue of their knowledge of methods and content are qualified to advance knowledge in ways that amateurs are not). In all five cases, a teacher introduces an opinion into the marketplace of ideas (in some cases the classroom and in other cases the general public) and the civil libertarian hopes to defend the teacher's right to do so in an environment of free inquiry. But why should the academic marketplace of ideas be free and open to unpopular, even hated and pernicious ideas?

Free inquiry has been defended on a variety of grounds, including self-realization or fulfillment, the promotion of democracy, maintenance of the balance between stability and change, and even as a value in itself.[31] However, for pedagogical reasons I limit my discussion to John Stuart Mill's popular four-pronged argument appealing to the pursuit of truth and knowledge.[32]

First, closing the marketplace of ideas to certain ideas assumes a degree of certainty we cannot have. No individual or group is infallible, and to compel an opinion to remain in silence is to assume certainty of the banned opinion's falsity or perniciousness. For example, the slaveholding states were so certain that abolitionist speech was evil that it was banned; Alabama even provided the death penalty for those convicted.[33] Thus a professor at the University of North Carolina was fired by the trustees, repudiated by his fellow faculty, burned in effigy by students, and demonized in the press when he refused to withdraw his support for John Fremont, the antislavery 1856 Republican presidential candidate.[34] The contemporary—and patently absurd—equivalent would be for a school district or university to fire a teacher for supporting the 2004 presidential candidacy of George W. Bush or John Kerry.

Second, views and theories most commonly contain a portion rather than the whole of the truth, and it is only through the collision of theories that the remainder of truth is discovered. For example, the public goods and services that we enjoy today, including municipal water and sewage and interstate highways, would never have come to be if defenders of laissez-faire capitalism had succeeded in silencing academic critics such as Richard T. Ely. So, too, the benefits of modern medicine, including inoculations and anesthesia and even hand washing, would never have emerged had opponents succeeded in censoring "naturalistic" science.[35]

Third and fourth, even when the "settled" opinion is the whole truth, it is only through its collision with other views that its full meaning and the grounds of its truth will remain evident and avoid decaying into a mere prejudice or dogma. For example, the full meaning and evidence supporting the historical facts of the Nazi Holocaust has been deepened through the efforts of Professor Deborah Lipstadt of Emory University in her painstaking rebuttal of Holocaust deniers and subsequent legal vindication in winning a libel lawsuit brought against her by the Nazi-sympathizing British historian David Irving.[36] It is in this spirit, too, that some First Amendment scholars, such as Gerald Graff, are now arguing that the full meaning and evidence supporting the scientific theory of evolution can be deepened by discussing (rather than ignoring or dismissing) the theory of intelligent design in science classes.[37]

To be sure, civil libertarians must go beyond such generalities to offer specific principles by which they identify expression that goes beyond the pale, because they too accept some restrictions on speech. One such principle involves a distinction between mere "offense" and genuine "harm."[38] Nonactionable "offense" is, roughly, an individual or group of individuals experiencing outrage or anger or even righteous indignation by the expression of another individual or group of individuals. Actionable "harm," on the other hand, involves some clear and direct impingement on some individual or group right—although establishing harm does not automatically establish a conclusive case for speech regulation.[39] To illustrate offense and harm in an academic setting, consider the case of George Lincoln Rockwell, the former commander of the American Nazi Party, who did a "tour" of college campuses in 1966 and 1967, including at least three campus visits in my home state of Wisconsin.[40] In each case, a student group invited Rockwell to speak while stressing that they did not agree with Rockwell but were interested in hearing his views. In every case there was significant public objection that made news headlines. Interestingly, most objectors acknowledged Rockwell's legal right to speak and the university's legal right to invite him; they objected, however, on moral grounds, maintaining that the university ought not to give Rockwell a pulpit to preach his message of hate and discrimination, ought not to financially support him or his organization, and ought not to contribute to an already volatile racial environment. But one of the legal and moral justifications for allowing Rockwell's speech was that although his speech was certain to offend many people, it would not clearly and directly harm anyone, that is, violate anyone's rights. The desire to restrict speech on campuses on grounds of partisan morality is a constant issue,

as illustrated by the University of Colorado's Ward Churchill controversy in 2005 and many other academic speakers throughout history.[41]

Some distinction between offense and harm is necessary because if
offense *simpliciter* were actionable, no one would be allowed to express
anything—not even the most banal truisms, because those deeply offend some people too! As a federal judge wrote in striking down the
campus hate speech code at Central Michigan University:

> It is not much of a stretch to imagine a treatise (or a student's term paper or even
> a cafeteria bull session) which explores the source of conflict among residents
> of some middle-eastern region and posits one tribe involved in the conflict is the
> more blameworthy due to some ancient ethnic traditions which give rise to bar-
> barian combativeness or a long-standing inability to compromise. When and if
> it were complained of, would such a treatise (or term paper or conversation) be
> judged to violate the CMU policy . . . ? It would be a good fit with the policy lan-
> guage. . . . *Any* behavior, even unintentional, that offends *any* individual is to be
> prohibited under this policy.[42]

Lest you think the judge's worry was far-fetched, consider the fact that
more than 200 kinds of books used in public school grades K–12 have
been objected to, including those teaching psychology, critical thinking skills, scientific inquiry, self-esteem, black literature, mythology, science fiction, sex education, values clarification, basal readers that do not
champion phonics only, histories that mention the United Nations, stories that portray conflicts between parents and children, books that portray children making their own decisions, books that do not promote
the "work ethic," books that have negative statements about people in
authority, and stories that seem to favor disarmament, gun control, or
pacifism.[43] What would be left on the bookshelves if offense were sufficient to justify censorship? Only unread books.

A second way in which the civil libertarian conception is clarified is
through the distinction between "speech" and "conduct," or, better, between verbal or nonverbal behavior that is primarily expressive in purpose and verbal or nonverbal behavior that is not primarily expressive
in purpose.[44] Civil libertarians grant expressive behavior more freedom
than nonexpressive behavior at least in part because the First Amendment of the U.S. Constitution singles out "speech" and "press" for special protection. For the civil libertarian it is one thing to advocate or describe an act or set of actions; it is another to perform the act or actions,
and context matters. Consider the case of hostile environment sexual
harassment. Some teachers and professors have been exonerated of accusations of hostile environment sexual harassment when it has been

determined, among other things, that they engaged primarily in "expression" rather than "behavior," whereas other teachers have been punished when it was determined that they engaged primarily in "behavior."[45] Or, consider the numerous academic critics of the legal concept of hostile environment harassment who express their opinions through reputable academic presses but would be subject to legal action and penalties were they to perform the actions they defend.[46] Such critiques of existing law and doctrine are necessary both for legal education and legal reform.

The civil libertarian conception also appeals to such legal notions as overbreadth, vagueness, arbitrary enforcement, and chilling effect in order to distinguish acceptable from unacceptable regulations on academic expression. Each of these concepts addresses the practical evils of restricting or closing the marketplace of ideas. A speech regulation is overbroad if it prohibits broad classes of speech, some of which may be regulated, if in doing so a substantial amount of constitutionally protected speech also is prohibited.[47] A speech regulation is vague when "men of common intelligence must necessarily guess at its meaning," thereby allowing public officials to arbitrarily enforce the regulation;[48] however, the potential "chilling effect" of the regulation must be real and substantial and a narrowing construction unavailable to the court. These notions rightly played an important role in the 1989 federal court decision that struck down the University of Michigan hate speech code.[49] The code was overbroad on its face because it included expression protected by the First Amendment as well as overbroad in its application because it penalized protected speech on at least three occasions.[50] The code was unduly vague because its key terms lacked operational definitions, making it "impossible to discern any limitation on its scope or any conceptual distinction between protected and unprotected conduct."[51] That is, a civil libertarian will accept restrictions on academic expression only if the policy narrowly targets unprotected speech, is clear enough to avoid arbitrary enforcement, and does not result in any significant chilling of legitimate expression.

Of course, many further principles may pertain to a case depending on the circumstances,[52] but the basic nature of and justification for the civil libertarian conception now should be fairly clear. Civil libertarians do not oppose all restrictions on academics; rather, they seek a framework of moral and legal principles that minimize nonacademic interferences and maximize the pursuit of truth and discussion of the meaning and grounds of truth. In conclusion, I should note that the civil libertarian conception is not a politically partisan one. The ACLU and

FIRE, for example, have defended Democrats, Republicans, Libertarians, Communists, and others. Nor should the conception be identified with any particular moral or jurisprudential basis, for it can be defended on both consequentialist and nonconsequentialist grounds[53] and using both categorical and balancing approaches.[54]

The Legal Moralist Conception

Both historically and in the post-9/11 context the main competitor to the civil libertarian conception is what I call the legal moralist conception. The core of legal moralism is that public education should be subject to strict moral and legal constraints which frequently override the pursuit and dissemination of knowledge in an environment of free inquiry—that academic freedom is, in fact, a narrow rather than a broad category. Consider this (partial) characterization:

> Academic freedom is the privilege of a researcher to study unsettled issues within his profession. This is a narrower concept than freedom of thought and freedom of speech. It is narrow, because many issues within any academic field are now settled, and the questioning of these issues . . . is at best a waste of time and at worst destructive of the profession.[55]

Thus, although legal moralists agree that knowledge is valuable and that universities ought to seek knowledge and truth, they emphasize that teachers also are public servants responsible to the taxpayers who pay their salaries and fund their institutions. They insist that the right of the community through its legitimately appointed authorities to decide curriculum and set rules for teachers and students outweighs the rights of individual teachers and students to speak or act as they please. Thus the legal moralist believes teachers are rightfully subject to political interference and penalties when they criticize "settled" truths in or out of the class or make controversial public statements outside their field of expertise. People at the extreme end of the legal moralist spectrum oppose a great many freedoms that civil libertarians support because they do not oppose in principle a "political" interest restricting academic expression, even though no violation of professional norms has occurred.

Let us reconsider from the legal moralist's perspective the five cases described earlier. Why is a school board correct to reject a Communist classroom speaker when taxpayers object? Why is a community college justified in disciplining a professor for controversial course content and methods? Why can a university legitimately fire an instructor for burning a flag in a classroom demonstration? Why is a parent correct to seek a professor's dismissal for questioning the state endorsement of Christianity? Why should an unrepentant teacher be fired for a reading assignment containing a vulgarity? Because in each case the teacher challenges a "settled" belief. "We" know that Communism is wrong and has failed, that vulgarities should not be used in class, that flag burning and pornography are immoral, and that Christianity is the truth and the United States is a Christian nation. The community (majority) has a right to define itself in such a way that trumps the rights of individuals and minority groups. Accordingly, administrators of public academic institutions are obligated to teach "settled" truths, to use course content and methods acceptable to community norms, to shield students from harmful and vulgar expression, and to hold teachers up to high moral standards of personal and professional behavior. And if Communism, confrontational teaching styles, flag burning, and criticisms of Christian orthodoxy do not violate professional norms, then so much the worse for the profession!

Of course, the contrast between civil libertarianism and legal moralism is not always so sharp. Consider, for example, Bible reading in public schools (grades K–12). It was common in the 1700s and 1800s for teachers in public schools to read verses from Protestant Bibles during the school day, usually at the direction of the local elected school board. As more non-Protestants, especially Catholics and Jews, began attending public schools, they began to object to the practice. Thus the question eventually arose: Does the community and school board's authority to set curriculum outweigh the student's right to be free from religious indoctrination? The standard legal moralist line maintained that (1) reading "universally accepted" Bible verses was not "sectarian," (2) the Bible was a state-approved textbook, (3) the Bible was approved by the local school board, which is duly formed by legal process in a proper manner and in accordance with the wishes of the majority of school families, and (4) only the Bible itself can truthfully present biblical history and morals that are essential to a proper education because the United States is a "Christian nation."[56] Such legal moralist thinking led five state courts to find the practice of Bible reading in public schools acceptable,[57] and Wisconsin became the first state to ban Bible reading (for religious instruction) when its Supreme Court in 1890 found that the Edgerton School District policy violated the state constitution's ban on "sectarian" school materials.[58]

The dispute over Bible reading in public schools is hardly over—

witness the 2002 decision by a federal court banning the Rhea County (Tennessee) Bible Education Ministry, a voluntary weekly 30-minute Bible class for K–5 students[59]—and this is where the debate takes a twist: Some defenders of Bible reading even in 1890 Edgerton appealed to civil libertarian themes, maintaining that (1) the policy did not require teachers to read from the Bible but rather merely allowed those who chose to do so in accordance with their individual rights to freedom of speech and freedom of religion as protected by the Wisconsin State Constitution; (2) the policy did not require pupils to remain in class or school during the reading of Bible passages but allowed them to withdraw without punishment during such readings if they desired to do so; and (3) teachers read from the Bible without comment and thus were not indoctrinating or even teaching at all.[60] Thus, although the natural assumption would be that civil libertarianism would support the teacher's right to choose course content and freely express relevant opinions and legal moralism would oppose it, civil libertarianism often has supported restrictions on religious academic expression through the so-called establishment clause and its "separation of church and state,"[61] thereby opening the door for defenders of religious expression in academic contexts to insert the wedge of civil libertarian rhetoric. Consider, for example, the case of Kenneth Roberts, a fifth-grade teacher who allotted fifteen minutes of silent reading to his students each day. Although students read the items of their choice, Roberts himself usually sat at his desk and read from the Bible he kept there. Eventually the principal and school board learned about this and ordered Roberts to stop reading from his Bible in his classroom. Roberts then appealed in court (unsuccessfully) his rights to the free exercise of religion, freedom of speech, and academic freedom.[62] On the other hand, consider the more recent case of a theater student at the University of Utah who dropped out of the Actor Training Program and (successfully, at least on procedural grounds) sued her professors when, contrary to her religious beliefs, they demanded she read assigned lines she found offensive.[63]

Tensions between the free speech and free exercise clauses and the establishment clause within the First Amendment ensure that courts will remain busy adjudicating the proper scope of religious expression in public academic institutions. Here are two current examples. First, contemporary advocates of teaching creationism or intelligent design in grades K–12 and post-secondary public school science classes increasingly appeal to the teacher's right to free speech and/or to choose course content and/or the need to present "all the evidence" in the "collision of ideas" in pursuit of the truth.[64] The First Amendment Center reports that recent religious challenges to evolution have been mounted in thirteen states, that only 35 percent of Americans believe evolution is supported by evidence, and that although the scientific community has been winning court cases excluding creationism and intelligent design from the science curriculum (at least so far),

> shutting down debate isn't good for academic freedom or critical thinking. Moreover, it doesn't work. Without understanding the controversy (and some of the historical and philosophical reasons for it), many students will continue to resist or distrust the claims of science.[65]

Second, the University of Wisconsin, Eau Claire (UW-EC) requires students to earn thirty hours of so-called service learning credit. Several years ago the UW-EC service learning office decided not to award credits for "religious-exclusive" activities such as teaching Sunday school or distributing religious literature door to door for fear that such activities would violate the establishment clause. However, this policy came under close scrutiny during the 2004–05 academic year in faculty committees, student and faculty senates, and the local media. Defenders of religious expression sought to overturn the ban, citing the free exercise clause, freedom of speech, and academic freedom, and they successfully recruited letters of support from the Foundation for Individual Rights in Education and the American Center for Law and Justice.[66] Since the university has continued the ban on service credit for religious expression (although not, for example, for political or artistic expression), it won't be surprising if the policy is challenged in court.

It is noteworthy that this same strategy (appealing to civil libertarian themes) is being exploited by political conservatives such as David Horowitz to attack the "liberal" university and to argue for an "academic bill of rights."[67] Some have argued that the academic bill of rights reduces rather than increases freedom of speech by mandating that certain speech be offered on a campus and in the classroom, but my present point is simply that when such proposals are examined, we must be mindful of reasoned legal and moral precedent. For example:

> In asserting their right to criticize, students must also understand the limitations of such rights. The classroom is a bounded educational environment. It is not, except at the invitation of a professor, an opportunity for those not enrolled in a course to attend and participate in classroom discussions. Additionally, students cannot expect, through the use of a grievance procedure or otherwise,

that the university administrators will call professors to account for the content of their lectures or their ideological assertions within the classroom.[68]

Because I do not have the space to try to explicate and defend a position on the issues involved here, I will simply point out that the problem in many of these cases is that people take a partisan—as opposed to principled—stand. Many defenders of religious expression seek to deny that same right of expression to secular humanists, and vice versa. Many political conservatives seek to deny freedom of expression to their opponents, and vice versa. As the journalist Nat Hentoff has so aptly put it, most people are interested in "free speech for me, but not for thee."[69]

This reveals an important problem in legal moralism (in addition to its failure to adequately distinguish harm and offense, expressive and nonexpressive behavior, etc.): It necessarily is applied in a politically partisan manner, or in legal terms, it lacks viewpoint neutrality.[70] Endorsing politically motivated censorship on professionally unrelated grounds allows you to censor or punish those you hate; on the other hand, it necessarily also opens the door for those you hate to censor or punish you. For example, if it is permissible for a local school board to require that biblical creationism be taught along with evolution in a science class, it must also be permissible for a local school board to require Hindu or Native American creationism and exclude Christian creationism. But on the basis of what educationally related principle would one nonscientific creation view be included and another excluded from a science class? If it is permissible for the University of Colorado at Boulder to fire Ward Churchill for publications and speeches expressing his "radical" or "left-wing" criticisms of U.S. foreign policy, then it also is permissible for the City College of New York to fire Michael Levin for publications and speeches expressing his "conservative" or "right-wing" criticisms of affirmative action.[71] If the University of Nevada, Las Vegas, can discipline economics professor Hans-Herman Hoppe for using a generalization about the tendency of homosexuals to spend more and save less than heterosexuals during a lecture on the "time preference" theory of the Austrian School of Economics to an upper-level undergraduate money and banking class,[72] then look out gay and lesbian and "queer" theorists! As the old saw goes, censorship is a two-edged sword.

Not only can legal moralists be faulted for viewpoint bias and relying on the civil libertarian position only when it is expedient, but also their reliance on "settled" truths cannot be sustained in the moral and political disputes they most like to intervene in, for it is exactly the lack of "settlement" that causes the dispute. It hardly works to say the matter is settled when in fact there is significant dispute about the matter. The fact that I, or the group I identify with, thinks a moral issue is settled beyond dispute does not make it so, and even if it did, to deny expression to my opponent is to put us on the road to losing the full meaning and justification for the "settled" truth.

Thankfully, against viewpoint discrimination and the two-edged sword of partisan moral and political truth stands Carl Schurz, a German immigrant to this country before the Civil War who became a major American political figure in the late 1800s. The eternal flame of Lady Liberty inspired Schurz to say in an April 18, 1860, speech in Boston's historic Faneuil Hall:

> I wish the words of the Declaration of Independence "that all men are created free and equal, and are endowed with certain inalienable rights," were inscribed upon every gate-post within the limits of this Republic. From this principle the Revolutionary Fathers derived their claim to independence; upon this they founded the institutions of this country, and the whole structure was to be the living incarnation of this idea. This principle contains the [program] of our political existence. . . . *From the equality of rights springs the identity of our higher interests; you cannot subvert your neighbor's rights without striking a dangerous blow at your own. And when the rights of one cannot be infringed without finding a ready defense in all others who defend their own rights in defending his, then, and only then, are the rights of all safe against the usurpations of governmental authority.* This general identity of interests is the only thing that can guarantee the stability of democratic institutions. (emphasis added)[73]

The "identity of interests"—what an excellent idea! An idea now being recognized, for example, in the coalition of "right" and "left" organizations resisting portions of the Patriot Act that infringe or chill individual rights[74] and in the coalition of "right" and "left" individuals directing and advising the Foundation for Individual Rights in Education in resisting university policies and decisions that infringe on individual rights.[75]

But beware, legal moralist thinking and its flaws are not the exclusive possession of any one political party, and all political parties ought to resist it, perhaps especially in times of crisis and controversy.

The Egalitarian Conception

As universities became more diverse learning communities throughout the 1970s and 1980s, an increasing number of scholars and activists became worried about an increasing verbal and nonverbal backlash against women and various minorities. By the mid to late 1980s a group of legal scholars, including some First Amendment experts, were arguing that campus "hate speech" ought to be banned.[76] Why? Essentially, the claim was that hate speech denies victims equal teaching and learning opportunities. Out of sympathy with the egalitarian cause as well as some combination of fear of legal penalties and/or bad press and/or student rebellion, hundreds of universities throughout the country quickly adopted nearly identical "hate speech codes."[77] But defenders of the codes and their allies had a broader vision of the academy and a different conception of academic freedom, which I call the egalitarian conception. Roughly, the egalitarian conception of academic freedom holds that the cause of educational equality and its prerequisites (perhaps political and economic equality) are compelling enough to warrant restrictions on academic life that civil libertarians and legal moralists do not accept. So even though the egalitarian conception of academic freedom has an agenda affecting many academic areas— curriculum and university structure to name just two examples—I restrict my comments to the issue of so-called hate speech codes. Advocates of campus hate speech codes had three major arguments supporting their position, involving the notions of deterrence, fighting words and harassment, and university mission.

First, being familiar with the civil libertarian distinction between offense and harm, advocates of hate speech codes attempted to articulate the harms to victims of hate speech, including psychological, physical, and pecuniary harms.[78] If scholars could establish that the harms were serious and that codes were necessary to deter the harm, then courts working with civil libertarian precedents might defer to institutional academic freedom even where it restricted individual academic freedom.

Second, being familiar with the civil libertarian acceptance of bans on "fighting words"[79] and some forms of racial and sexual harassment,[80] egalitarian advocates attempted to show that hate speech in effect was a form of unprotected fighting words or harassment.[81] If scholars could show that those legal categories permitting restrictions on speech were well-founded and applicable, then First Amendment objections to the speech codes could be overcome.

Finally, being familiar with the civil libertarian appeal to the pursuit of truth as a core mission of education, advocates attempted to show that equal opportunity too was a core mission of education and in fact trumped free speech in the case of hate speech because of three constitutional amendments and myriad federal and state statutes protecting and/or promoting equality, including the Civil Rights Act.[82] If scholars could show that equality was a substantial state interest and that codes were a necessary way of furthering that state interest, then here too courts might defer to institutional academic freedom.

These arguments were met with a torrent of criticism and the debate between supporters and critics of speech codes elicited several important new studies of free speech and academic freedom.[83] The codes often were written and applied as broad *speech* codes rather than as narrowly defined and applied *hate speech* codes, and when the codes and related speech cases were scrutinized in the courtroom, judges rightfully and consistently eviscerated campus speech codes on the kinds of civil libertarian grounds introduced earlier in this chapter in a series of cases, including *Doe v. University of Michigan*, 721 F. Supp. 852 (E.D. Mich. 1989); *UWM Post Inc. et al. v. Board of Regents of the University of Wisconsin*, 774 F. Supp. 1163 (E.D. Wis. 1991); *Iota XI Chapter of Sigma Chi Fraternity v. George Mason University*, 773 F. Supp. 792 (E.D. Va. 1991); *Dambrot v. Central Michigan University*, 55 F.3d 1177 (6th Cir. 1995); *Robert Corry et al. v. Stanford University*, County of Santa Clara Superior Court, No. 740309 (Feb. 27, 1995); *Cohen v. San Bernardino Community College*, 92 F.3d 968 (9th Cir. 1996), *cert. denied*, 117 S. Ct. 1290 (1996); and *Silva v. University of New Hampshire*, 888 F. Supp 293 (D. N.H. 1994). As Committee A (the Committee on Academic Freedom and Tenure) of the AAUP states: "Free speech is not simply an aspect of the educational enterprise to be weighed against other desirable ends. It is the very precondition of the academic enterprise itself."[84] Again, Judge Warren in the University of Wisconsin system case wrote, "The problems of bigotry and discrimination . . . are real and truly corrosive of the educational environment. But freedom of speech is almost an absolute in our land."[85]

Although it was obvious that civil libertarians could not abide the broad speech codes that many universities adopted, it may be less obvious why legal moralists opposed the codes because it is a "settled" American view that all people deserve equal educational opportunity and that racist and sexist speech are wrong, and the codes were enacted and enforced through proper channels of legitimate authority. On what grounds, then, would a legal moralist oppose egalitarian restrictions on academic life? I am forced to make an educated guess here, as opponents of hate speech codes of all sorts found it convenient and effective to line up behind the civil libertarian objections. For example, even conservative news columnist George Will and former president George H. W. Bush, hardly close friends of civil libertarianism, found it politic to rail against campus censorship and "political correctness" on grounds of free inquiry.[86] I would conjecture, however, that a distinctly legal moralist objection might be aimed at the elitist and/or progressive elements of egalitarianism because the reliance of legal moralism on the rights of the dominant moral community with its "settled" views has an inherent tendency toward populism and conservatism. That is, a legal moralist may well oppose campus speech codes (and other egalitarian or "progressive" proposals) as tools invented and enforced by an academic elite seeking to advance their own extremist political agenda or to "indoctrinate" or "change" students and may maintain thereby that such rules are not part of or inconsistent with some other "settled" truth.

But the egalitarian conception of academic freedom faces the same problem of political partisanship and viewpoint bias as the legal moralist conception of academic freedom, for it too seeks to "license one side of a debate to fight freestyle, while requiring the other to follow Marquis of Queensbury Rules."[87] Double standards—one for progressive egalitarians, another for their opponents—abound, and necessarily so, for egalitarians are essentially legal moralists only with regard to equality (or at least their conception of equality) rather than some other value. For example, the Washington State University Office for Campus Involvement sponsored the 2005 productions of *The Vagina Monologues* and *Tales of the Lost Formicans* but bought tickets for forty students to disrupt *Passion of the Musical* by repeatedly standing up, shouting about being offended, and verbally threatening audience members and the cast.[88] Moreover, campus security refused to take action against the hecklers, instead demanding that a line be changed in the production and WSU president V. Lane Rawlins commended the hecklers for exercising "their rights of free speech in a very responsible manner." This is not an isolated incident. In a recent forum on academic freedom, three historians noted, "When campus administrators enforce speech codes and related rules, conservatives and libertarians often bear the brunt of the attack."[89] Most disturbing, however, is Jon B. Gould's finding that despite the court decisions striking down campus hate speech codes, they are "far from dead"; indeed, only 11 percent of schools with an illegal policy removed it, and 25 percent of schools nationwide failed to comply with the court decisions.[90] Why? Gould found that campus administrators often calculated that the symbolic importance of keeping the illegal policy outweighed the likelihood of being legally challenged, and some even actively adopted policies contrary to legal precedent out of a belief that such policies were the norm in higher education.

Note well that civil libertarians do not oppose narrowly drawn regulations on campus speech (although they have become so narrow that it is deceptive to call their proposals a speech code) [91] and recognize that there are plenty of hard cases in which public school and university authorities seek to defend an institution's academic freedom against a faculty or student's individual academic freedom. But one mistake we must not make is to seek to resolve the controversies by pursuing the sterile and impossible kind of "equality" that the UW-EC Student Senate imagined in the spring of 2005 when it voted to ban any student-organized activity that promotes a "particular ideological, religious, or partisan viewpoint" from receiving student-fee funding.[92] As Greg Lukianoff put it:

> It is astounding and absurd that any student government would adopt the viewpoint that a student group having a point of view is a bad thing. In the past few years, FIRE has seen a disturbing trend in which students and administrators seem willing to restrict all expression rather than contend with a single point of view they dislike. As long as students harbor such a clear hostility to the marketplace of ideas, free speech is in serious jeopardy.[93]

Such people need to read the stirring words of Carl Schurz, who had the courage to respond to the objections of a hostile crowd hoping to silence Boston abolitionists:

> But you say that fanaticism and demagogism, if armed with the power of speech, may pervert the popular mind, and in appealing to the passions or the imagination of the multitude mislead their reason. . . . *But I say, "Where speech is not free, there people are most apt to swallow the unjustly forbidden fruit unexamined. . . .* History is full of examples which show the highest oratory cannot move the popular mind from the ground of strong moral conviction. . . . *Why not by free speech counteract the mischief that free speech threatened to accomplish?* Why not call a meeting on their side? . . . This nation has undertaken to be the great guiding star of mankind, and to show the people of earth how man can be free if left to himself. . . . *If liberty fall here, where can we expect to see it maintained?* (emphasis added)[94]

Reasons for Declining Support

As a result of civil libertarian moral and legal arguments, U.S. educators enjoy greater academic freedom than many of their colleagues around the world (see Chapters 6–8); however, the civil libertarian conception faces serious practical if not theoretical challenges in the twenty-first century arising from a great variety of factors, including national security concerns, political correctness, the increasing use of nontenured teachers, the increasing reliance on corporations for funding, stricter regulations on access to information and archives and foreign academics entering the country, the need to "teach to the test," and fear of controversy and challenges. Because many of these concerns are addressed in other chapters in this book, I want instead to discuss three different— albeit interrelated—practical challenges to the civil libertarian conception that are perhaps more fundamental.

The Education Problem. The professional and personal lives of administrators, teachers, and students are defined largely by the degree to which they have academic freedom. It affects course content, teaching materials, teaching strategies, and speakers, assemblies, and plays as well as the expression of opinion and freedom of action outside the classroom. Indeed, one commentator has said:

Academic freedom is the most significant concept a teacher can embrace. The freedom to study, learn, teach, and express ideas is the defining characteristic of the concept of academic freedom for teachers and students. A society that intends to be free requires teachers who are willing and able to exercise academic freedom and provides a strong support for it.[95]

In 1986 the AAUP Commission on Academic Freedom and Pre-College Instruction emphasized in its report that "academic freedom is indispensable to college and university teaching and research, but the professor's free expression and free inquiry are unlikely to be fully achieved if the student's development at the pre-college level is incomplete."[96] Yet most people, even the teachers and students most directly affected by the conditions of academic freedom, have little understanding of what their rights and responsibilities are and why they are legally protected.[97] Consider just a small sample of the empirical evidence.

A 2005 John S. and James L. Knight Foundation survey of 100,000 high school students, nearly 8,000 high school teachers, and more than 500 administrators at 544 high schools across the United States found that nearly three-fourths of high school students either do not know how they feel about the First Amendment or admit they take it for granted; 75 percent erroneously think flag burning is illegal; half believe the government can censor the Internet; and more than one-third think that the First Amendment goes too far in the rights it guarantees.[98]

Nearly half think newspapers need governmental approval of stories, nearly four in ten do not know if they take the First Amendment for granted, and one in four does not know if people should be allowed to express unpopular opinions.[99] Knight Foundation president and CEO Hodding Carter III says, "These results are not only disturbing; they are dangerous. Ignorance about the basics of this free society is a danger to our nation's future."[100]

The First Amendment Center's "State of the First Amendment 2005" survey found that few Americans can name any of the five specific rights guaranteed by the First Amendment, only 58 percent believe newspapers should be allowed to freely criticize the military, and 67 percent believe public school students should not be allowed to wear T-shirts that others might find offensive, 50 percent believe people should not be allowed to say things in public that might be offensive to religious groups, and 43 percent believe people should not be allowed to say things in public that are offensive to racial groups.[101]

A 2004 survey of Wisconsin adults found the same abysmally low ability to identify any First Amendment rights; the survey also found that one in ten Wisconsin adults thinks people should be punished for protesting on public property or for criticizing the government during wartime, one in four thinks the government should censor journalists, nearly half think government should violate religious freedom in the fight on terrorism, six in ten think people should be punished for burning the flag in political protest, and eight in ten think schools should punish offensive speech.[102]

Finally, and most telling, the 2003 Foundation for Individual Rights in Education (FIRE) surveys found that "college and university students are woefully ignorant about freedom of speech and freedom of religion," that "administrators who govern student life on campus fared no better," and that "freedom of speech and freedom of religion are undergoing a frightening and powerful assault."[103] For example, one out of every four undergraduates is unable to mention any freedoms protected by the First Amendment, and one in four administrators believes that they have the legal right to prohibit a student religious group from actively trying to convert students to its religion.

Is it any wonder that a 5-year-old elementary school student was ordered by school officials not to say a prayer over her lunch on the (bogus) grounds that it violated the separation of church and state?[104] That a high school junior in Michigan was (illegally) ordered not to wear an antiwar T-shirt to school, that the valedictorian of another Michigan school had her yearbook entry (illegally) deleted because it included a biblical passage she found meaningful, and that a Minnesota student was (illegally) prohibited from wearing his "Straight Pride" sweatshirt in school?[105] Is it any wonder that such repression continues on the college campus? Has the spirit of "continual and fearless sifting and winnowing" in the pursuit of truth been lost or subdued? What a catastrophe this would be given the centrality of that purpose to the mission of public education.

The Exceptions Problem.   People like the idea of freedom much better than the practice of it. In particular, we prefer our own freedom of expression to the freedom of others.[106] Thus, even when people do have some understanding of their rights and responsibilities, they find it easy to support—whether actively or passively—restrictions on freedom when it conflicts with other values they hold. Unpopular moral and political expression is conveniently described as "low-value" speech (e.g., egalitarians describing hate speech) or "not really speech at all" (e.g., legal moralists describing flag burning in political protest). Consider, for example, the nationwide rash of campus newspaper confiscations, which even struck my own institution (University of Wisconsin, Stout) when someone confiscated the April Fool's edition of our campus newspaper from several building distribution sites when he or she saw that it contained some crass criticisms and caricatures of our senior administrator. Consider the willingness of a majority of Americans to tolerate infringements on religious freedom in the fight against terrorism—how many of the people who support that do you suppose think it is their own religious freedom that will be infringed? According to the Wisconsin survey, they are much more worried about the government sneaking a peek at their own library records![107]

It is possible to recognize and combat hypocrisy and unjustified restrictions on speech. I came to see it in myself when I examined more closely my initial sympathy for campus hate speech codes. Even in the heat of war, Americans have spoken out against double standards. For example, during the Civil War, U.S. Representative Charles Augustus Eldredge (D-Wis.) concluded his argument against a resolution calling for the expulsion of a colleague, Mr. Long of Ohio, for expressing criticisms of the war and the Lincoln administration during legislative debate with these remarks:

Finally, the resolution should be rejected because it is hypocritical. Republicans such as Mr. Conway of Kansas, Mr. Washburne of Illinois, Mr. Stevens of Pennsylvania, even Mr. Walker of President Lincoln's own administration, have expressed similar and even worse opinions about the war, but we don't see any resolutions being proposed against them. But Mr. Long, a Democrat, says it, and the Republicans are quick to condemn. Where is [the] consistency? This blatant pursuit of party interests shows disregard for both law and morals. Some of the Republican papers in the country are frank and manly enough to see and declare the folly of this farce. The *New York Times* of yesterday, which I hold in my hand declares the resolution ". . . neither right nor expedient." The *New York Evening Post* . . . says, "Long's [speech] was a perfectly legitimate expression of opinion."[108]

Through such appeals, Rep. Long was saved from expulsion, although not censure. Again, in the censorship-crazed days of World War I, Senator Robert "Fightin' Bob" La Follette delivered one of the finest speeches in American history defending the right of free speech and attacking the hypocrisy of his censors in his speech, "Free Speech in Wartime," delivered to Congress on October 6, 1917.[109] Are we willing and able to expose and overcome the hypocrisy of actual and would-be censors at the dawn of the twenty-first century?

The Organization Problem. There are powerful organizations dedicated to distorting and destroying the civil libertarian conception and practice of academic freedom. As far back as 1985, Edward B. Jenkinson had identified at least 2,000 organizations that systematically attacked civil libertarian academic freedom in public schools, including the American Education Association, the American Education Coalition, the John Birch Society, Daughters of the American Revolution, the Eagle Forum, the Heritage Foundation, the Ku Klux Klan, the National Association of Christian Educators, Posse Comitatus, the 700 Club, and Concerned Women of America.[110] To give just one example, Tim La Haye, author and one of the founders of the Moral Majority, writes, "Our public schools have become conduits to the minds of our youth, training them to be anti-God, anti-moral, anti-family, anti-free enterprise and anti-American."[111] Numerous other examples can be given— indeed, some describe this as a "hate the school" book industry.[112] In addition to such publications, more direct methods are still used at times, including, for example, book protests, book burnings, court challenges, and harassment. Nor are such challenges limited to the K–12 environment.

Given such threats, we would do well to remember the tenuousness of the civil libertarian conception of academic freedom. Public education departments and administrators as well as elected officials and judges recognize academic freedom only to the extent that they deem it right or in their interest, that high-minded rhetoric in one decision does not require a high-minded decision in another case, and that expansive language in cases from the 1960s gets narrowed as courts grapple with conflicts between the academic freedom of teachers, students, and institutions.[113] As one court put it in 1982, "While academic freedom is well recognized, its perimeters are ill-defined and the case law defining it is inconsistent."[114] More recently, in 1995 a court wrote, "The concept of academic freedom, however, is more clearly established in academic literature than it is in the courts."[115] Worse, even a legal victory can in effect be a loss, as when, for example, the financial or emotional or reputational costs of defending academic freedom are excessive.[116]

What can defenders of the civil libertarian conception do to combat the interrelated problems of education, inconsistency, and organization? To ask the question is really to answer it. They will have to organize, educate, and take both political and grassroots action with as much or more vigor than their opponents. There is room for hope: Nine in ten Wisconsinites surveyed agreed that "public schools should require instruction on First Amendment rights."[117] But this is easier said than done in an already overcrowded curriculum and media market. Fifteen years ago, Jack Nelson wrote:

The war over ideas has not been resolved in favor of teachers and students. So long as teachers remain docile and "less vigorous" than they should be in their defense of academic freedom, the censorious and doctrinaire elements of society have unbridled opportunity to stifle dissent and de-professionalize teachers.[118]

These words are just as true, if not more so, in the twenty-first century. Certainly there have been strong efforts at education by some individuals and organizations, but unless supporters of the civil libertarian conception can increase their base of support through increased organization, education, and politicking, I see little reason to be optimistic and considerable reason to be pessimistic about the future of academic freedom.

Conclusion

In this essay I hope to have made plausible three main claims: (1) Whether or not we consider a particular action or set of actions a violation of academic freedom or not depends largely on whether we use the civil libertarian, legal moralist, or egalitarian conception; (2) although each conception appeals to important values to support its perspective on academic freedom, there are overriding legal, political, moral, and historical reasons why we ought to support the civil libertarian conception over the legal moralist and egalitarian conceptions; and (3) without an aggressive, organized movement to educate the public and academics about the virtues of the civil libertarian conception, it will (continue to) weaken through complacency, ignorance, inconsistency, and an ambivalent judiciary.[119]

Perhaps the most important point to make is that although academic freedom for teachers and professors is a set of rights (and responsibilities) assigned to individuals, the rights (and responsibilities) are justified not through their value to that individual but through their value to society. As the faculty member at the University of Southern Florida put it, this kind of academic freedom is really "the right of society to honest expert advice and counsel."[120] It is for this reason that the 1957 *Sweezy* decision took a decisively civil libertarian turn despite the fact that Sweezy was a journalist invited to speak to a class rather than a teacher or professor:

> To impose any straitjacket upon the intellectual leaders in our colleges and universities would imperil the future of our Nation. No field of education is so thoroughly comprehended by man that new discoveries cannot yet be made. . . . Scholarship cannot flourish in an atmosphere of suspicion and distrust. Teachers and students must always remain free to inquire, to study and to evaluate, to gain new maturity and understanding; *otherwise our civilization will stagnate and die.* (emphasis added)[121]

A democratic government and people must actively support a robust civil libertarian conception of academic freedom for teachers and professors because it is in the public's own long-term self-interest, as indicated in the many historical examples presented here. A first step is for academics themselves to better understand and appreciate academic freedom, but for public education to flourish, academic freedom must live in the hearts and minds of Joe and Jane Public too.

PART TWO

Academic Freedom and American Universities

CHAPTER 3

Academic Freedom in the Post–September 11 Era: An Old Game with New Rules

Robert M. O'Neil

IN SPRING 2003, a Senate subcommittee released long-sealed transcripts of hearings that Senator Joseph McCarthy had conducted behind closed doors a half-century earlier. The focus of these hearings was a group of witnesses, including some college professors, whom the 1950s subcommittee eventually decided not to summon in public. One of those who was to be spared such a public humiliation at McCarthy's hands committed suicide before he learned of his reprieve.

This startling revelation evoked quite varied responses on Capitol Hill. Senator Carl Levin, who had chaired the successor subcommittee, ventured that a repetition of such excesses was most unlikely. "There's a greater awareness," he explained, "of McCarthyism and what tactics can be used by people who are trying to quiet dissenters." And, he added, "There's greater resistance against those who would try to still voices that they disagree with." But Levin's colleague, Russ Feingold, who had cast the only Senate vote against the USA PATRIOT Act, offered a less benign view. "What I'm hearing from constituents," he insisted, "suggests a climate of fear toward our government that is unprecedented, at least in my memory." And, lest we miss the symbolism, Feingold added, "Don't forget that I *am* the junior Senator from Wisconsin."[1]

The central question before us is which view—Levin's optimistic assessment or Feingold's bleaker prognosis—better reflects the current condition of, and prospects for, academic and intellectual freedom in times of stress. Senator Levin knows whereof he speaks. During his undergraduate years in Ann Arbor, the University of Michigan carried out one of the most egregious purges of tenured faculty, summarily dismissing three professors who either were suspected of disloyalty because of their political affiliations or simply refused publicly to accuse colleagues of suspect associations. For the past decade, the university has sponsored a lecture series honoring the three victims of the anti-Communist hysteria. Other institutions that acted in similarly shameful fashion during those dark days have also made amends. The University of Washington, Rutgers, and Harvard, among others, have in various ways recognized the sins of the past, and, although few of the victims survive to appreciate such atonement, the universities have offered apologies to the academic community at large. In all, nearly seventy tenured or tenure-track faculty members were dismissed during the McCarthy era for political activity or recalcitrance on such matters, according to Ellen Schrecker, who has most closely chronicled this tragic era.[2]

Are we confident that such a travesty could not happen again? Or is Senator Feingold justifiably concerned about a possible recurrence, especially if there were to be another attack of September 11 magnitude? The returns so far tend to support Levin's view, although with one notable exception. A brief review of the evidence at hand will invite speculation about the causes for what has, to date, been a national response strikingly different from the hysteria of the 1950s.

The Landscape Changes After September 11

The weeks immediately after the attack on the Pentagon and the World Trade Center saw several events that could well have brought out the worst in university administrators, governing boards, alumni, and legislatures—although curiously they did not. On the afternoon of September 11, University of New Mexico history professor Richard Berthold joked to his first-year survey class that "anyone who can blow up the Pentagon gets my vote."[3] Despite strong pressure from some legislators and irate citizens to dismiss Berthold on the spot, the university suspended him with pay and began a careful but quiet investigation. The outcome, several months later, was an official reprimand, suspension from teaching first-year students, and the prospect of an intensive post-tenure review. Berthold readily accepted such relatively mild sanctions, and the planned review became moot the next semester when he took early retirement after the filing of a sexual harassment charge.

A week after the attacks, Orange Coast (California) Community College professor Kenneth Hearlson was placed on leave for comments made during a September 18 introductory political science class. Several Muslim students claimed that Hearlson had pointed at them, accusing them of being "Nazis" and "terrorists," because "you drove two planes into the World Trade Center." A careful internal inquiry concluded that Hearlson had indeed been less than fully sensitive to his Muslim students, although the specific allegations were not substantiated. He was reinstated for the spring semester, with a letter of reprimand in his file the only formal sanction.[4]

Several weeks after September 11, a teach-in occurred at the City University of New York (CUNY). Several faculty members sharply criticized U.S. foreign policy, specifically blaming "American colonialism" for the attacks. Response within and outside the CUNY system was immediate and intense. The chancellor took the faculty critics to task, publicly faulting those who had made "lame excuses" for the terrorists. One trustee labeled the speakers' conduct "seditious," and another declared that the board should censure the aberrant professors.

Shortly before the board meeting at which such action might have occurred, CUNY's vice chairman (now chair), Benno Schmidt, educated his colleagues on some basic principles of free speech and academic freedom—drawn from his strong First Amendment academic background and his years as Yale University's president. "The freedom of thought to challenge and to speak one's mind," Schmidt reminded the other trustees, "is the matrix, the indispensable condition of any university worthy of the name." That seemed to end the matter, with the censure motion vanishing from the agenda.[5]

Strikingly similar events were to take place at Columbia University a year and a half later, with a comparably benign outcome. Nicholas De Genova, an assistant professor of anthropology and Latino studies, took part in a teach-in at the height of the war in Iraq. Among several provocative comments, De Genova said he wished for "a million Mogadishus"—recalling the tragic ambush of U.S. troops in Somalia, graphically portrayed in the film Black Hawk Down. This challenge was not the professor's first; the previous spring he had expressed deep hostility toward Israel at a campus rally.

Although word of De Genova's comments did not become public for several days, they evoked instant reaction as soon as the media did report them. Columbia alumni around the world demanded De Genova's dismissal. More than a hundred members of the U.S. House of Representatives called for his resignation. The leader of the petition drive, Rep. J. D. Hayworth, insisted that the issue was not "whether De Genova has the right to make idiotic comments . . . but whether he has the right to a teaching job at Columbia University after making such comments."

That issue soon came before another highly respected First Amendment expert, Columbia's new president, Lee Bollinger. He declared that he was personally "shocked" by De Genova's remarks, noting that "this one has crossed the line, and I really feel the need to say something." On several occasions later that spring, however, Bollinger declared that, however reprehensible, such an outburst did not forfeit a faculty member's position and that "under the principle of academic freedom, it would be inappropriate to take disciplinary action."[6]

While tempers were cooling slightly at Columbia, the De Genova incident became fodder for Fox News's *O'Reilly Factor*. President Bollinger was invited to appear and defend his stance, but understandably he declined. I agreed to appear in his stead and (as former chair of the American Association of University Professors [AAUP] Committee A) to explain the role of academic freedom. After a few opening parries, and my host's repeated charge that Bollinger was "hiding under his desk," Mr. O'Reilly concluded with this quite extraordinary statement: "I'll tell you what I would do if I were Bollinger. . . . I wouldn't fire this guy; I wouldn't fire this De Genova. OK? Because I agree with you. You've got to tolerate this kind of speech." O'Reilly offered, instead, his preferred solution: "I'd shun him. I wouldn't invite him to any faculty things." After a closing word of appreciation from the normally contentious host—"Thank you very much for your point of view—very provocative"—we went to a commercial break.[7]

The fact that this exchange took place during the tensest period of combat in Iraq—March 31, 2003—gives added impetus to Mr. O'Reilly's possibly extemporaneous, although widely noted, concession. It seems inconceivable that, a half-century earlier, Walter Winchell or Westbrook Pegler could have made a similarly tolerant statement about a highly visible academic target of Senator McCarthy's scrutiny. For this reason more than any other piece of recent evidence, the Levin view of the current condition of academic freedom seems closer to the mark.

Such a sanguine view seemed briefly at risk during the first week of February 2004, but within a few days it had been restored. A federal grand jury in Des Moines issued subpoenas to Drake University, demanding detailed information about an antiwar conference held there in late 2003 and about the event's sponsor, the local student chapter of the National Lawyers Guild. Included among the subpoenaed records were lists of all conference attendees and reports that the student group had filed with the university during the past several years. The apparent basis for such requests was the belief that the conference had spawned a physical protest at a nearby military base, which had piqued the grand jury's interest. News of the subpoenas brought immediate expressions of concern from civil libertarians and academic groups. Several comments noted that such intrusive inquiries had not been seen for nearly a half-century and could presage a return to McCarthyism. Drake's president took a firm stance in opposition, and the Lawyers Guild filed a motion to quash the subpoenas.

Within a few days, an obviously embarrassed United States attorney withdrew the demands. His initial explanation—that his office was concerned about the catalyst for a physical trespass at the military base and did not "prosecute persons peacefully and lawfully engaged in rallies which are conducted under the protection of the First Amendment"—satisfied nobody. Yet the fact that a federal prosecutor would feel compelled to offer such a disclaimer suggests the degree to which the landscape has indeed changed during the past half-century.[8]

Before celebrating too openly, however, we should recognize that some limited basis does exist for Senator Feingold's more cautious assessment and prognosis. There is one major faculty personnel case that warrants deep concern. The University of South Florida (USF) first suspended, and later dismissed, tenured computer science professor Sami Al-Arian. Al-Arian was indicted by a federal grand jury and in December 2005 was acquitted on eight charges of aiding and abetting terrorist organizations. The jury deadlocked on nine other charges, leaving open the question of whether Al-Arian will eventually be retried on the unresolved issues remaining after the first trial. For some years, Al-Arian had been active in Middle Eastern affairs, and he headed an institute at USF with a strongly Palestinian bias. During a late 2001 appearance on *The O'Reilly Factor*, Al-Arian acknowledged that he had once said to a sympathetic group, "Death to Israel." Because his institutional affiliation appeared on the screen, the university was soon flooded with calls from angry alumni, anxious parents, and concerned citizens. At that point, he was placed on paid leave, pending an investigation relating to his safety and that of others.

Just before the end of 2001, the administration and the board of trustees notified Al-Arian of their intent to seek his dismissal. When the spring semester began, however, the university's approach changed markedly. The president announced the filing of a suit seeking a declaration that Al-Arian could be discharged with impunity—a case that a federal judge eventually dismissed because, in her view, the dispute belonged back on the campus within the grievance procedure established by a collective bargaining agreement. The matter remained in limbo throughout 2002, with Al-Arian suspended and facing the prospect of dismissal.

Early in 2003, Al-Arian was arrested on federal charges of raising funds and providing material support for terrorist organizations— offenses specified by a 1996 statute, long before the September 11 attacks. Less than a week later, the USF administration, relying not only on the federal indictment but also on related charges that the grand jury had not invoked, announced that Al-Arian had been dismissed from his tenured position. The parties then agreed to postpone internal proceedings on the dismissal hearing until the criminal charges were resolved—a matter that will probably occupy several years.[9]

Despite his partial acquittal on the most serious federal criminal charges, it may yet turn out that other suspect activities could warrant Al-Arian's suspension and even the seeking of his dismissal for cause. There are, however, two crucial flaws in the university's handling of the case. For one, no hearing has ever been held at any level within the USF structure, and thus no opportunity was ever afforded for exculpatory arguments or extenuating evidence. Equally disturbing is the manifest frailty of the explicit basis for initial suspension—whatever darker fears or hypotheses the administration may have harbored. The university's formal announcement of its action in the late fall of 2001 relied entirely on concerns prompted by phone calls or other messages from angry alumni (whose financial support for the university might suffer if Al-Arian remained on its faculty), anxious parents (some of whom apparently worried about their children's' safety after watching the O'Reilly program), and other concerned neighbors and citizens.

So tenuous a stated basis for an adverse personnel action simply does not comport with basic principles of academic freedom and tenure. Even if some of the university's worst suspicions are eventually confirmed through the criminal process, we should not confer the benefit of hindsight, just as we should not validate Senator McCarthy's totally irresponsible charges in the 1950s on the basis of information about actual Communist infiltration that recently came to light with the unsealing of the KGB files.

The rest of the record on academic freedom since September 11 is somewhat mixed. Many relevant concerns, relating to restrictions on research, access of foreign students and visitors, and a host of other constraints, are beyond the scope of this chapter, which focuses chiefly on faculty personnel actions and policies and related developments. These subjects are touched on elsewhere in the book. On the positive side, efforts to cancel two highly controversial conferences in the fall of 2002—one at the University of Michigan and the other at the University of North Carolina, Chapel Hill—were notably unsuccessful. Suits were filed in both cases—and protests were held—to prevent these events from taking place on the ground that most of the speakers were unacceptably pro-Palestinian.

The administrations of both institutions, and their lawyers, took and maintained a strong defense of academic freedom, enabling the conferences to take place as scheduled, while protestors remained free to convey their displeasure. Earlier, several University of Colorado campuses refused to withdraw invitations to Palestinian spokesperson Hanan Ashrawi despite sharp criticism from legislators, one of whom charged that her appearance would be "a slap in the face to all who have died and suffered as a result of 9/11."[10] Indeed, with one notable exception—a cancellation at the College of the Holy Cross—visiting speakers have been able to appear and speak as planned.

On the other hand, several commencement speakers fared less well. In December 2001, *Sacramento Bee* publisher Janis Heaphy was shouted off the stage at California State University, Sacramento, by angry parents and friends of graduates after she made comments that revealed a liberal bias. A year and a half later, *New York Times* reporter Chris Hedges was unable to complete his Rockford College graduation speech because of audience anger apparently triggered by the speaker's reports from Iraq. Even talk show host Phil Donahue barely made it through his May 2003 commencement address at North Carolina State. Nevertheless, three such encounters represent a tiny fraction of the probably 10,000 or more graduation speeches that have taken place since September 11, more than a few of which might have become targets for disruption and cancellation.[11]

Much more could be said about the uncertain state of academic freedom since the attacks on the World Trade Center and the Pentagon. Restrictions on scientific research have expanded ominously (see Chapter 5), access of foreign students and even visiting scholars to the United States has been inhibited and at times blocked (see Chapters 6, 7, and 8), potential enforcement of certain Patriot Act provisions endangers free inquiry and scholarship, and in other respects there can be little doubt that the climate for academic freedom has deteriorated significantly in the past two and a half years. This is not, however, the time or the place to undertake such a broad assessment—and indeed it is probably far too soon to attempt that task with any reliability. The critical question is not whether academic freedom is less fully protected today than it was on September 10, 2001—it would be startling if that were not the case, even under the best of conditions.[12] Rather, the issue to which I now return is the debate between Senators Levin and Feingold.

What's Different Today—and Why?

Although it would be premature and incautious to look back at McCarthyism and say "it could never happen again"—nor did Senator Levin advance such a myopic view—the current situation seems to warrant mild optimism. For one thing, the present political spectrum seems to include no claimant to the McCarthy mantle—that is, no prominent public official who has yet yielded to myriad temptations to blame university professors for the nation's ills. Those few lawmakers who did urge the resignations of outspoken professors in New York and New Mexico or the cancellation of controversial speakers in Colorado and North Carolina spoke with considerable restraint—and dropped the issue after initial public response suggested limited popular support for faculty bashing. It would be difficult to imagine McCarthyism again without another McCarthy, or Jenner, or Velde, or Thomas.

There is much more about the current climate that seems very different. Recall exactly what Senator Levin said upon the release of the subcommittee transcripts that had been sealed since the 1950s: "I think there's a greater awareness of McCarthyism and what tactics can be used by people who are trying to quiet dissenters. And there's greater resistance against those who would try to still voices that they disagree with."

Several factors do appear to support Senator Levin's assessment. The "greater resistance" reflects a major difference between the two eras. When the AAUP announced the creation of the Special Committee on Academic Freedom and National Security in Time of Crisis, the organization noted the absence of similar action a half-century earlier—even though the AAUP had created special groups to study the potential impact of U.S. entry into both world wars on academic freedom. By any standard, as the Special Committee noted in its report, the AAUP's response to McCarthyism could be characterized as "tardy but categorical."[13] The AAUP did eventually take the lead in challenging campus speaker bans and disclaimer loyalty oaths. But its voice was neither as loud nor as clear as it should have been—or has been in later decades—during the early days of McCarthyism, an era that actually began with the dismissal of three tenured professors at the University of Washington in the spring of 1948, fully two years before Senator McCarthy's first charges of Communist infiltration of the State Department.

Nor was the AAUP alone in what now seems like undue reticence; the response of other protective groups, such as the American Civil Liberties Union (ACLU), did not match the prompt and bold defense of civil liberties that emerged immediately after September 11. Groups that play a major part in the current challenge to government attacks on civil liberties—most notably, People for the American Way—are creatures of the post-Vietnam era that did not even exist a half-century ago. Thus there seems to be ample support for Senator Levin's view that we are today blessed with "greater resistance against" would-be censors or red-baiters reminiscent of the McCarthy era.

That factor opens the discussion but surely does not conclude it. I need also to explain Bill O'Reilly's unexpected receptivity to the academic freedom claim advanced on Professor De Genova's behalf—"I wouldn't fire this guy. . . . You've got to tolerate this kind of speech." Surely Mr. O'Reilly is unlikely to have been influenced by the AAUP, the ACLU, People for the American Way, or any other such liberal organization. Yet he and many others who have taken a relatively moderate view of incidents that could have been highly inflammatory may reflect Senator Levin's "greater awareness of McCarthyism and what tactics can be used" by repressive forces. Thus the university governing boards at CUNY, New Mexico, Columbia, and elsewhere may have reacted as they did in part because they either recalled or had learned about those perilous times and were not anxious to trigger a repetition of such dark days.

There is another providential and closely related factor. Those university governing boards received unusually sage advice from academic leaders who happened to be in the right place at the right time. One could not overemphasize the happy coincidence that Benno Schmidt was about to chair the CUNY board at the time of the teach-in while Lee Bollinger had just assumed Columbia's presidency when De Genova spoke out. Indeed, the community of First Amendment scholars deserves credit for a third post–September 11 victory. Mark Yudof, renowned along with Schmidt and Bollinger for his writing and teaching on free speech, returned to the University of Texas (as system chancellor) just as a mandatory background check for all new employees was about to take effect. Conceding that some new hires might deserve such scrutiny, Yudof publicly wondered whether "every Chaucer scholar" needed to be vetted in this way. He sharply narrowed the new policy, limiting background checks to senior administrators, people entering security-sensitive posts, mainly those dealing directly with children or patients, and those who handled pharmaceutical and other controlled or dangerous substances.[14]

It would be hard to imagine a more felicitous match of people, positions, and policies than these three incidents in which critical judgments fell to several of the legal world's most eminent champions of free speech and academic freedom. Not only did they, in each case, make the right choice, but they also used the occasion to enlighten their colleagues about the principles of unfettered inquiry that lie at the core of academic freedom.

One could not fairly imply that leaders of comparable stature were missing entirely during the McCarthy era. There is clear evidence that matters would have been far worse at many campuses without the heroic intervention of wise presidents and chancellors. Indiana University's longtime president Herman B Wells, for example, managed to avoid any adverse personnel actions throughout this period—in a state that sent Homer Capehart and William Jenner to the Senate and Harold Velde to the House.

For that matter, notably absent from the casualty list of the 1950s was the premier public institution in McCarthy's home state; the University of Wisconsin escaped the worst under the protective leadership of a wise and independent board of regents and presidents such as E. B. Fred and Conrad Elvejhem. Even where faculty purges did occur, credit should be given to the efforts of leaders such as Harvard president James Bryant Conant and Michigan's law school dean (later academic vice president) Allen Smith, who did the best they could under impossible conditions. Yet when one looks back to the 1950s, there are few antecedents of today's fortunate placement of such strong champions of free inquiry as Schmidt, Bollinger, and Yudof.

It would be tempting to add to this ameliorative mix such diffuse factors as the general political climate. It is true that today's junior senator from Wisconsin, the only member of the upper house to vote against the Patriot Act, is a far cry from his predecessor of a half-century ago. Yet there are enough conflicting differences in the political environments of these two epochs to qualify any such sweeping generalization. There may, however, be a related factor that partially explains the more favorable current environment. In the McCarthy era, the targeted enemies were all on the left—Communists, radicals, fellow travelers, "pinkos," and others so described. From the moment of the September 11 attacks, identifying the enemy has proved elusive—both at the international level and within the United States. So it has been within the academic world.

Recall in this regard the diversity of the first two potentially explosive academic personnel cases. Professor Berthold ("Anyone who can bomb the Pentagon gets my vote") reflected one viewpoint, and Professor Hearlson ("You [Muslims] drove two planes into the World Trade Center") certainly spoke from a very different perspective. The faculty critics at the CUNY teach-in did not represent either side of that debate but were simply disenchanted with U.S. foreign policy—quite as much in Latin America or Asia as in the Middle East. Although more controversy on Middle Eastern issues seems to have been generated by the pro-Palestinian side, it is well to recall that strident efforts to block the Ann Arbor and Chapel Hill conferences came from pro-Israeli groups.

Those who disrupted commencement speakers in Sacramento, Rockford, and Raleigh did not unambiguously reflect any cause or viewpoint and were apparently as much aggrieved about liberal comments about domestic issues (e.g., racial profiling at Sacramento) as about foreign policy. And the lawmakers who tried to bar Hanan Ashrawi from speaking at Colorado campuses surely had no brief for Israel; they simply felt that inviting a controversial Palestinian so soon after September 11 was insensitive, if not downright unpatriotic. Thus we have moved from a time in the 1950s when no scorecard was needed to tell the good guys from the bad guys to a situation where such delineation is uncertain even with the most detailed of scorecards. The greatest perceived threats to our security and national welfare do not come today, as they did a half-century ago, from a single source or even from one side of any given debate. In that sense, the ambiguity of the current situation may represent a vital difference between the 1950s and today and may account for what seems like a somewhat happier state of affairs.

The Courts Embrace Academic Freedom

Among the array of possible reasons that Senator Levin's hopeful view lies closer to the truth, one factor seems compelling: The state of the law that defines and protects academic freedom has improved so markedly in the past half-century that, without considering any other elements in the equation, we would be disposed to share Senator Levin's view that McCarthyism is unlikely to recur in anything like its original form. At the time of the faculty purges in the late 1940s and early 1950s, there really were no legal precedents protective either of academic freedom or of public employee speech. The *Scopes* case had been a disaster for teachers at all levels. And even when the Supreme Court ruled that states could not bar private schools from teaching non-English languages, that ruling rested on general notions of due process rather than on anything resembling academic freedom. Thus if Senator McCarthy had asked Roy Cohn, his chief counsel to the Senate Subversive Activities Committee, for guidance on the state of the law as he embarked on his poisonous quest in 1950, the resulting advice would have given the senator virtually carte blanche.

Fifty years later, the situation is profoundly different. Indeed, only a decade after the McCarthy era began and barely a year after it ended, the legal landscape was changing dramatically. Since the 1960s, a beleaguered or embattled professor has been able to seek refuge or support from many legal doctrines and principles. The change in this branch of the law, as in many others, has been momentous. It is worth tracing several strands of this fabric in our quest for understanding of how things have changed since the McCarthy era.

The first mention of academic freedom in Supreme Court jurisprudence, notes Professor William Van Alstyne, appeared in a dissent by Justices Black and Douglas in 1952.[15] Later that same year, Justice Frankfurter was to add his recognition of academic freedom, concurring on just such grounds with a judgment that (for the first time) invalidated a state loyalty oath, albeit for due process reasons.[16] However, it took five more years for academic freedom to garner the endorsement of a majority of the justices. By 1957, they were ready to hold that a state attorney general had not properly sought to compel testimony by a visiting professor about the content of his lectures—although the majority rested that ruling on narrow and essentially procedural grounds.[17] It was in this 1957 case, however, that Justice Frankfurter expanded greatly upon his earlier recognition of academic freedom, speaking eloquently of "the spirit of free inquiry" and warning of "the grave harm resulting from government intrusion into the intellectual life of a university."[18] Significantly, this momentous ruling coincided closely in time with the Senate's censure of a now politically crippled (and terminally ill) Senator Joseph McCarthy.

After the late 1950s, the evolution of protective principles proceeded along several parallel paths. Reliance on academic freedom as a protected constitutional interest has expanded well beyond academic personnel matters. When in 1978 the Supreme Court validated universities' use of race in the admissions process, deference to academic freedom proved more persuasive to Justice Powell (the key vote) than did diversity, an interest that became more prominent when the high court revisited race-based admissions in the summer of 2003.[19] In other contexts, such as funding for the arts and allocation of student activity fees, the justices have also found in academic freedom a useful desideratum.[20] Thus not only is the doctrine now firmly embedded in the defense of outspoken college professors, but it has also proved useful in other, fairly remote, settings.

Soon after recognizing academic freedom, the Supreme Court began to strike down disclaimer-type loyalty oaths, mostly in cases brought by university professors, relying first on due process but shifting later to freedom of expression. Finally, in 1967, the justices removed any lingering doubt about the power of states to compel such a disavowal of belief or affiliation, by striking down on First Amendment grounds both New York's and Maryland's loyalty oaths.[21]

The central role of academic freedom was beyond question in Justice Brennan's opinion for the Court: "Academic freedom is of transcendent value to all of us and not merely to the teachers concerned. . . . That freedom is therefore a special concern of the First Amendment, which does not tolerate laws that cast a pall of orthodoxy over the classroom."[22] Thereafter, no serious claim could ever again be made that states may require any person—least of all a university professor—to disclaim the very political affiliations and activities that had been at the heart of the McCarthy subcommittee's intrusive questions.

The loyalty oath cases drew heavily on the concurrent evolution of a constitutional doctrine of even broader import. Although there had long been due process limits on states' power to impose onerous conditions on out-of-state companies as the price of doing business in the state, it was not until 1959 that the high court applied the doctrine of "unconstitutional conditions" to individual rights and liberties. This time it was not a college professor but a California veteran who objected to being forced to disavow political ties as the condition of keeping a property tax benefit granted to all persons honorably discharged from the armed forces.

In striking down this requirement as a clear abridgment of the veteran-taxpayer's free speech, the justices made clear that individual rights and liberties were now as fully protected as was corporate migration—and that basically what government could not accomplish directly with the stick, it could not achieve indirectly with the carrot.[23] The continued refinement of unconstitutional conditions and its application to an ever-expanding range of rights and liberties, continued at least until the early 1990s. Since then, the fortunes of this doctrine have varied, although its central premise has not been abandoned.

Academic freedom as a constitutionally protected interest did not, of course, evolve in a vacuum. Its emergence was accompanied by several other complementary developments. Notably, the First Amendment says nothing about the right to associate, affiliate, or belong. It does mention "freedom . . . peaceably to assemble," but that is about as close as the text comes. It was not until 1958, in fact, that the Supreme Court first recognized as necessarily implicit within the First Amendment a right to associate with others for political purposes and, as a corollary, the right not to be forced to divulge an unpopular affiliation.[24]

Initially, that recognition protected organizations such as the NAACP from being compelled to disclose membership lists—the revelation of which would not only jeopardize the individuals whose affiliation thus became public but would also obviously impair the organization's capacity to recruit and retain members. Eventually freedom of association has extended to less obviously political affiliations and to subtler forms of intrusion and restraint. What is striking is that no such liberty could claim constitutional protection until the year after Senator McCarthy ceased to be a serious threat.

Not long after recognizing freedom of association and entertaining loyalty oath challenges, the Supreme Court began to curb a governmental power that was even more central to McCarthyism, by restricting the scope of legislative inquiries into political beliefs and associations. In a series of cases that involved witnesses summoned before both federal and state investigative bodies, the justices reshaped that relationship from the highly skewed dynamic that McCarthy's victims faced.[25] One of the major congressional investigation cases had been argued, and had actually been decided in conference, at the time Justice Brennan (appointed while the Senate was in recess) crossed the street for his confirmation hearing before the Senate Judiciary Committee.[26] McCarthy was still a major force on the committee, even though his power was clearly waning.

Repeatedly McCarthy asked Justice Brennan whether the particular case had been argued, an affirmative answer to which question was clearly a matter of public record. But when the senator pressed the justice to reveal how he had voted, a polite demurrer followed and was patiently repeated as the inquiry lengthened. The justice politely but firmly refused to divulge either the Court's inclination or his own. Eventually a chastened McCarthy gave up, and Brennan was confirmed. The Brennan experience deserves to be cited to anyone who believes that the Bork and Thomas hearings marked the first truly contentious or adversarial nomination proceedings.

Through a series of cases during the 1960s, the Supreme Court enhanced greatly the rights of those called before legislative committees and asked about their political affiliations or those of others. Most notably, a 1963 decision held that an NAACP officer could not be compelled by a Florida legislative committee even to bring membership lists with him to the hearing.[27] In the absence of a "compelling interest" in demanding such information—at which the state had made not even a pretense—such a demand abridged First Amendment rights of the witness and of the organization on whose behalf he appeared. Quite clearly, therefore, any attempt to revive what technically constitutes McCarthyism—the abuse of the congressional investigative power to probe beliefs and associations—would founder at the first badgering of a recalcitrant witness.

Last but surely not least among the beneficiaries of expanded First Amendment jurisprudence has been the speech of public employees. Justice Oliver Wendell Holmes, then still a Massachusetts state court judge, upheld the firing of a Boston policeman named McAuliffe because he had campaigned publicly for a friend. Explained Holmes: "A policeman may have a constitutional right to talk politics, but he has no constitutional right to be a policeman."[28] Three-quarters of a century later, it was not clear that Officer McAuliffe would have fared much better in most courts. But in 1968 the Supreme Court declared that public employee speech, although not as fully protected from agency reprisal as is the speech of citizens from criminal prosecution, enjoyed substantial protection.[29]

Even though a public worker's statements might be inaccurate, speaking out on a matter of public concern would now cause the loss of a government job only if done with actual knowledge that the statements were false or with "reckless disregard" of their truth or falsity. Although this doctrine has gone through many refinements in the past three and a half decades, the central premise that public employee speech deserves substantial First Amendment protection remains intact—and constitutes one of the key ingredients in a radically changed environment. (Whether state college and university professors enjoy greater protection under this doctrine than do custodial and clerical employees at the same institution remains an intriguing issue.)

Although most of the constitutional doctrine that supports a more sanguine view of current prospects has First Amendment roots, there are at least two complementary developments with quite different origins. There is a time-honored maxim that, unlike private parties who may be legally required to continue on a course they voluntarily undertook, "estoppel does not apply to government." Thus, if a public entity changes policy in ways that citizens find more favorable, it is usually free to revert to its former and less benign policy even though the public may to some degree have relied on the improvement.

In the late 1950s and early 1960s, however, a sensitive Supreme Court qualified that doctrine in cases that posed major implications for civil rights and liberties. Thus a congressional investigating committee in the post-McCarthy era had provided under its own rules a hearing opportunity for certain witnesses, even though no constitutional claim of due process would have availed under such conditions. When that hearing option was denied to a particular witness whose case a hostile committee wished to expedite, the Supreme Court ruled that the gratuitous hearing right could be abolished prospectively but could not be denied or diminished in a pending matter.[30] At the core of this judgment was one of the best of Justice Holmes's maxims, "Government must turn square corners."

Turning square corners means that, although government is of course free to alter and even rescind benign policies that are not constitutionally compelled, it may not do so to the detriment of a citizen caught up in a proceeding to which the policy would have applied at the outset. The rules may be changed after the game ends, in other words, but where civil liberties are at stake, they may not so readily be altered while the game is under way. Although this doctrine has been sparingly applied, and even lacks a legal designation (e.g., "unconstitutional conditions"), it remains a crucial element in the legal framework that would surely constrain any attempted revival of McCarthyism.

Finally, one nonconstitutional safeguard deserves recognition. Until the mid 1960s, government had essentially unfettered power to decide what information it wished to disclose or conceal. Public bodies and agencies could also control with few limits the access of the public and the press to most proceedings, hearings, trials, and the like. Not until 1980 did the Supreme Court first recognize a constitutional right of the public to attend criminal trials—a right that of course included the news media as members of the public. By that time, however, the federal government and virtually all states had passed freedom of information laws that opened the doors and the files of most government records and proceedings. Although such laws are riddled with exceptions—for personnel matters, legally privileged communications, land transactions, and many other sensitive topics—they do create a presumption of openness and access that simply did not exist until well after the end of the McCarthy era.

Although the national response to the events of September 11 has closed many doors and files and has created secrecy where transparency prevailed in less troubled times, the continuing force of the Freedom of Information Act as a safeguard of an informed citizenry is even now a major element in the post-McCarthy legal environment. Whatever administrative resistance may greet those in the public and the news media who seek access to sensitive information and proceedings, repeal or renunciation of freedom of information policies seems most unlikely—on grounds that are probably more political than principled.

Beyond September 11

I return to the issue with which I began: Was Senator Levin justified in his premise that McCarthyism remains a grim specter of the past? Or was Senator Feingold, sole Senate opponent of the Patriot Act, on sounder ground in offering a darker prognosis? Most of our experience in the more than two years since September 11 suggests a preference for Levin's more benign view—especially because those who might have wished to blame the academy and the professoriat for some of the world's current ills have not been reticent in these tense times.

For a variety of reasons, not least our dimming but still painful memories of the McCarthy era, the prospect of a recurrence seems remote. Apart from the abiding lessons of history, we now have in place a quite elaborate and complex set of constitutional safeguards for academic freedom, free inquiry, and due process that are not likely to be displaced or undermined, even by a Supreme Court that might well not have created such safeguards as an original matter. Whether the issue is a criminal suspect's *Miranda* rights, or *Roe v. Wade*'s recognition of a woman's right of choice, the doctrine of stare decisis accords great durability, if not permanence, to principles often at variance with the dominant views of the current Supreme Court justices. Thus as we look ahead through an undoubtedly difficult and perilous time, there are some vital sources of promise.

CHAPTER 4

Political Mobilization and Resistance to Censorship

Donald A. Downs

THE ATTACKS OF September 11, 2001, dramatically changed American life. For the first time in memory, national security was seriously endangered and new governmental measures to protect the country on the home front were called for. The need for new security measures has revived the old question about the proper trade-off between liberty and security. On the one hand, we need the government to protect us from a historically unprecedented threat: terrorist acts that could include the use of weapons of mass destruction that have fallen into the hands of nonstate actors who cannot be deterred by traditional policies premised on rational self-interest. On the other hand, many citizens fear that the expansion of government power and the rise of patriotic pressures threaten civil liberties. Once again, the nation confronts the classic constitutional dilemma that James Madison articulated under different circumstances in the *Federalist Papers*: The first "difficulty" in framing a government is to "enable the government to control the governed" (or, in our present dilemma, to control would-be terrorists). The second difficulty is "to oblige it to control itself."[1]

Critics of governmental policies and pressures to be patriotic recall how the United States has dealt with civil liberties in some past eras riveted by national security crises. They point to such governmental actions as the imprisonment of thousands of antiwar protesters during World War I, the internment of Japanese Americans during World War II without any consideration of due process, and the hysteria associated with the McCarthy era.[2] And these periods also witnessed unprincipled attacks on academic freedom in institutions of higher education.[3]

A Chance to Find Common Ground
on Academic Freedom

One of the most important questions of our time is whether a similar threat to academic freedom grips our own post–September 11 era. Emphasizing the pro–free speech and civil liberty legal environment that has arisen in the decades since McCarthy's decline, Robert O'Neil's essay in this volume (Chapter 3) presents a plausible case that universities are doing a pretty good job of protecting academic freedom against claims of national security and patriotism. But O'Neil does not address the repression of politically incorrect thought and speech in higher education that has been taking place over the course of the last fifteen to eighteen years. (This omission is surprising, given that O'Neil has long been a leading critic of speech codes and related policies, progressive censorship's most important weapons in the contemporary campus wars.) O'Neil is correct that institutions of higher learning are doing a better job than in the past of protecting academic freedom from attacks in the name of national security. This state of affairs is to be celebrated. But it does not mean that the quite different type of censorship does not continue to harm higher education.

If I am right, higher education has missed a chance to correct its ways. Exposure to the new threats to academic freedom and free speech stemming from the war on terror could have presented universities and colleges with an opportunity to reconsider the legitimacy of any form of censorship, whether it emanates from the left or from the right. This assessment reflects a classic fact about the politics of censorship and rights: Individuals and groups tend to be most concerned about censorship when their own rights are in jeopardy—that is, when their own ox is being gored. With the rise of the war on terror, the threats to academic freedom that were already being exerted inside universities from the left were joined by new threats to academic freedom, this time wielded by outside forces on the right. (The right was less alarmed by censorship during the McCarthy era than the left because it was not the target of repression; these postures were reversed in the 1990s, as censorship changed direction and content.) With the academic freedom of both sides now under attack, an opportunity existed for each side to see beyond its own interests and to establish a common ground in support of intellectual freedom.

An example of precisely this type of process and logic recently took place at the national level. Consider the fate of the independent counsel law at the end of the 1990s. For two decades the law allowed the attorney general to call for a special, independent prosecutor to investigate executive branch officials suspected of breaking the law. In theory, the new position was designed to ameliorate concerns about the executive branch investigating itself, which would constitute a conflict of interest. In practice, however, the position often became a way, in effect, to criminalize political or policy differences. Regardless, Democrats supported the law in the 1980s when it was applied against Republicans, who controlled the White House; for their part, Republicans opposed the law as unjust and biased. But Republicans changed their tune during the various scandals surrounding President Clinton during the 1990s, when the roles of the parties were reversed. After the dust of the Clinton scandals settled, however, both parties realized the law's potential to harm each one equally and mutually agreed to let it die a merciful death.[4]

There are two ways to envision this type of move toward common ground. The first way is simply as a matter of mutual self-interest: Each individual agrees to respect the basic rights of others in order to ensure that his or her rights will also be respected.[5] Borrowing a term from political scientist Theodore Lowi (who uses the term pejoratively), we could call this model the model of *interest group liberalism*. In interest group liberalism, policy is produced not by some conception of the public interest but rather because of interest group pressure.[6] The second model embodies something more substantive or principled than this sort of self-interested agreement. It recognizes that the equal protection of such basic rights as academic freedom and free speech is essential to basic justice and the flourishing of free societies. Protecting rights equally is an end that should be pursued for its own sake. I call this the *citizenship* model. In the field of free speech, the citizenship model has had many champions, including such thinkers as Alexander Meiklejohn, Louis Brandeis, and John Stuart Mill.[7]

In truth, such cardinal rights as free speech, freedom of conscience, and due process are inherently universal in nature; they are important to all individuals regardless of the content of their beliefs. Universal rights have two dimensions: deontological and consequentialist. In a deontological sense, possessing rights is an inherent aspect of justice and human nature; rights are morally meaningless unless they apply to all citizens equally. (As free speech champion Alan Kors has written, "Liberty of opinion, speech, and expression is indispensable to a free and, in the deepest sense, progressive society. Deny it to one, and you deny it to all.")[8] The consequentialist aspect of rights speaks to the way in which honoring equal rights promotes such goods as the pursuit of truth, self-determination, and social progress. The universalism of rights is necessary to both justice and a good society.[9]

Universities are prime examples of the importance of universalism. Their primary mission is the pursuit of truth, which is furthered by respecting the freedom of speech and inquiry of all faculty and students, regardless of their political orientation. As Jonathan Rauch has remarked, universities' "moral charter is first and foremost to advance human knowledge." Consequently, "If governments stifle criticism, then they impoverish their citizenry; if universities do so, then they have no reason to exist."[10]

The citizenship model is preferable to the interest group liberalism model for universities, because it represents common commitment to the intellectual freedoms that are the sine qua non of higher education. But we should not sell the interest group liberalism model short, for its basic features are characteristic of the history and politics of rights. Practical conceptions of rights and civil liberty are often forged out of the cauldron of politics and adversity. In *The American Language of Rights*, Richard Primus links the discourse and law of rights in U.S. history to political rhetoric and practice. The discourse of rights is, among other things, a discursive device used to help political actors frame and justify underlying political and normative objectives, and to respond to what they perceive as violations of their right to equal respect. Primus writes, "The major pattern of development in American rights discourse has been one of concrete negation: innovations in conceptions of rights have chiefly occurred in opposition to new adversities, as people articulate new rights that would, if accepted, negate the crisis at hand."[11]

Accordingly, personal experience is important to the appreciation and conceptualization of rights. Along these lines, civil liberties attorney James Weinstein claims that there is no substitute for experience when it comes to fully fathoming the First Amendment implications of policies and actions. Courts have fashioned the modern doctrine of speech (as epitomized by the reigning content and viewpoint neutrality doctrines) in reaction to historical conflicts and claims. "Free speech doctrine is more a product of experience than theory," Weinstein maintains.[12] A historical example is John Dewey and his allies, who did not fully appreciate the importance of free speech to democratic self-governance until they were exposed to the widespread unprincipled suppression of dissent during World War I.[13]

The experience of having to defend one's rights against pressure can prompt one to consider the broader implications and applications of rights claims. Tocqueville envisioned a somewhat similar process in *Democracy in America* in his discussion of "self-interest rightly understood." This attitude entails a balance between self-interest and empathy for the rights of others based on a reflection of the links between one's self-interest and the plights of others.[14] American constitutionalism is, in part, premised on this principle of mutually reinforcing self-interest. For example, checks and balances and other restraints on power are designed to further the protection of minority rights and to weaken the power of moral or political consensus, which is inherently predisposed to repress the rights of those who dissent from whatever orthodoxy happens to reign.[15]

Thus both interest group liberalism and the citizenship model are germane in their own distinct ways to the move toward the universalism of rights. In the rest of this essay, I want to look at some suggestive evidence (admittedly anecdotal) concerning the status of academic freedom on campus in the United States after September 11. To what extent has higher education made the move toward equal protection and universalism? And which model is most relevant to the tentative conclusions that we can reach in this exploratory paper? Let me begin this inquiry by looking at the rise of the type of "progressive" censorship and by discussing why it is harmful to the idea of a university.

Rights on Paper, Rights in Practice:
The Rise of Progressive Censorship

Rights have two lives. There are the rights that exist on paper and the rights that exist in actuality or in practice. In a similar vein, it is one thing to have a right declared by a court and another to have this right respected by those who have power over others. One branch of political science is replete with literature on the gap between what constitutional courts hold and what authorities and citizens actually do.[16] A number of reasons help to explain such gaps. For example, classic civil liberty attitudinal research teaches us that there is generally more support for rights in the abstract than in individual cases.[17] Everyone loves free speech, but not always the free speech of those who fall too far outside the mainstream. In Nat Hentoff's words, it is a matter of "free speech for me, but not for thee."[18] And, as Alexis de Tocqueville portrayed so hauntingly in *Democracy in America*, Americans love liberty at the same time that they are prone to the "tyranny of the majority."[19]

Tocqueville delineated several "remedies" to the soft despotism posed by tyranny of the majority, one of the most important of which is the nurturing of such "free institutions" as local government, private associations, rule of law, and a free press.[20] Institutions of higher learning perform a similar political and normative function. Universities have a fiduciary obligation to promote respect for dissenting thought and freedom of inquiry and to instill the intellectual skills that foster critical, independent thinking.[21] Yet history has shown that universities and colleges have not always lived up to this responsibility.

The question of the post–September 11 status of intellectual freedom is interesting because, as already mentioned, a different kind of threat to free speech, academic freedom, and civil liberty had already gained a foothold in higher education during the late 1980s and the 1990s. This challenge came about when censorship became a tool for promoting progressive and egalitarian goals on campus (what is now known, in the spirit of the philosopher Herbert Marcuse, as "progressive censorship," or censorship designed to promote social justice).[22] The most important reforms included speech codes, broad antiharassment codes, orientation programs dedicated to promoting an ideology of sensitivity, and new procedures and pressures in the adjudication of student and faculty misconduct. Although these measures were laudably intended to foster civility, tolerance, and respect for racial and cultural diversity, they too often had illiberal consequences. Rather than improving the campus climate, the new policies often provided tools for moral bullies to enforce an ideological orthodoxy that undermines the intellectual freedom and intellectual diversity that are the hallmarks of great universities. Many books have chronicled the extent of this problem, most notably *The Shadow University: The Betrayal of Liberty on America's Campuses*, by Alan Charles Kors and Harvey A. Silverglate. I also have a book, *Restoring Free Speech and Liberty on Campus*, that deals with these issues from the perspective of political mobilization and resistance.[23]

Several infringements of basic rights took place on my own campus during the 1990s (soon after the university adopted student and faculty speech codes), events that led me to join in organizing the Committee for Academic Freedom and Rights, an independent, nonpartisan academic freedom and civil liberty group at the University of Wisconsin, Madison. What happened at Wisconsin was typical of many other schools. For example, an anonymous e-mail sent by a senior-level judi-

cial administrator at a "top ten institution" in July 2001 to Thor Halvorssen, chief executive director of the Foundation for Individual Rights in
Education (FIRE)—a leading academic freedom organization in the
United States today that was established to promote the principles es-
poused in *The Shadow University*—suggests the considerable extent of
the problem in the realm of due process and adjudication:

Mr. Halvorssen,
   I spoke with you last week for a while before I got cut off (I was on a pay
phone). I am a senior level administrator and director of judicial affairs at a top
10 institution, and have information that I would like to share with you. Believe
me, FIRE has barely scratched the surface regarding university/college judicial
affairs, and while reading the testimonials on your website is interesting, I notice that none are from professionals in the field. I believe that information from
someone in the field would add greater legitimacy to your good work. Obviously, I don't want to lose my job, but after many years in the field, I believe the
public needs to know what really goes on, from a perspective you rarely, if ever,
hear from. Can you suggest a next step?[24]

One indicative example of universities' commitment to progressive
censorship and related policies is their reaction in the 1990s to actual
court decisions that attempted to circumscribe speech codes. Federal
courts struck down the student speech codes at Michigan and Wisconsin, and a state court invalidated Stanford's code.[25] And in 1992, the
United States Supreme Court issued a decision that many thought
would sound the death knell of speech codes, *R.A.V. v. St. Paul*, which
declared St. Paul's hate speech ordinance unconstitutional for being
viewpoint based.[26] Most new college codes resembled the ordinance
in *R.A.V.*

Perhaps surprisingly, *R.A.V.* had little impact on universities' treat-
ments of speech codes. As Jon B. Gould shows in an innovative and
thorough empirical study, the number of speech codes actually *increased*
after *R.A.V.* Gould attributes this reaction to several factors, including
ideological commitment and institutional political pressures.[27] In fact,
Gould probably understates the extent of the resistance to anticensor-
ship court rulings, because he does not deal with institutions' increasing use of harassment codes to limit or investigate free speech. Originally, such measures were not intended to be used as expansive speech
codes but rather to prohibit such clearly unacceptable conduct as quid
quo pro sexual harassment, repeated unwanted sexual advances, and
environments laden with sexual expression and prurient appeal. Over
time, however, many administrative authorities began to apply harass-

ment codes much more broadly, making such codes the most important source of censorship on campus.[28] In one recent case, an ill-fated "civility" policy at Edinboro University in Erie, Pennsylvania, maintained that criticizing someone's political views could constitute prohibited harassment. Similarly, the University of Massachusetts code prohibited, among a long list of offenses, demeaning someone's "political belief or affiliation."[29] By the end of the 1990s, the spirit of progressive censorship was alive and well, regardless of what the law said.

A final example of "progressive" policies that point to thought control is the recent rise of "social dispositions" requirements. Under the sway of these policies, students or faculty members will graduate or be promoted only if they demonstrate the proper attitudes toward "social justice." Education programs at Brooklyn College and Washington State University have adopted these policies as certification requirements, to name just two examples. In the fall of 2005, the program at Brooklyn College accused K. C. Johnson, a prominent historian, of violating academic freedom simply because he wrote an essay in a national forum that criticized the "social justice" policy at that institution. Johnson was informed of the charges and asked to respond. Brooklyn College dropped the investigation only after FIRE exerted national pressure on the school. And recently the University of Oregon considered making the "correct" attitudes toward cultural differences a requirement for tenure and promotion for faculty. Such programs invariably define "social justice" in a narrow ideological way.[30]

The Return of Classic Censorship: An Occasion for Free Speech Universalism?

With the advent of September 11, a more familiar, traditional challenge to academic freedom returned. After all, the era of speech codes and progressive censorship represented something relatively new under the sun. The main periods in which attacks on academic freedom were unleashed include the suppression of religious dissidents before the late nineteenth century, charges against progressive professors during the Gilded Age, crackdowns against leftists and antiwar activists during and after World War I, and the multitudinous suppressions of the McCarthy era.[31] Two factors stood out in these previous disputes that distinguish them from the recent era of progressive censorship: (1) The attacks came from the right, and (2) they came largely from *outside* institutions of higher education. The threats posed by speech codes reversed this state of affairs; they stemmed largely from the left and, as often as not, from *inside* the university itself, where, according to studies, the left is disproportionately represented.[32]

Post–September 11 free speech cases involve both traditional and progressive forms of censorship. As Robert O'Neil relates in Chapter 3, there is evidence that institutions of higher learning have done a fairly good job of protecting freedom of inquiry and speech from attacks by governmental and social forces motivated by national security and patriotism concerns. O'Neil's example of Drake University's successful resistance against a federal grand jury subpoena demanding information about antiwar protesters is an illustrative example.[33] In fact, there is also some anecdotal evidence that progressive censorship is starting to retreat (however haltingly) in the face of mobilizations by a new generation of free speech and civil liberty activists at the local and national levels who have exerted internal and external pressure on administrations. These movements were already in full swing before September 2001. At this point in time, these movements appear to represent the model of interest group liberalism rather than the model of campus citizenship. There is little evidence that institutions of higher education have turned a corner in any systematic way; but some of the institutions that have been exposed to political pressure by activists have begun to change their ways.

The Post–September 11 Era: Has the Pendulum Swung?

Well-known legal scholar Kermit Hall recently proclaimed that the era of political correctness is "pretty much dead."[34] This claim is no doubt quite overstated, as several conflicts dealing with progressive censorship are still being waged. I cite only a couple of examples for reasons of space. The best source of information about recent cases of both progressive and traditional forms of censorship on campus is the website for the Foundation for Individual Rights in Education (FIRE).[35]

One indicative example is the case of a student at California Polytechnic Institute, who was charged in 2003 with "disruption" for simply placing a poster, on a bulletin board next to the multicultural center, that advertised a talk by a conservative black speaker. The talk was based on the speaker's book, which criticized welfare policy for perpetrating a "plantation" mentality in both whites and blacks. Students opposed to the speech complained to the administration that the posting constituted actual harassment. (One of the tenets of progressive censors is the claim that politically incorrect speech actually constitutes an act of discrimination. Speech and action are not fundamentally distinct in the minds of the new censors.)[36] The administration then subjected the student to a Kafkaesque set of hearings. At one point a key administrator told the student that he should have been aware of how his reputation for conservatism made his actions even more harassing in nature. The university dragged the case on for several months, dropping it only after being exposed to intense pressure exerted by such outside groups as FIRE, the American Civil Liberties Union (ACLU), and the Center for Individual Rights (CIR).[37]

Another example of continued progressive censorship is the denial of official campus recognition to several conservative Christian groups on the grounds that their beliefs and membership policies are discriminatory. A recent FIRE hornbook on the freedom of religion on campus exposes a number of such cases, as does David Bernstein in a new book on the status of free speech and associational rights on campus and elsewhere.[38] In a recent case in point, in December 2003, the president of Gonzaga Law School banned a Christian pro-life group because it restricted its membership to those who shared its beliefs—a sine qua non of the right of association.[39]

In addition, some of the cases that arise under the umbrella of post–September 11 censorship also fit the preexisting model of progressive censorship. Consider the case of a professor at Orange Coast Community College a few weeks after September 11. Several Muslim students accused the professor of calling them "terrorists" and "Nazis" when he complained about Muslims being silent about such things as the suicide bombings against Israel. Although he was vindicated in the end, the administration placed the professor on administrative leave without a hearing and sanctioned him with a reprimand.[40] There is also the case of Zewdalem Kebede, the Ethiopian student at San Diego State University who overheard some Saudi Arabian students laughing in Arabic about what happened in New York and Washington on September 11. Kebede challenged them and asked them why they did not "feel shame." A heated exchange ensued, and campus police had to order the students to disperse. In what appears to be a parody of the spirit of progressive censorship, the campus Center for Student Rights wrote Kebede a letter accusing *him* of engaging in "verbally abusive behavior to other students." Eventually, the case was dropped, but only after

Kebede was criticized in public and authorities had placed a warning letter in his file.[41] There are also cases in which institutions of higher learning cracked down on individuals who displayed patriotic symbols, flags, or statements after September 11. These cases and others suggest that Kermit Hall's statement about the demise of political correctness is either wrong or premature.

But there are some encouraging signs that free speech is making a kind of comeback in this domain on campus. Two reasons could be responsible for this turn. First, threats posed by the war on terror could be compelling universities to be more appreciative of free speech as a universal right. Second—and more plausibly—progressive censorship has been thrown on the defensive over the course of the last few years from another source. In a recent column in *U.S. News and World Report*, the arch-critic of progressive censorship, John Leo, wrote, "campus censors" are "in retreat."[42] He cites some of the cases mentioned here but points out how campus administrators are now recoiling in the face of the legal and political pressures being exerted by such advocacy groups as FIRE, the Center for Individual Rights, the Alliance Defense Fund, and the American Civil Liberties Union.

Leo's emphasis points to the second reason for a possible pendulum swing: the intensification of political and legal mobilization by civil liberty and free speech activists who have forced some institutions of higher learning to defend their policies in light of public scrutiny—a domain where double standards are harder to defend than behind the closed doors of academe. As seen, institutions of higher learning largely ignored the signals that the U.S. Supreme Court sent in *R.A.V. v. St. Paul* in 1992.[43] A major reason for this state of affairs was the lack of organized mobilization on campuses to compel these institutions to respond in a proactive way to this decision. Meaningful legal change often requires sufficient political mobilization to compel change in actual social practice.[44] As Timothy Shiell stresses in his thorough book on speech codes, the absence of organized opposition was partly responsible for the rise of speech codes in the first place at the schools that pioneered the speech code movement, such as Yale, Michigan, Stanford, and Wisconsin.[45]

Two types of mobilization have been most effective. First, FIRE, the CIR, the ACLU, and other groups have created pressure at the national level by deploying publicity and political action and by bringing legal challenges by attorneys associated with these groups. FIRE, in particular, has waged powerful attacks in a large number of cases.[46] As Leo points out, this pressure is having some impact. For example, the guidelines accompanying the new "civility" code at Edinboro University declared that simply offending someone for almost any reason constituted "harassment." A faculty member trained in First Amendment principles informed his department chair that the code was seriously overbroad, and the sympathetic chair then conveyed the colleague's points to the university's office dealing with harassment and discrimination. With the help of these insights, the officer recognized the problem and changed the policy to make it consistent with free speech. In thanking the individuals who enlightened her, the officer told my source that she was grateful because "we would have been sued, especially after what FIRE has done over at Shippensburg."[47] (In September 2003, a federal court ordered Shippensburg University to stop enforcing its speech code, which was drastically overbroad. The case was among the first in FIRE's "Declaration of War on Speech Codes.")[48] The victories for free speech being won by these groups shows the importance of creating an infrastructure of legal mobilization in the actualization of rights.[49]

The second domain of action is less well known but also effective: local campus mobilization. This type of mobilization took place at the University of Pennsylvania in the 1990s, sparked by the notorious case in which a student was subjected to Kafkaesque formal proceedings for calling some African American students "water buffaloes," a term that had no racial meaning. Alan Kors leveraged this case to create a resistance movement that led to the president's abolition of the code and far-reaching libertarian reform at Penn.[50]

Another example is the University of Wisconsin, at one time a pioneer in the pro–speech code movement. There, a privately funded, nonpartisan group called the Committee for Academic Freedom and Rights (CAFR) and its student allies have spearheaded a free speech and civil liberty movement that has won several important battles.[51] In fact, CAFR served as the model for FIRE after FIRE's co-founder, Harvey Silverglate, witnessed the key role that CAFR played in the process that led to Wisconsin's abolition of its faculty speech code by a vote of the faculty senate in March 1999. CAFR has provided legal assistance to several faculty and staff members and students who have come under questionable investigations and sanctions; and it has led the way on many political fronts, including the following: leading the drive to abolish the faculty speech code in the classroom in 1999 (Wisconsin remains the only case of a code being abolished at the hands of a political movement on campus); organizing the opposition that led to the dismantling of a comprehensive system of anonymous complaint boxes in 2000, a system replete with unavoidably Orwellian implications; initiating due process reform in the university rules governing the disciplining of faculty members; providing support for groups whose free speech has come under attack, often the student newspapers; and pressuring departments into modifying their own internal speech codes based on the concept of "professional conduct standards."[52]

The Wisconsin initiative had to be accomplished politically because the Wisconsin branch of the ACLU would not take the code to court. Although this decision upset opponents of the faculty code at first, it proved to be a blessing in disguise because it necessitated building a political mobilization organization that has proved to be an invaluable resource in recent years. Most commentators believe that a corner has been turned at Wisconsin in terms of free speech and civil liberty, because the norms of free speech now enjoy widespread public presence on the campus (backed by mobilization power).[53] Because the Wisconsin movement has led to actual pro–free speech and academic freedom votes in the faculty senate, it is fair to say that the Wisconsin mobilization comes close to the citizenship model of free speech and academic freedom, for a large number of campus citizens now accept academic freedom as a bedrock principle of the institution. In winning the speech code battle and other cases, the Wisconsin movement has often publicly drawn on the tradition of academic freedom that is such an important part of the university's heritage.[54]

Universities and the War on Terror

In discussing the reaction to the war on terror, I rely on an extensive study of the American Association of University Professors (AAUP), titled "Academic Freedom and National Security in a Time of Crisis," and reports in the press and on FIRE's web page.[55] I also refer the reader to the essay by Robert M. O'Neil in this volume (Chapter 3), which covers these cases in more depth. I do not have the space to discuss the full range of reported cases or the broader aspects of the new powers that the government has amassed in the war on terror, particularly those pertaining to the USA PATRIOT Act. But I should stress that the new laws involve significantly expanding surveillance and searches of libraries and other campus programs, extensive record keeping and background checks on students and university workers in sensitive areas, and gag orders against disclosing government inquiries and surveillance to third parties, including the targets. Whatever one's position on the balance between liberty and security in the post–September 11 world, there is reason to be guarded and vigilant about the potential abuse of government power.[56]

Although the AAUP report provides grounds for guarded optimism on the academic freedom front, it does cite several examples of chilling effect on academic freedom related to the war on terror. According to the report, several universities have expanded background criminal checks on new faculty members.[57] In addition, some schools have issued broad warnings to their faculties about talking about the war in Iraq unless "directly relevant" to the class. Although it is not improper to require faculty members to stick to relevant material in class, at least one such warning (at Irvine Valley College in California) amounted to a prior restraint on such expression across the board.[58] In another notorious case, a writing instructor at Forsyth Technical Community College lost her job for criticizing the war in Iraq in March 2003, even though the war was the subject of the writing assignment that day.[59]

Conflicts over curricula and speakers have also been reported on a number of campuses. In the summer of 2002, a University of North Carolina professor in charge of the summer reading program for incoming students required them to read Michael A. Sells's *Approaching the Qur'an: The Early Revelations*. A private group brought a lawsuit against the program, which a federal court dismissed, and the state legislature later dropped an "equal time" provision after a pitted battle. As the AAUP reported, "Chapel Hill and University of North Carolina officials stood their ground."[60] Later, the administration at North Carolina stood firm in the face of protests against "Islamic Awareness Week." Similarly, the University of Michigan administration resisted vehement calls to cancel a conference on the Middle East that included some controversial speakers. But the State University of New York at New Paltz succumbed to pressure and canceled a panel discussion that outside groups considered "unbalanced in its criticism of Israel." A similar result took place at Rutgers University, when the administration yielded to claims by pro-Israeli groups and state politicians and refused to host the "Third National Student Conference on the Palestinian Solidarity Movement."[61]

Visiting speakers and scholars have also encountered some major problems in the post–September 11 context. In late 2002, the University of Colorado and Colorado College stood up to pressure and allowed a pro-Palestinian speaker to come to campus; around the same time, Harvard University ultimately resisted pressure to disinvite Irish poet Tom Paulin, who had written that "Brooklyn-born Jews" who resettled on the West Bank should be "shot dead." The College of Holy Cross, however, revoked an invitation to a prominent British clergyman when faculty members opposed his visit on the grounds that he was an anti-Semite.[62] Many visiting scholars have also had a hard time getting into the United States. (This, of course, is not the decision of universities, so it is not directly relevant to the concerns of this chapter. See Chapters 6, 7, and 8 for more discussion of this topic.)

An important set of cases involves faculty free expression. Such private groups as Campus Watch and the American Council for Trustees and Alumni have begun monitoring classes and denouncing faculty whose views they consider unpatriotic. This is their right. But such action can contribute to making the climate hostile to free speech, so it needs to be critically evaluated. And some institutions of higher learning have jeopardized academic freedom by the way they have responded to public pressure exerted against faculty members who have made intemperate statements after the September 11 attacks. O'Neil and the AAUP report cite several such cases, which have typically entailed statements by faculty blaming the United States for the attacks, or denouncing the United States as the real villain in the world. Despite strong pressure from trustees and the public, I know of no case, other than the Forsyth case discussed earlier, in which a faculty member has lost his or her job for simply expressing an unpopular viewpoint; but some faculty have received reprimands, which do represent formal sanctions. And one case involving alleged association with terrorists led to dismissal.

Two clear victories for academic freedom are discussed by O'Neil: the case of Nicholas De Genova at Columbia University, who called for "a million Mogadishus" during the war against Iraq in 2003; and the case at the City University of New York, in which several faculty members made similar statements. Despite intense outside pressure to fire or seriously sanction the speakers for decidedly unpatriotic speech, campus leaders stood up and openly supported the dissidents' free speech rights. In the latter case, Benno Schmidt, vice chair of the board of trustees, spoke eloquently that "the freedom to challenge and to speak one's mind [is] the matrix, the indispensable condition of any university worth the name."[63] In the end, the board dropped the matter. During the 1990s, Schmidt gained a national reputation as probably the nation's leading administrative champion of free speech in the face of the challenges posed by speech codes and similar policies. (Among other positions, he served as president of Yale.) His stance in the City University case shows that he is not selective in applying his principles.[64]

The one case the AAUP calls "grave" is the Sami Al-Arian case at the University of South Florida, also discussed by O'Neil (see Chapter 3). Al-Arian was arrested in February 2003 for providing material support for terrorism. Although dismissal would certainly be merited if such claims were substantiated or had a sufficient basis in evidence, the administration decided to dismiss Al-Arian well before such evidence became known because of the public furor that had arisen surrounding the case. (The furor was triggered by a campaign conducted by Bill O'Reilly on *The O'Reilly Factor* television show.) Both the AAUP and FIRE have opposed the university's actions in this case.[65]

Those who maintain that the faculty in these cases should be immune to criticism misunderstand the concept of the marketplace of ideas. Taking verbal heat for making controversial statements is itself an indispensable part of the very matrix of free speech. It is part of the give and take of debate.[66] But free speech principles dictate that no one should be sanctioned for saying controversial things in appropriate forums and that institutions with which such speakers are associated should make it clear, as Schmidt did, that such rights will be protected.

An Occasion to Affirm Universalism

Although the record is less than sterling, the AAUP report on the status of academic freedom in relation to the war on terrorism concludes that universities today appear to be doing a better job of protecting controversial faculty and speakers than they did during previous eras in which national security fears were paramount, such as the McCarthy era and the Red Scare following World War I. "Incidents involving outspoken faculty members have been fewer than one might have expected in the aftermath of so momentous an event as September 11. Moreover, with few exceptions—at least one of them grave—the responses by college and university administrators to the events that have occurred have been reassuringly temperate."[67]

Whether institutions of higher education have turned a corner regarding respect for equal protection and the universality of free speech and civil liberty remains to be seen. More rigorous empirical work is needed to answer this question with any confidence. What the present evidence does suggest is that O'Neil is right: Institutions of higher learning are protecting antiwar free speech and liberty more than in previous eras in which concerns about national security were high. One reason could be that universities are more likely to "circle the wagons" in defense of academic freedom and free speech when the threat is from the right and from outside the institution. When calls for censorship emanate from sources other than those beholden to political correctness, institutions of higher learning do not fail to recognize the threat that impends.

Another possible reason for this posture is more historical. O'Neil writes about the development and entrenchment of free speech and liberty principles in constitutional law. This is important. But broader political and legal forces are at least equally important. Free speech norms are now widely supported by various forms of organized and mobilized power, such as library associations, First Amendment law firms, broadcasters and publishers, constitutional law doctrine, free speech interest groups and advocates, and even universities (depending on the cause), to name just a few. Key to this development is the rise of advocacy groups who have mobilized to pressure courts and the government to enact policies favorable to the protection and promotion of rights. According to Charles Epp, a leading scholar on the politics of the rights revolution, this movement has involved "a support structure for legal mobilization, consisting of rights-advocacy organizations, rights-advocacy lawyers, and sources of financing, particularly government-supported financing."[68] In a similar vein, Richard S. Randall has written about the rise of the "free speech society" in which norms supporting free speech have permeated society.[69] If so, institutions of higher education enjoy societal support in resisting calls for censorship and the punishment of anti-American discourse. (Higher education's hypocrisy in this regard should not be ignored.) As O'Neil points out, even though he was outraged at De Genova's unpatriotic speech at Columbia University, Fox News's Bill O'Reilly ultimately bowed before the gods of free speech in his show dealing with that incident.

At the end of the day, however, we are left with a powerful exception to the norms of the "free speech society": universities practicing progressive censorship. In the era of progressive censorship, universities have been busy repressing speech that enjoys widespread protection in the real world. In a recent article in which he criticized universities' intolerance of speech deemed politically incorrect, Jonathan Yardley of the *Washington Post* commented, "The American college campus is a foreign country; they do things differently there."[70] Although the war on terror might be reminding educational leaders of the importance of free speech universalism once again, the evidence still supports the view that universities' support for free speech and academic freedom remains selective—except when pro-academic freedom groups mobilize to resist affronts to academic freedom motivated by progressive censorship.

In my view, the revival of academic freedom and free speech as universal community principles would be an occasion, in Alexander Meiklejohn's words, for dancing in the streets.[71] The politicization of speech policy launched by progressive censorship has not served institutions of higher learning or the United States well. The mobilization of such groups as FIRE, the CIR, and CAFR on behalf of free speech and academic freedom is a promising start. Promotion of these principles based on the practice of interest group liberalism is better than letting them dangle in the wind. But the time has arisen for taking the next step, which is the true renewal of academic freedom, free inquiry, and free speech as the bedrock principles of higher education. What is needed is the political and moral will to take the next step in the process.

CHAPTER 5

Censoring Science: Lesson from the Past for the Post-9/11 Era

M. Susan Lindee

AT A 1949 MIT SYMPOSIUM on the social implications of scientific progress, the physicist Lee A. DuBridge spoke of academic freedom with a vague discomfort. His comments reflected the emerging tensions of an intense period of the cold war, as he observed that "an enlightened government will always encourage the search for truth and the teaching of truth." Unfortunately, DuBridge noted, there were two difficulties. First, one cannot always count on having an enlightened government, and, second, it is not always crystal clear just what is true. "That dictatorial governments do arise, and that their first line of action is the suppression of free speech, free thought and free education is a fact which needs no argument in the year 1949."

He was referring of course to Hitler, Stalin, and Mussolini, but he also suggested that "we might not have to wait for a dictatorship in this country."[1] A prominent government scientist had recently been publicly attacked by the House Committee on Un-American Activities, and DuBridge wondered, "What would be happening today if all the professors of all our colleges and universities of this country were paid in whole or in part by Federal tax money. What a witch hunt might be in progress right now. Academic freedom is not something which is destroyed only by concentration camps and firing lines. It can be withered to a shadow merely by the threat of economic insecurity, of unearned disgrace, of unsupported public attacks."[2]

The witch hunt DuBridge hypothesized was of course already in process; the scientist he referred to obliquely, without mentioning him, was Edward Condon, a physicist at the National Bureau of Standards whose sustained and unjustified persecution became something of a cause célèbre in the scientific community. Cold war threats to the academic freedom of scientists were both real and substantial. In 1949 they might have looked tentative and potentially troubling. By 1953 they had produced a crisis of tragic dimensions for the scientific community. And today threats to academic freedom and scientific integrity continue from more than one direction. University ties to private industry shape tenure decisions; many believe that the Bush administration chooses scientific appointees based on their sympathy to administration positions; and the "war on terror" justifies new kinds of scientific witch hunts, as in the case of Thomas Butler. In the post-9/11 world, scientists face new challenges and new threats to academic freedom.

In this chapter I explore the roles of scientists and other technical experts in the cold war and also in the war against terror, suggesting in the process that our current war hauntingly mirrors the cold war. Like the cold war, the war against terror often focuses on technical secrets (e.g., about weapons of mass destruction). It involves ground wars by proxy in geographic locations that may be of limited relevance to the central issues, and it seems to require the vigilance of individual citizens, who need to be watching their fellow passengers and reporting overheard conversations in restaurants. I focus on several cases of individual scientists who were subject to reprisals of one kind or another, and I consider how self-censorship and political censorship have operated both during the cold war and in the present. My larger goal is to explore the roles of technical knowledge, both then and now, as a resource for the state. I am interested in the intersection of political demands with the culture and practice of science.

War and Technical Knowledge

It is important to recognize that biologists, physicists, engineers, psychologists, and other scientific experts have been critical to the practice of war over the last century. Indeed, war has arguably become the dominant scientific enterprise in the industrialized world, absorbing more funding, time, and personnel than any other single technically driven domain. Nuclear, biological, and chemical weapons, now feared for their potential use by terrorists, are all products of scientific expertise. Meteorology, which still cannot quite predict the weather, became a discipline in response to the demands of air power and was invented as a science to help plan bombing runs. Ornithologists played a role in

Pacific weapons testing; the shape of modern bullets reflects laboratory research in wound ballistics; missiles use advanced computing technologies; and the high quality of care now available in an urban emergency room reflects medical experience with battlefield trauma. War, science, and the healing arts of medicine are bound up tightly together in twentieth-century history.

At the same time, science has generally occupied a paradoxical political location. The disinterested pursuit of pure knowledge has been widely recognized as a political resource—that is, as reflecting and reinforcing *interests*. Scientists have deployed their status as neutral arbiters of truth to lend support to a particular state or a particular political approach, thereby leaving behind neutrality. For example, at the start of World War I a group of prominent German scientists signed a statement (the Statement of the 95 Intellectuals) proclaiming that Germany was right and that international outrage at German actions was not justified.

As an enterprise, then, science is presumed to produce apolitical truths—absolute statements about the way things really are in nature. These dispatches from the front lines of the campaign to understand and control the natural world are presumed to be uninflected in any way by power politics, by the excesses of tyranny, or by the blindness of prejudice or propaganda. At the same time, such natural truths are often absolutely central to the needs of the state. In some cases this centrality has been notorious. Scientists were the authors of "Aryan Physics," as contrasted with "Jewish Physics." Aryan Physics was the name for a scientific movement organized by German scientists critical of Einstein and relativity in interwar Germany.[3] Aryan Physics was promoted as Newtonian, mystical, modest, and German, whereas Jewish Physics was theoretical, abstract, mathematical, and internationalistic.[4] The attributes of the science reflected the broader cultural struggle over German identity in the twentieth century.

Scientists were also active participants in the development of Nazi racial hygiene, a form of biological reasoning that justified the dismissal of Jewish scientists from German academe and eventually played a role in the Holocaust.[5] Nazi racial hygiene has been attributed to the social tensions produced by Germany's rapid industrialization in the second industrial revolution, to the professional traditions of German medicine, and to the intellectual interest in social Darwinism spurred by the work of two prominent German biologists, Ernst Haeckel and August Weissman. Weissman's work in particular suggested that eugenics was the only practical strategy to avoid species decline. Such ideas had currency in Germany long before 1933, but they took on a more virulent meaning with the rise of National Socialism. In the end many technical experts facilitated the Holocaust, including engineers, physicians, and chemists. Scientists are thus a critical political resource even in a fascist state. Their views about nature and about human experimentation can be expected to mirror those of the broader culture.

In another case, supposed facts about nature were critical to the state enforcement of Soviet Lysenkoism, which was a movement that characterized the Mendelian genetics of Columbia University's T. H. Morgan as bourgeois and capitalistic. Trofim Lysenko was an agricultural scientist who in 1926 proclaimed that crops could be transformed rapidly by changes in their environment. This was a version of Lamarckism, the idea promoted by the early nineteenth century French biologist that evolution occurred as a result of the inheritance of acquired characters. But in the Soviet case, this expectation had disastrous consequences for agriculture, because Lysenko's beliefs about "winter wheat" were enforced as state policy. Stalin favored Lysenko's theories and saw elements of "class struggle" in Lysenko's models of nature. Chromosomes, Lysenko said, were reactionary, idealist, and metaphysical. The great Russian geneticist Nikolai Vavilov died in a Soviet prison at least partly because he believed in such chromosomes.[6]

Facts about nature have also provided technological forces that could permit a state to emerge as a world power of the first rank, as at Los Alamos. The atomic bomb, completed in 1945, was both a technical and a political achievement, a physical sign of U.S. dominance and strength.[7] The abundant resources that were turned to the production of the atomic bomb, which cost roughly $2 billion to build in 1945, were the products of the economic and industrial strength of the United States at this pivotal moment in the nation's history. The bomb itself preserved the "American Lake" by, ironically, cementing U.S. ties to Japan: The United States was able to maintain fleet strength in the Pacific at least partly because of its secure control of the Japanese islands after 1945. Had the Soviets been more involved in the defeat of Japan, that control would presumably have been much less secure.

At mid-century, the scientific community was further understood by many to provide a model of how a state should operate. Harvard president James Conant believed that science was just what secular culture needed. It expressed, he said, the "finest values that had once been carried forward by Christianity—sober, rational, deliberate, unprejudiced." Science, Conant said, made "impartiality a heroic routine." A political leader who could adopt the mores and standards of science and apply them in the world of power and sovereignty would be an enlightened leader of the first rank in Conant's configuration.[8]

This imbrication of "the American century" and the development of American science and technology has been understudied by historical scholars. It is impossible to understand twentieth-century American history without attention to technical knowledge, its development, and its use. Science and politics are tangled together at multiple levels. Scientists have sometimes operated in a mirror world of objectivity and neutrality that flips over easily to utilitarianism and political relevance. Indeed, some observers have proposed that science is politically useful precisely because it has the status associated with neutrality and objectivity. The introduction of scientists into the U.S. diplomatic corps in the 1950s drew explicitly on the idea that technical experts, as neutral intermediaries, could help the United States achieve its political goals. Conant's own fears in 1945 that scientists would become "intellectual slaves of the state" were perhaps legitimate as the cold war unfolded over the next 20 years, for, as the Cornell physicist Philip Morison later put it, during the cold war the military "bought American science on the installment plan."[9]

What did this mean in practice? First, it meant that knowledge produced by technical experts was a valuable military commodity. And second, it meant that technical experts were subject to high levels of surveillance and suspicion that had consequences for the practice of science in general. Technical secrets were at the heart of the cold war. The Rosenbergs were executed over technical secrets; and the arms race was fueled by ever-escalating projections of technical secrets that the other side might possess.[10] Scientists were therefore part of the battle, as the case of Edward U. Condon suggests.

McCarthyism and Science

President Harry Truman's Federal Loyalty Program was enacted in March 1947. The program affected the estimated 60,000 scientists who were federal employees in many different agencies. Industrial and university scientists were also subject to reprisals in the process of security clearance approvals, but those who worked for the federal government itself were particularly vulnerable. Loyalty issues became a common fact of life in the scientific community, partly because disloyalty was defined so broadly. Scientists could be viewed as disloyal if they supported civil rights, labor unions, the international control of atomic energy, or (perhaps especially) scientific cooperation with the Soviet Union.

As Jessica Wang's work has demonstrated, in such a climate Condon was extremely vulnerable. In 1947 he was a prominent theoretical physicist, a veteran of both the radar and the atomic bomb wartime research projects, and the director of the National Bureau of Standards. That March, J. Parnell Thomas, chair of the House Un-American Activities Committee, told several journalists that Condon had allowed his name to be listed among supporters of what the committee believed to be a Communist front organization, called the Southern Conference for Human Welfare. A few days later, other newspapers reported (accurately) that Condon was a member of a society that promoted open scientific exchange between the United States and the Soviet Union. Condon was a strong proponent of open publication in science and free international exchange and had indeed met with Soviet physicists to discuss scientific questions. He was a prominent figure in the postwar atomic scientists' movement, the group that promoted international control of atomic energy. Like many other scientists of his generation, he was opposed to secrecy in science, and he thought that internationalism was the only way to avoid a full-scale nuclear war.[11]

For J. Parnell Thomas, such views were suspicious and dangerous. Thomas believed that there was a specific "atomic secret" that could be withheld from the Soviet Union. He thought that atomic energy should be under complete military control. Any exchange of scientific information with other countries would, in his view, threaten the United States. Most scientists by 1948 took the position that there were no "atomic secrets." Everything that had made it possible to build the bomb was known in the scientific community, and any competent physicist would be able to figure it out. Engineering and manufacturing problems might delay Soviet acquisition of the bomb, but the technical secrets, the secrets produced by scientific knowledge, were already out of the bag. Thomas, however, believed in the "great secret," and this shaped his interpretation of Condon and other scientists.

In 1947 Thomas identified Condon as a major security risk, "one of the weakest links in our atomic security." Condon famously replied that if he were one of the weakest links, then "that is very gratifying, and the country can feel absolutely safe, for I am completely reliable, loyal, conscientious and devoted to the interests of my country, as my whole career and life clearly reveal." Condon also warned that scientists were growing increasingly reluctant to work for the federal government, given the "mounting threat of purges, spy-ring exposures, publicity attacks and sudden dismissals without hearings."[12]

Condon was publicly supported by the American Civil Liberties Union (ACLU), the National Academy of Sciences, the Federation of American Scientists, the American Association for the Advancement of Science, and many individual scientific luminaries at Harvard and other institutions. A special dinner organized to show support for Condon attracted Einstein, Linus Pauling, Hans Bethe, Karl Compton, Leo Szilard, and Edward Teller, among others. Clearly the case had become a rallying point for the scientific community. Unfortunately for Condon, such support did not protect him. For the next decade or so he was subject to intermittent claims by anti-Communists inside and outside government that he was a dangerous scientist. His security clearance renewals, which had been approved unproblematically all through the war and the immediate postwar period, began to be denied. When clearance was finally approved for him in 1954, he was working in private industry, at Corning, and applying for clearance so that he could work on a project that Corning was carrying out at the request of the navy. But publicity about the approval led to its revocation. Condon had become a de facto Communist threat, regardless of the nature of the evidence against him.

Condon never applied for clearance again and never worked for the government again. He moved to academe, eventually the University of Colorado. But Condon's experience, and the experiences of hundreds of others like him, had a cumulative impact on the scientific community, creating a climate of fear and discouraging scientists from working on federal projects or for the government.

The security clearance hearing of J. Robert Oppenheimer in 1954 did not improve the climate. In the 1950s Oppenheimer was director of the Institute for Advanced Study at Princeton University and also a major adviser to the government on nuclear policy.[13] He was a high-profile public figure. Oppenheimer opposed development of the hydrogen bomb, and he supported, in an influential report in February 1953, easing cold war secrecy, which he believed made war more likely rather than less. His views and his public visibility made him particularly dangerous, and the Atomic Energy Commission (AEC) suspended his security clearance in December 1953. The following summer the Personnel Security Board held a month-long hearing to assess whether

Oppenheimer was a security risk. In direct violation of AEC policy, the transcript of this hearing was released to the public. This was one of the most infamous security cases of the period, remarkable both because of the prominence of the scientist and the unusual circumstances surrounding his career, stretching back to the 1930s, when he was in fact involved with groups sympathetic to the Communist cause. One of the case's most compelling lessons was that any scientist who disagreed with the direction of government policy risked the same kind of retaliation. Oppenheimer was personally and professionally devastated by the hearing and the permanent denial of clearance. He never fully recovered.[14]

Science and the War Against Terror

Now I want to move forward to early 2003, when rather different circumstances produced another remarkable and puzzling investigation of a scientist, the plague researcher Thomas Butler. Butler, a Texas Tech microbiologist, was tried in federal court in fall 2003 as a result of a Department of Justice investigation that led to sixty-nine criminal charges, many of them related not to his work on plague bacteria but to his taxes, medical consulting practices, and contracts with biotech firms. That December he was found guilty on forty-seven of these charges, although not on the crucial charges relating to biological materials.

The case began on January 14, 2003, when Butler called the FBI to report that thirty vials of plague bacteria were missing from his laboratory. Overnight, after a panicked search turned up nothing and after many hours of questioning, Butler signed a handwritten statement saying that he had accidentally destroyed the samples. Butler has since said that he does not know what happened to the vials, and many of his supporters have claimed that the signed statement was merely dictated by an FBI agent to an exhausted Butler, who had no legal counsel and who had been questioned all night.

These events, in themselves puzzling, led to a full-scale investigation of Butler and his professional life, including audits of his tax returns, assessments of his contracts with private industry, and, in particular, assessments of the practices surrounding his transportation of plague materials either by express mail services or on commercial airlines over the previous four or five years. In January 2004, Butler resigned his professorship at Texas Tech. He agreed to pay the university where he was employed $300,000 to settle their dispute with him. Butler was sentenced on March 10, 2004, to twenty-four months in prison for defrauding Texas Tech and for illegally transporting plague samples.[15] Butler must also pay $19,700 in federal fines and assessments and $38,675 in restitution to the university. He is not eligible for early parole because none is allowed in the federal justice system. As a journalist for *The Scientist* reported, the 62-year-old scientist refused to speak to reporters after the sentencing, except to say, "I would like to talk to you but I'm kind of disabled." Earlier, during a break before the sentence was announced, he said, again only to *The Scientist*, "I'm sitting here trying to endure it. I don't have any comment." [16]

During the trial, Butler's supporters pointed out that a technique he developed for hydration of children with diarrhea, a massive global health problem, saved the lives of 2 to 3 million children under the age of 4 every year. The judge reportedly took into account Butler's contributions to science and public health in his sentencing. But Butler's conviction and imprisonment mark the effective end of a biomedical career that had involved extended field research on infectious diseases in Vietnam, Bangladesh, and Tanzania and collaborations with the Centers for Disease Control and Prevention and the biological weapons program at Fort Detrick.

Butler's case became not only a major media event but also a major cause in the scientific community. A leading bioterrorist scientist, D. A Henderson, who led the Bush administration's first emergency response program after the anthrax mailings, was harshly critical of the Department of Justice and its campaigns against Butler and another scientist. Henderson said that the questioning of Butler for more than ten hours without a lawyer was "unbelievable," that the FBI had "lost all perspective" and was "out of control," and that the scientific community as a whole was likely to refuse to work with the FBI in the wake of these events.[17]

Four Nobel laureates, one of whom had been Butler's student and protégé, wrote a letter in his defense, suggesting that the lesson of the Butler case was that those who were most devoted to the U.S. cause—those willing to take the risks involved in working on biological pathogens—were most likely to become victims of punitive federal investigations. Butler's student, Peter Agre, who won the Nobel Prize for Chemistry in 2003, compared the events to McCarthyism and vowed to use some of his $600,000 in Nobel cash to help Butler and his wife. Similarly, the New York Academy of Sciences said in a formal statement that the government was using "selective prosecution" and "piling on" extra charges that resulted in blowing "the whole episode out of proportion." The National Academy of Sciences similarly came to Butler's defense and sent an August 2003 letter of protest to Attorney General John Ashcroft.[18] Such public protests, however, had no effect. Butler's expertise in biological weapons research and his problematic contractual arrangements came at a moment of public hysteria about biological weapons. Butler became the symbolic focus of fears about biological weapons, secrecy, technical knowledge, and war that have long shaped microbiology as a discipline.

Of the many forms of scientific knowledge crucial to war, microbiology has been subject to more sustained and intense governmental scrutiny. Even physicists have been able to speak more openly about their research in many periods. Microbiologists are the possible creators of knowledge that is widely understood to be morally problematic, and most uses of biological weapons have been carried out in secret and later denied by those governments that used them. Unlike guns or bombs, biological weapons are illegitimate, and any country using them will be accused of conducting illegitimate war. The scientists who make such weapons are therefore uniquely problematic for the nations that employ them in secret programs.

The use of biological weapons is usually dated to besieged medieval castles. The bodies of plague victims would be catapulted into the castle to spread disease and death and to hasten the defeat. Later, a famous incident in 1763, in which British officers gave blankets infested with smallpox to Native Americans in western Pennsylvania, conforms more closely to the modern notion of biological weapons as stealthy and secretive. But the scientific notion of biological weapons as industrialized technology grounded in laboratory research is a product of the twentieth century. Disease was always around as a possible weapon, but weaponized disease requires laboratory expertise.

In 1915, the German army was accused of using cholera against Italian troops and of using anthrax in Bucharest. The 1925 Geneva Protocol banned the use of biological weapons but did not ban research and development of such weapons. Participating nations created biological weapons research centers in the interwar period. The Soviet Union built a biological weapons laboratory in 1929, the United Kingdom and Japan built theirs in 1934, and the United States and Canada built theirs in 1941. The motivations for this sudden surge in scientific biological weapons research programs included the many rumors and accusations about biological weapons during World War I and during the colonial wars in the 1930s, the general fear that an enemy would have biological weapons first, and some enthusiasm about the potential of biological weapons to transform battlefields or warfare. Like all military technologies, biological weapons had supporters who believed that the pathogens might lead to a more humane form of war, in which people were merely sickened rather than killed.

Rumors about biological weapons use persisted throughout the twentieth century. In late February 1952, for example, the North Korean foreign minister claimed that the United States had used biological weapons in Korea. This charge drew worldwide attention after some American pilots who were prisoners in China confessed to having used biological weapons, although these Americans were prisoners of war at the time and later retracted their claims. Subsequently, some researchers claimed to have found evidence that biological pathogens were in fact used in Korea.[19] Certainly in 1951 and 1952 the United States was embarking on a major biological weapons crash program to develop new and usable weapons, and the United States had reached an agreement with Japanese researchers who had been at the infamous Ping Fan camp to share data on biological weapons.[20]

In seeking to keep its biological weapons research secret and conceal its possible use of biological weapons, the behavior of the United States was consistent with that of many other nations. The standard description of biological warfare as "public health in reverse" explains why most nations have sought to use biological weapons only when they could do so secretly and why so many strategic plans for biological weapons use include as a part of the plan subterfuge and dissimulation. Indeed, secrecy was sometimes incorporated into plans for biological weapons use in the 1950s. One proposal called for U.S. agents to spread rumors that a particular agent for which a vaccine was available was about to be used. Such rumors would presumably spark a public panic, with enemy civilians demanding the vaccine and refusing to leave their homes. The social and economic chaos thus produced would be the point of the attack, and no biological weapon would ever need to be used, because the same effect (interfering with work and production) could be achieved without any actual pathogens. Rumor could disrupt a society as readily as disease, and in the new industrialized warfare of the twentieth century, as in terrorism, social disruption was an important military goal.

Biological weapons are also rather different from other weapons systems because they require medical expertise. Laboratory work in microbiology produces medical knowledge and depends on medical knowledge. Medicine is in theory focused on healing, but in biological weapons research the focus is on producing more bodily injury. For microbiologists, this equation has long posed a moral dilemma. The American Society for Microbiology (ASM) is one of the largest scientific organizations in the United States, with about 40,000 members. Of its ninety-one presidents, twenty-one have worked at the Fort Detrick biological weapons laboratory.

The ASM has gone back and forth on the question of whether microbiologists should be involved in biological weapons research. In 1942 the group supported international control of biological weapons, although members continued to work closely with Fort Detrick scientists. In 1955 the ASM set up an advisory committee to help Fort Detrick plan a biological weapons program, but the committee was dissolved in 1968 after many microbiologists became concerned about the close ties between their profession and biological weapons research facilities. In a famous statement in 1970, the head of the ASM said that biological weapons research could create human weapons, could lead to the prevention or cure of disease, and would not be a problem if it were published and open. The secrecy of the research was the real issue. The 1985 Code of Ethics of the ASM made this explicit: Any microbiologist could do research on biological weapons so long as that research was open and public.

Self-Censorship and Government Censorship

After the anthrax scare in 2001–2002, scientists themselves began to consider voluntary self-censorship, at least partly to forestall more draconian government censorship. In February 2003 the editors of *Science*, *Nature*, and other major scientific journals announced that they would evaluate incoming articles to determine whether they could be useful to terrorists seeking to use chemical or biological weapons. These major scientific publications agreed that if a scientific paper seemed to be directly relevant to the production of biological weapons or other terrorist technologies, the editors would either eliminate some of the technical details or reject the paper. The move was a reaction to both government censorship and to the emerging potential of new biotechnologies that could make it possible to construct new biological weapons of unprecedented power.

New gene splicing technologies, for example, have made it possible to transform diseases such as smallpox; an effective vaccine exists for smallpox, but the smallpox genome could be modified in ways that reduced the efficacy of the vaccine. In recent studies a single gene substitution in mousepox causes mice that have been vaccinated to contract the disease. Scientists began to speculate that the same kind of simple gene splicing technique could be applied in human populations. In addition, scientists recently cobbled together an entirely new virus from DNA drawn from two existing viruses. This seemed to open the possibility that a disease such as Ebola, which spreads only with direct contact, could be imbued with the infectious properties of the common cold. The potential to build an organism from the bottom up, by using a DNA tinkering process, could mean that biological weapons specialists could use a published DNA sequence to literally build a pathogen without ever having acquired it from an existing stockpile. The new molecular genetics, then, suggests that scientific publication itself could pose real risks to populations around the world. Secrecy and self-censorship, in this case, reflect both technological and political realities.

Yet it is also true that a group determined to make biological weapons does not need advanced science to do so. Many pathogens readily available can be used as weapons, just as passenger planes could stand in for bombs in the 9/11 attack. The arguments against self-censorship focus on the importance of free and open exchange to scientific practice, the idea that it will be impossible to develop defensive technologies if results of biological weapons research are kept secret, and the idea that science moves step by step toward solutions that might well depend on an intermediary step that seems unproductive at first. Most scientists resist censorship, including self-censorship, and in fact the most serious risk to the scientific community comes not from such modest efforts to prevent certain data from being published but from governmental policies that systematically seek to control and manipulate scientific data.

In the spring of 2004, for example, the Union of Concerned Scientists charged that the Bush administration was systematically distorting and censoring scientific findings. The organization claimed that data were manipulated and ignored in order to support the policies of the Bush administration. Scientific panel nominees were expected to pass various litmus tests and were chosen based not on their stature in the scientific community but on their loyalty to administration policy. Underqualified individuals with industry ties were being appointed to crucial oversight committees, and many scientific advisory committees were being disbanded summarily, particularly if they had reached conclusions that were unsympathetic to the Bush administration.[21] "Today we are witnessing a political censorship in what is considered the temple of democracy, the White House," said one critic.[22]

Results that contradicted the Bush administration's policies, the Union said, were covered up or "revised" to suit whatever claims the administration sought to make about global warming, environmental protection, endangered species, mercury emissions, HIV/AIDS, and lead poisoning. "When scientific knowledge has been found to be in conflict with its political goals, the administration has often manipulated the process through which science enters into its decisions," the report states. "This has been done by placing people who are professionally unqualified or who have clear conflicts of interest in official posts and on scientific advisory committees; by disbanding existing advisory committees; by censoring and suppressing reports by the government's own scientists; and by simply not seeking independent scientific advice. Other administrations have, on occasion, engaged in such practices, but not so systematically nor on so wide a front." [23]

One particularly egregious case involved the Bush administration's handling of an Environmental Protection Agency (EPA) report in June 2003. The White House itself tried to make a series of changes to the EPA's draft report on the environment. [24] After the *New York Times* reported that the White House was attempting to suppress some evidence, the White House backed down. Apparently the key issue was over the question of whether human activity contributes to global warming, an issue that had been addressed in a substantive report from the National Academy of Sciences that the White House wished to see ignored in the EPA report. [25] The specific data that troubled the White House focused on a temperature record covering 1,000 years. The EPA staff was asked to leave out this record in order to focus on "a recent, limited analysis [that] supports the administration's favored message." [26] The White House also insisted that the EPA report include a reference to a study of temperature records funded by the American Petroleum Institute [27] and asked the EPA staff to eliminate a closing statement that "climate change has global consequences for human health and the environment." [28]

Eventually any mention of global climate change was dropped from the report. "According to internal EPA documents and interviews with EPA researchers, the agency staff chose this path rather than compromising their credibility by misrepresenting the scientific consensus." [29] And like many others who have sought to manipulate science, Bush has exaggerated uncertainty and called for further research. In Robert Proctor's study of the disinformation of the tobacco industry, he demonstrates how "trade association science" consistently calls for further research ad infinitum. Such calls are not grounded in technical necessity. They are part of a well-recognized pattern in the political management of science.[30]

Censorship of science can also take other forms, as it has in the case of Ignacio Chapela, an assistant professor at the University of California, Berkeley, who was denied tenure apparently because of his skepticism about genetically modified crops.

Censorship, Industry, and Academe

The Chapela case is particularly compelling and troubling because it makes manifest the deep effect of industrial ties on academic life and because it suggests that the biotechnology industry can effectively silence scientific critics. Chapela, an ecologist, received notice in November 2003 that his contract would not be renewed and that his tenure had not been approved. But Chapela and his colleagues had good reason to find this decision problematic. Chapela had been a vocal critic of the university's contract with the biotech firm Novartis (now Syngenta). The deal gave Novartis control of the research funding and the results for five years, in exchange for $25 million. It was widely viewed as a symbol of the erosion of academic independence. Furthermore, Chapela had published a paper, in the journal *Nature*, that documented the contamination of Mexican maize by genes from genetically modified corn. His data showed what was widely known to be true, namely, that genes from genetically modified crops could move into other crop populations. But the data also suggested, in a further elaboration, that genetically modified crops were unstable and that the transgenic sections of the genome were fragmenting in both the genetically modified crops and their neighbors. This was a much more threatening finding than mere contamination, which was widely known to occur.[31]

Later observers tracked the e-mail outcry about Chapela to a marketing firm hired by the biotechnology industry. Chapela's colleagues had voted overwhelmingly in his favor (thirty-two for tenure, one against, three abstentions), and it would be unusual for tenure to be denied in such cases. In December 2003 Chapela hosted a public discussion of "scientific freedom in the age of the biotech industry," where he was joined by other scientists whose work has threatened the industry. These included Arpad Pusztai, whose contract at Berkeley was terminated after his work indicated that genetically modified potatoes adversely affected young rats; Tyrone Hayes, whose study showing that levels of a certain herbicide lower than what was permitted in drinking water turned frogs into hermaphrodites was suppressed by the agrochemical industry; and John Losey, whose study showing that monarch butterfly larvae died after eating genetically modified maize pollen was attacked by the biotechnology industry.

Conclusion

The National Academy of Sciences letter defending Texas Tech microbiologist Thomas Butler was modeled on a letter sent to Attorney General Janet Reno three years earlier in defense of Wen Ho Lee, the Los Alamos scientist who spent nine months in solitary confinement after an FBI investigation on charges of spying. Lee was eventually released with the judge's apology because it became clear that he had done nothing to further Chinese research on nuclear weapons.

The case against Lee, which reached a hysterical pitch at times, intersected with tensions in the political and scientific relationship between the United States and China during the 1980s and 1990s.[32] In the same way, the case against Butler intersected with public fears of biological weapons and uncertainty about who could be trusted in the new world of terroristic warfare. And in the cases of both Condon and Oppenheimer, expectations about the Soviet Union were as important as any of the details of the individual lives of these scientists.

What do these cases, spanning more than fifty years, suggest about the relationships between science, the state, and military priorities? Certainly they indicate the ways that "security" constitutes state power, not only in international affairs but also in domestic management of people, society, emotions, and ideologies. They also suggest the impact of the expansive support of twentieth-century science by the Department of Defense, the Office of Naval Research, the Atomic Energy Commission, and other agencies that constitute the military system. None of the scientists I have discussed seem to have actually been spies or traitors or to have been disloyal to the United States. There have been technical experts who sought to aid enemies of the United States, but Oppenheimer, Condon, Lee, Chapela, and Butler were not among them. Yet they suffered personal and professional humiliation because their technical expertise threatened either government interests or private industry.

Scientists perhaps have not become "intellectual slaves of the state," but they have been critical to the practice of war in the twentieth century. The "normal science" of the twentieth century has often been secret, or potentially secret, and scientists have often been subject to state control even when they worked in academic settings. In 1962, Alvin Weinberg called MIT a "cluster of government labs, with a very good educational institution attached to it." Indeed, MIT in 1968 had $100 million in military contracts, more than some large private defense contractors at the time.[33] What does "academic freedom" mean under such circumstances?

The scientific enterprise is a site, then, at which we can see what is contradictory, quizzical, sometimes incoherent. The scientific community valorizes freedom and autonomy and also participates in self-censorship, secrecy, industrial ties, and state-sponsored research. Scientists enjoy public respect, even veneration, and the scientific method remains a model for clear thinking, the key to the resolution of public disputes about everything from AIDS to global warming. At the same time, scientists appear to be uniquely dangerous, subject to public reprisal that can, at times, produce tragic injustice. Technical truths are politically valuable because they are presumed to be outside politics; scientists are politically threatening because they are presumed to create knowledge that is outside politics. Expectations of neutrality and bias work together to position technical knowledge in a network of contradictions and ironies.

To close, I return to DuBridge and his difficulties. He suggested that "an enlightened government will always encourage the search for truth." But one cannot always count on having an enlightened government, and it is not always clear, as DuBridge knew only too well, just what the truth is.

PART THREE

Academic Freedom in Global Perspective

Academic Freedom in the Middle East, Africa, and Asia: Looking Toward the NEAR Future

John Akker

THE TERRIBLE EVENTS of September 11, 2001, reverberated throughout the entire world, including the academic world. As Antonio Brown and Enrique Desmond Arias discuss in the next two chapters, a major effect of the tragedy on academic freedom was to hamper the ability of scholars from developing nations to access the vast resources of U.S. universities and institutes. This occurrence certainly is problematic, but we must not forget the far more serious limits to academic freedom in nations around the world. The primary purpose of this chapter is to serve as a warning that academic freedom cannot be taken for granted. As I detail in this chapter, throughout much of the developing world free intellectual thought and discourse are far more of a dream than a reality. Much of the oppression of academic freedom has been justified by the sort of national security rhetoric that has been heard in some quarters in the United States following the 2001 attacks on the World Trade Center and the Pentagon. When one reads of more than 100 members of Congress calling for the firing of a faculty member for anti-U.S. comments or the federal government issuing subpoenas to university officials to find out which students engaged in an antigovernment protest, one feels the need to remind citizens what a precious gift true academic freedom is and how fragile it is in much of the world. What follows, then, is a brief description of the Network for Education and Academic Rights (NEAR), the UNESCO-sponsored international academic freedom organization of which I am privileged to be the executive director, and a discussion of some of the most telling examples of violations of academic freedom in the developing world. Unfortunately, the cases discussed here are but a small sample of violations of academic freedom throughout Africa, Asia, and the Middle East.

NEAR and Its Commitment to Academic Freedom

NEAR is a membership-based, nongovernmental organization that facilitates international collaboration between organizations active in issues of academic freedom and educational rights, and it is committed to promoting an understanding of and respect for the values enshrined in the Universal Declaration of Human Rights. NEAR was founded on the principle that academic freedom is essential to the development of open, stable, and democratic societies and that members of the education community have a special responsibility to assist and support those for whom these freedoms are threatened. NEAR believes that freedom of expression in higher education is a core value in a civil society and that it matters not only to those who work at academic institutions but also to all members of a society.

NEAR also believes that it is especially important to recognize the application of academic freedom across all education levels. In countries where literacy rates are low and access to education is difficult, teachers and high school students often have vital leadership roles in their communities, yet discussions about academic freedom often focus on tertiary education to the exclusion of primary and secondary educators.

Academic Freedom in a Civil Society

In the United States discussions of academic freedom often come back to the First Amendment of the U.S. Constitution. The idea that academic freedom stems from the same pool of constitutional rights as the First Amendment has some weight. Certainly, there is no mention of academic freedom in the First Amendment, but the Supreme Court has inferred as much in stating that universities have the right to determine the structure of their teaching.[1] Nonetheless, throughout much of the world there is little correlation between a nation's constitution and its genuine commitment to academic freedom. As a result, in this overview of the current world situation I use the test of what freedom exists in practice, not on paper. Many will argue that I am using a standard that does not apply in a formal sense in the established universities of the West. This critique misses the point because I believe that the concept of academic freedom is established as part of German, British, and American cultures. It certainly is provided for in some domestic legislation in a variety of countries in Europe, where there is a right for faculty members to pursue scholarship without restraint, although it is also fair to say that this right is not unlimited. Concerns of this kind prompted the British Parliament to pass an academic freedom amendment to the Education Reform Act of 1988. This amendment was proposed by Lord Roy Jenkins and protected "the freedom within the law of academics to question and test received wisdom, and to put forward new ideas and controversial or unpopular opinions without placing themselves in jeopardy of losing their jobs or privileges they may have at their institutions."[2]

A common theme throughout this chapter is that the notion of academic freedom has been breached. I take violations of academic freedom to mean where institutions, staff, or students have their freedom of independent action limited by others or where pressure by others creates a feeling of restraint. With these standards in mind, it is clear that academic freedom from a global perspective is under serious attack. Universities and those that work in them are often confronting economic, social, and political issues that affect governments and other powerful institutions within nation-states that bring about uncomfortable situations. Whereas in some countries this is tolerated to varying degrees, in other countries academic freedom is much more constrained. Some of these countries can be regarded as significant and important nations that have much influence in the current world.

It is appropriate, then, that we continue to highlight the importance of academic freedom at a time when, all over the world, academics and students are being harassed, imprisoned, tortured, and murdered for voicing opinions and undertaking research. Universities are mostly set up to be centers for independent thought. However, often academic work and student opinion prove uncomfortable for governments and state-based agencies, leading to the repression of academic freedom and education rights. I say "mostly" because there are, of course, universities that are created for a particular purpose. Their functions could either be to provide selective education to a ruling elite and/or to act in a symbolic way as an example of the cultural mission of that country. But even at such universities, issues of academic freedom are still relevant. In 1966, Lord Lionel Robbins (former chair of the most important U.K. inquiry into the future of higher education) gave a noteworthy lecture at the British Academy titled "Of Academic Freedom." He stated, "I am clear that academic freedom . . . is a matter of great importance to the welfare of our community." Dealing with those academics who had fled Nazi domination of Central Europe in the 1930s, he said "It has also been very much in my mind that it was to escape a state of academic unfreedom, and worse, that many of those who contributed to its endowment left the lands of their birth and came to these [U.K.] shores."[3]

During the 1930s, thousands of academics fled to the United Kingdom and the United States, and some of them became the distinguished academics of their time. For instance, in the United Kingdom at least eighteen became Nobel Prize winners and countless others became members of the British Academy and Royal Society. Unfortunately situations similar to the one in Nazi Germany exist today. It is true that in Iraq and Iran, to name just two countries, many academics have left their positions and fled the country. Academic life in these countries was subject to so many restrictions and censorship that it became impossible for them to teach and conduct research. NEAR estimates that more than 700 scholars from each country have fled. The Council for Assisting Refugee Academics (CARA) assists them in the United Kingdom, and the Scholars at Risk Network, based at New York University, also provides some assistance in the United States. It is not uncommon, however, to find such academics driving cabs in Chicago, as I once did, or being employed as security guards.

Lord Robbins had more to say about the notion of academic freedom:

Simple definitions [of academic freedom] are by no means easy. When we think of the rules and duties essential to the proper conduct of any academic enterprise involving the co-operation and division of labour, still more if we think of the complications which arise if such enterprises are financed at least in part by contributions compulsorily levied by the state, it is not easy to provide any simple statement of what constitutes academic freedom. . . . But at least we can recognize the negative.[4]

Like Robbins, I believe that academic freedom is a notion that many consider desirable and a special kind of freedom that can transcend other forms of freedom. Numerous examples today make it quite clear that, in a civil society, academic freedom is not divisible from other freedoms. In a recent case in Egypt in which a professor was arrested for allegedly misusing funding, not only the research institution in question but also the electoral rights and key values in the government of that country were affected (I discuss this case in greater detail later).

For academic freedom to be protected, universities must have considerable powers of academic and administrative self-government. This goes to every aspect of a modern university, although it is accepted that not all universities carry out research. Still, many countries refuse to uphold academic freedom. Often those in control see students as a major radical force and believe that lecturers are able to influence the students to think about regime change. In my examination of events in Ethiopia (presented later in this chapter), I draw attention to the massive involvement of the police and state agencies in the University of Addis Abba, which resulted in the death of forty-one people and the imprisonment of two lecturers because they discussed academic freedom in a university lecture.

Academic freedom is important because any impingement on it detrimentally affects the purpose of a university or education provider— to provide the tools that encourage and facilitate thought, debate, intellectual criticism, the dissemination of knowledge, and creative problem solving. In turn, these skills directly influence the growth and development of a country—politically, socially, and economically. Hence it is important to analyze the effects of the nonobservance of academic freedom on individual countries or regions.

Several key issues that affect academic freedom need to be addressed. Reference has been made to the large number of cases in which governments refused to protect even the most basic academic freedom. We know of these cases because information technology has, of course, brought the rapid transfer of information. On average, NEAR posts eight cases a month on its website that document violations of academic freedom.[5] Each of these cases underlines the threat that academic freedom suffers worldwide. In the next section I provide a sampling of these cases, which illustrate how prominent the threat to academic freedom really is.

Threats to Academic Freedom

The first example of such a situation relates to the imprisonment of an Egyptian sociology professor, Saad Eddin Ibrahim. Ibrahim was employed at the American University in Cairo and was the cofounder and director of the Ibn Khaldun Centre for Development Studies. He was accused of using funding from the European Union dishonestly. The Egyptian government claimed that the funding had been used in unintended ways, but the European Union denied this charge. The professor was researching Egyptian election practices and discovered some significant issues that were critical of the governing party. Ibrahim and several other staff employed at the Centre were imprisoned; Ibrahim remained in prison for more than twenty months.

Ibrahim and his team were eventually released, but only after an international campaign by the United States, Great Britain, and the European Commission that put pressure on the Egyptian government. It is fair to say that there was considerable concern—by what after all are the most powerful governments in the world—about an incident that was clearly an affront to academic freedom by any standards. Without the pressure from the United States and Great Britain, Ibrahim would not have been released. The governments of the United States and the United Kingdom sent observers to the court in Cairo where Ibrahim was tried and for the subsequent appeals. The secretary of state for the United States and the British foreign secretary became involved, and, through NEAR, academics throughout the world learned of Ibrahim's case and acted to bring their own pressure on the Egyptian authorities. Also, journalists within Egypt played a major part in drawing worldwide attention to this case.

Actions taken by Egyptian security forces in apprehending students have also demonstrated a lack of commitment by the government to academic freedom. In 2003, three students were arrested after they took part in a demonstration at the Press Syndicate in Cairo. One student told Human Rights Watch that he and the others held at State Security Investigations (SSI) headquarters had been beaten at the time of arrest and during the interrogation sessions. Describing his beating during interrogation, the student declared, "One of them was holding my arm behind my back so I couldn't protect myself. One hit me in the groin, one hit me in the stomach, one on my chest, and one around the thighs."[6] The Cairo-based Nadeem Center for the Treatment and Rehabilitation of Victims of Violence examined this student and confirmed testicular congestion, contusions, and bruises on the back.

If such blatant violations of academic freedom can happen in Egypt, they could easily occur elsewhere. With the exceptions of the Iraq War and the Israeli-Palestinian conflict, the Egyptian government is not one that is unfriendly to core issues expressed by the U.S. and Europeans governments. Yet Egyptian authorities seemed to NEAR representatives to be puzzled by the interest shown particularly in the Ibrahim case and resented it. Moreover, it was Egypt's belief that this case was an internal matter and that their university autonomy was not an issue for others. Simply put, academic freedom was not a matter the Egyptian government either recognized or supported. The interests of the government were paramount. The reactions of the Egyptian government should be of great concern to everyone who supports academic freedom. If the Egyptian view of academic freedom is common, then clearly the principle of academic freedom is threatened.

Zimbabwe also provides examples of blatant disregard for academic freedom. NEAR has published a considerable amount of information on the effect that the existing government is having on Zimbabwean students' rights of freedom of expression. All the evidence points one way: The internal police harass student leaders who express concern about government interference in the universities. In some cases this has lead to the imprisonment and even death of student leaders. NEAR financed legal aid for the family of one of the students killed under suspicious circumstances.

The case of Tapera Kapuya, the former secretary general of the University of Zimbabwe Student Union, stands out. Along with twenty other students, Kapuya had been expelled from the university for protesting against government policy on higher education and the continued mismanagement of the country. According to Kapuya:

While at the University of Zimbabwe, I was abducted in the middle of the night and made to stand in a bucket of water for a day. When I was finally taken out, live electric wires were placed on my toes. In a later incident I was detained during a student protest, beaten with fists and sticks, and kicked as tear gas canisters were detonated where I lay. Pleas for medical attention were laughed aside, despite a deep cut on my head. I later received nine stitches.[7]

Kapuya is not the only student who faced the wrath of the Zanu PF "Green Bomber" militia that he claims runs university security. "Students are harassed and beaten with apparent impunity," writes Kapuya. "Members of the secret police watch dissident lecturers and students, and armed riot police are ready to pounce at any slightest show of discontent by members of the academic community."[8] Two cases resulted in the deaths of students and numerous other abductions have occurred.[9] That these grave abuses and disregard for the rule of law are allowed to happen at the university raises serious concerns about academic freedom.

No review of violations of academic freedom could take place without an examination of the situation in China. Human Rights Watch, the American Association for the Advancement of Science, and other learned societies have given major attention to the imprisonment of numerous scholars in the country. The governments of the West have joined the call to have the scholars released, and there has rightly been a great deal of attention to specific cases in the educational press and more widely in the major news outlets. As of March 2006 there were twenty-nine cases concerning the violation of academic freedom in China on the NEAR website, more than any other country.[10] One such case involved a biology professor, Yan Jun, who was sentenced to two years in prison for publishing several "subversive" essays on the Internet. In one of his writings the "cyber-dissident" condemned the lack of press freedom in China. In another essay Jun called for a review of the sentences against students who were arrested during the Tiananmen Square massacre in 1989. He also called for the release of Zhao Ziyang, the former Communist Party secretary general who was placed under house arrest after voicing support for students arrested during the 1989 events. While in prison, Jun was beaten by fellow prisoners.[11]

Jun is not the only cyberdissident arrested by the Chinese government. Liu Di, a psychology student at Beijing Normal University, allegedly criticized the jailing of a prominent Internet dissident, Huang Qi. She was held without charge from November 2002 to December 2003, when she was released. Nevertheless, several cases regarding cyberdissidents still remain unsolved.[12]

I referred earlier to the situation in Ethiopia, a country whose president is in regular contact with senior politicians in Europe and the United States. Nevertheless, the Ethiopian government has no commitment to academic freedom. There has been much civil unrest and imprisonment of leading intellectuals in the country. Alemayehu Teferra, a civil engineer and former president of Addis Ababa University in Ethiopia, was released from prison in 2003. Teferra was charged, in March 1997, by Ethiopia's Federal High Court for engaging in "aggravated genocide" through antirevolutionary activities committed under the government of President Mengistu Haile-Mariam in 1977–1978. During this period, commonly referred to as the Red Terror campaign, tens of thousands of people were killed, tortured, or disappeared. Teferra was the chairman of a local urban-dwellers association during the Red Terror campaign, but he denied committing any atrocities. The government had absolved him of any crimes in 1991. However, he was arrested in 1993 when the government stated that it had new evidence implicating Teferra in the atrocities of the late 1970s.

Despite testimony from other individuals that Teferra was innocent, he remained in jail without being formally changed until 1997. For the remaining six years, his case lingered in the Federal High Court, allegedly because of a lack of magistrates to hear the case. Many human rights organizations believe that Terferra's arrest was related to his criticism of the government following a brutal repression of Addis Ababa University students who were protesting a planned referendum on Eritrean independence. After the crackdown on the protestors, the government sent armed security agents to the campus. Teferra requested the immediate withdrawal of these forces. He was fired from his position as university president shortly thereafter and was arrested four months later.[13]

In addition to the Teferra case, groups such as the Ethiopian Human Rights Council (EHRCO) have criticized the Ethiopian government for the mass arrest of hundreds of students. The arrests, which took place in late January 2003, occurred following a dispute between students belonging to the Oromo ethnic group—Ethiopia's largest ethnic group—and university authorities at Addis Ababa University over a cultural show supported by the Oromo People's Democratic Organization (OPDO), one of four political parties in the ruling coalition, the Ethiopian People's Revolutionary Democratic Front.

During the event, riots broke out and hundreds of armed federal police stormed the campus, rounding up the Oromo students. According to EHRCO, the students were forced to march barefoot or on their knees along a gravel path for several hours. EHRCO also claimed that the university suspended the students after their detention without conducting any formal investigations. University officials asserted that security forces intervened only to quell the vandalism that broke out at the event.[14]

In conjunction with the student arrests, professor Mesfin Wolde Mariam, the former secretary general of EHRCO, and economist Berhanu Nega, a supporter of EHRCO, were arrested in connection with student unrest. They were accused by the government of "inciting the students to violence," although both men insisted that the controversial meeting in which they were arrested was simply a discussion of human rights.[15] Organizations such as NEAR, the U.K. Foreign Office, and Amnesty International criticized the arrests as being unjustified.

Because of the major violations to academic freedom in Ethiopia,

NEAR is keeping a close eye on events that unfold there. Unfortunately, it seems likely that the violence there will be repeated before too long, but it is clear that many organizations regard the government actions taken against lecturers and students in Ethiopia to be repressive.

Not all the cases that NEAR works on relate to academics or students working in their home countries. In September 2002, academic Lesley McCulloch, along with former health worker Joy Lee Sadler and their translator, was detained in the Indonesian province of Aceh because of her research on a separatist insurgency in the country, the Free Aceh Movement, a movement that is considered a terrorist organization by government officials. McCulloch was charged with carrying out "activities incompatible with tourist visas," an offense that carries a sentence of up to five years' imprisonment. According to International PEN, McCulloch reportedly complained of mistreatment in detention, including sleep and food deprivation, beatings, and being threatened with a knife.[16] After months of international pressure from outside governments, including Great Britain and the United States, and organizations, including NEAR and International PEN, McCulloch and her colleagues were finally released in June 2004.

Unfortunately, NEAR has not always been victorious in defending academic freedom. In August 2002, Seyyed Hashem Aghajari, a history professor at a Tehran college, made a speech that was seen as an attack on the country's Islamic establishment and the supreme leader, Ayatollah Ali Akbar Khamenei. The professor was sentenced to death in November 2002 for apostasy after he spoke out against Iran's mullahs and called for a "religious renewal." The sentence sparked the largest student protest in years and was overturned by Iran's Supreme Court in February 2003. Although Aghajari's death sentence was overturned, in July 2004 he was sentenced to five years in prison, an obviously disturbing result.

It would be simplistic to draw too many conclusions regarding the cases on which NEAR works. Often the situations vary to a great extent, and also we have to adapt and use the pressure points that are best able to get results in each situation. The pressures that can be applied are worthy of their own research. We would say, however, that there are a few common conclusions. The harassment and worse of university faculty and staff seek to intimidate not only those directly involved but also others within the universities, including students. In addition, the events discussed here send messages to journalists and others within the community that those with legitimate views contrary to the government's will be restrained. Furthermore, more often than not, those in charge of the universities acquiesce in the face of government intervention. As a result, it is imperative that organizations such as NEAR be created to provide support to those in need.

Wider Issues of Academic Freedom

I want now to turn to another issue regarding academic rights. It is not only physical threats that affect these rights but also wider considerations such as the well-being of universities. There is, of course, a wide disparity in the economic situation facing universities in countries throughout the world. Those in Europe and in North America have a degree of monetary support that is without doubt of a much higher order compared with countries, say, in Africa. NEAR receives substantial information that staff in many parts of Africa do not receive salaries, and when they do, it compares poorly even with the low level of payment of other professions. Salaries are only one aspect of the lack of funding; the provision of such basic requirements as books, computers, and buildings are often left wanting. We have become concerned, therefore, that "brain drain" may have a strong impact on many universities in the developing world, which will, in turn, affect academic freedom.

Professionals often quote economic opportunities, combined with sociopolitical factors, as the primary reason for leaving their home countries and seeking work elsewhere. For many academics disparities in salaries are a key factor in their attempts to seek employment elsewhere. Disparities in salaries are applicable not only between countries (i.e., comparative salaries between academics in the global north and those of academics in the global south) but also within countries over time. In certain African countries the salaries of professionals have decreased progressively over the last twenty years. For example, university sources reveal that, in some instances, a university professor earning $1,000 a month in 1980 earned $50 a month in 2004. A recent report by the U.S. Agency for International Development indicated that sub-Saharan Africa is the only region in the world in which average income has declined over the past three decades.[17] Between 20,000 and 23,000 professionals emigrate from Africa each year.[18] According to one estimate, 60,000 professionals (doctors, university professors, etc.) left Africa between 1985 and 1990.[19] The United Nations Commission for Trade and Development estimates that every time a professional leaves, the cost to the country amounts to a loss of $184,000.[20]

Reasons for the so-called brain drain are complex and cannot be reduced to a single cause. Some of the circumstances that prompt professionals to leave include economic factors, political instability, and social upheaval. For educators, especially academics, lack of resources in educational institutions and research centers and restrictions on academic freedom can be considered the major contributing factors. On the African continent there are only 300 institutions that can be classified as universities, making Africa the world's least developed region in terms of both institutions and enrollments.[21] Combined with the shortfall of primary and secondary institutions, this effectively means that there are few institutions in Africa where citizens can undertake or further their education—encouraging those fortunate enough to migrate to countries or regions where there is greater access to facilities. "The crème de la crème of our country in terms of skills, qualifications and financial resources has bled out," said the South African minister of home affairs, Mangosuthu Buthelezi, talking about the problems of brain drain. "This is a haemorrhaging of human capital which is difficult to replace, and which has enormous implications."[22] Not the least of these implications is an additional burden on education and health systems. International recruitment agencies directly target professionals in underdeveloped countries in order to meet the shortfall in professional staff in countries such as the United Kingdom. Crippling debt repayments, restrictive trade agreements, structural adjustment programs, and other characteristics of a global capitalist market system often mean that even if countries were willing to provide better opportunities to professionals, they are unable to do so.

Local instability and unaccountable leadership compound problems brought about by globalization. To arrest or reduce the phenomenon, states must undergo a number of internal reforms, multinational companies and world leaders must commit to fair and ethical trade agreements, and international and local nongovernmental organizations must continue to press for change at both the local and international levels. As was recently noted, "The trick is to raise the cost of migration, not by forcing people not to leave home, but by providing better opportunities at home."[23]

There are, however, some happy exceptions. According to a discussion forum on the brain drain in Africa, in Botswana the number of educated professionals who leave the country is comparatively low.[24] One of the reasons given for this anomaly is that "the country has one of the most efficiently managed economies in Africa and a political system that is accountable and responsive to the need of its citizens."[25] Also, South Africa is clearly an exception to the rule. According to Hugh MacMillan, the best universities in South Africa "are centres of excellence in teaching and research, which may be a model for the rest of the region."[26]

As a result of the problems of brain drain, NEAR presented a series of recommendations to the United Nations Education, Scientific, and Cultural Organization (UNESCO) regarding actions that should be taken in Africa to enable academics from other African countries to benefit from the extensive amount of work that has been done on the problems of higher education in South Africa. UNESCO should undertake research on the issue of intellectual property rights and its implication for academic freedom. Governments should consider ways to encourage independent research in the universities to help promote sustained economic growth. And governments should recognize the rights of academic staff unions and encourage regional cooperation between academic staff unions.

In particular, the involvement of governments and large multinational companies in determining the use of intellectual property and access to freedom of information is a major issue related to academic freedom. Regarding access to freedom of information, it is clear that access to the World Wide Web is being denied. China and Zimbabwe have recently taken action against unfettered use of the Internet. Amnesty International has expressed concern about the effect on expression and information of Cuba's new law restricting Internet access.[27] I believe that these cases are just the tip of the iceberg regarding restrictions on Internet use.

On commercial and intellectual rights relating to research, universities, particularly those that are involved in applied research, are facing restrictions on the unrestricted publication of research findings. Intellectual property rights of academic staff have attracted worldwide attention, particularly in key scientific areas. The ability of academics to determine how their invention can be utilized may not be regarded in the mainstream of issues affecting academic freedom, but it is clear that many universities, particularly the ones with a strong expertise in science, will increasingly seek to limit university staff abilities to have freedom in this regard. Faculty unions have shown some interest in resisting the restriction on publication of research, but the size of commercial royalties to universities might make it a difficult matter to oppose.

Also, academic freedom has the wider aspect of relating to access to education itself. As pointed out by UNESCO, academic freedom involves the fundamental human right to education. The head of UNESCO, Koïchiro Matsuura, has said, "I have personally committed myself to making it a priority, for education is a fundamental human right, set forth in the Universal Declaration of Human Rights and the International Human Rights Covenants, which have force of international law. To pursue the aim of education for all is therefore an obligation for States."[28]

A final key component of academic freedom is that governments must educate their citizens without discrimination through direct acts or indirectly by their omissions. A report by Human Rights Watch, based on its research in South Africa, demonstrated that the high incidence of rape and sexual assault of girls in schools constituted a serious obstacle to the education of girls in that country. The report found that the government of South Africa was remiss in addressing this violence.[29]

Gender inequality, especially relating to access to education, is a significant issue throughout the world. For example, women in Africa fortunate enough to have become professional academics are substantially discriminated against because of their lack of access to positions, official and unofficial patronage within educational institutions, and lack of opportunities for promotion. This discrimination results in women academics either seeking to leave academia and education sectors completely or emigrating elsewhere in the hopes of having better opportunities.[30] Some evidence also exists from other sources that the low number of female postgraduate students put forward to international scholarship programs has caused concern, and, in one case that is known to NEAR, the program concerned refused to consider any application until female postgraduates were also included.

Various in-depth studies relating to gender in African universities refer to the low esteem in which female academics are held. For example, Sylvia Tamale and J. Oloka-Onyango wrote, "Few people would dispute the fact that gender is an extremely significant factor in African institutions of higher learning. A woman lecturer instructing university students as well as a woman intellectual relating to her male counterparts are generally perceived through lenses tainted by their sexuality. Not only are they considered less knowledgeable than their male colleagues, but they also have to work twice as hard in order to legitimise their positions and authority."[31] Some regard the whole notion of academic freedom as suspect if it does not take on and seek to deal with the gender issue. It has been very eloquently discussed in Tanzania that the concept of academic freedom in the context of the changing socio-political landscape in Africa has had to be rethought. It has been suggested that the problem with the concept is not so much what it includes, but rather what it does not include. Can we, for instance, exclude policies that disempowered half the population of a nation; those which restrict their access to higher education; those which do not provide equal opportunities for the pursuance of any fields of study; practices which make it impossible for sections of students or academics to conduct their business in peace; those which limit the amount of time that those sections can spend on their work; and so on.[32]

Some Final Notes

Before concluding this chapter, I would like to refer to perhaps the most sober situation facing those in higher education. In Colombia, in 2002 alone more than 140 individuals connected with education were killed, many of whom were faculty members and students. I hope that this travesty places some of the matters I have commented on in some context. By any standards, this statistic is shocking, yet the tragic events in Colombia are not widely known.

According to the U.K.'s Foreign and Commonwealth Office:

The internal conflict is estimated to have caused the deaths of between 3,000 and 4,000 civilians during 2002. Only about 10% of violent deaths in Colombia are linked to the conflict, but the country also suffers high levels of common criminality, much of it linked to the drug trade. Colombia probably has the world's worst record for kidnappings. Though numbers decreased in 2002 (2,492 compared to 3,041 in 2001) they remain alarmingly high. There is a major humanitarian crisis in Colombia, with one study suggesting that over the course of 2003, an average of 1,000 Colombians could be displaced every day. The most reliable estimates suggest the total number of displaced may be around 2.7 million, 60% under 14.[33]

Army-backed paramilitary groups, such as the United Self-Defence Forces of Colombia, have made the threat to journalists and newspaper editors great because the members of the media have been accused by the group of having links to "subversive groups." According to Amnesty International, "Fears for the safety of these sectors of civil society are further heightened by the fact that members of the security forces have frequently labelled them as guerrillas or guerrilla collaborators. In the past, such accusations have often been followed by serious human rights violations committed by paramilitary groups."[34]

Finally, I have not commented on the post-9/11 situation in the United States regarding academic freedom that others have so eloquently addressed in this book. I would like to make one comment, though. I am concerned that foreign scholars, particularly from the Middle East and Africa, are finding new difficulties in obtaining visas to attend conferences in the United States. Organizations such as the National Academies of Science, Engineering, and Medicine were concerned about visa delays, which restrict collaboration between American and foreign scholars. The American Association of University Professors also found a significant decrease in the enrollment of foreign students in the United States and a substantial backlog of visa applications.[35] There are issues here that need to be confronted, as they are essential to the pursuit of knowledge worldwide.

CHAPTER 7

Academic Freedom in Western Europe: Right or Privilege?

Antonio Brown

> Academic freedom is a privilege not a right.
> —Cyril Smith, Dean, Trinity College, Dublin, Ireland

ACADEMICS ARE PERCEIVED TO BE among a privileged set of individuals who are free to pursue scholarly interests and communicate their concerns to a relatively broad audience of students, colleagues, and various segments of the general population. Considering this perception, and for the purposes of this chapter, I define academic freedom as the right of university faculty members and researchers to appropriately investigate fields of knowledge and express views without fear of restraint or reprisals.

Education is a highly influential source of political socialization and socioeconomic mobility.[1] Therefore professors and researchers are in a unique position to affect the attitudes, beliefs, and behaviors of sociopolitical actors. That is, although education may enhance the understanding and support of political systems, it may also stimulate critique and mobilization for social change. As such, I argue that as an extension of free speech, academic freedom is among the dilemmas of liberal democracies, which attempt to balance civil liberties and human rights with diffuse support for the political systems. Although academic freedom in American political culture is discussed elsewhere in this book, the challenges highlighted by the tensions between academic freedom, intellectual integrity, and free speech in Western Europe are also striking, and in some cases, as I discuss shortly, the consequences are dire.

On September 11, 2001, the United States experienced an almost unprecedented attack. The act of terrorism on U.S. soil awakened new fears and raised questions regarding the acceptable limitations of freedom, access, and civil liberties for a new generation, some of which are discussed throughout this book. Concerns for cherished liberties and required protections from its enemies have increased the challenges to academic freedom in the United States. However, for Western Europeans terrorist acts in their homelands are all too familiar. Likewise, compromises to civil liberties and academic freedoms have become de rigueur.

Terrorists from around the globe have chosen cities such as London and Paris as targets of bombings and other extreme acts to gain the attention of the world press and regional governments. For instance, early 1999 saw three bombings that targeted various communities and neighborhoods in London. These bombings were attributed to a single actor who chose to victimize ethnic and sexual minorities in his campaign of violence.[2] Before this spate of attacks, the IRA claimed responsibility for numerous antiestablishment-inspired bombings, including a 1993 explosion that rippled through London's financial district. In France, during 1995, radical Islamic operatives set off bombs in the Paris subways.[3] And, 1994 saw the capture of "Carlos the Jackal," who was linked to Saddam Hussein and Moammar Gadhafi and to whom many massacres and acts of terrorism beginning in the 1970s throughout Western Europe and beyond are attributed.[4] These are but a few examples of the terrorist activities that have threatened the daily lives of Europeans over the last several decades. Furthermore, local terrorist organizations such as the ETA in Spain and the IRA in Britain have focused their activities on their homelands, local governments, and, importantly, academics whose critiques are viewed as a threat to the belief systems and goals of some controversial groups. As I discuss later in this chapter, terrorist groups have targeted Western European academics and researchers routinely for decades. That history, in combination with new concerns raised after September 11, and the support of European nations in the U.S.-led war in Iraq have drawn more attention to the potential for terrorist threats in Western Europe and the need to monitor academic freedom as it relates to research, higher practices, and other issues relevant to continuing business as usual on university campuses in the region.

One of the major issues that I address is the role of constitutional and institutional support for academic freedom as a right in a liberal democracy. In addition, I examine the consequences of state involvement in relation to the cultivation of academic freedom. Finally, I look at the effects of academic freedom in stimulating responses to social conditions, government actions, and the informed critique of political cultures and political systems by the citizenry.

Throughout this chapter I review the major positions on academic freedom in Western Europe. Many argue that there is a clear need for academic freedom to exist as a right in free societies. Still others state that not only is academic freedom a privilege but also freedom of speech is not a universal good, particularly when it impedes the rights of others or derides social groups and erodes intergroup relations within the political culture. While observing the ongoing debate, I examine the necessary role of academic freedom as a right rather than a privilege that is constantly questioned and potentially revoked at will by gatekeepers positioned to define and preserve national interests. But first, I offer a bit of history.

Freedom Matters: The Origins of Academic Freedom in Western Europe and Beyond

Academic freedom did not originate as a concept in relation to teaching and research. Before the seventeenth century, intellectual activities at universities throughout the West were restricted by tradition and doctrine mostly related to religious interventions.[5] That is, conclusions, discussions, and presentations that conflicted with religious doctrines typically were condemned, and the representatives of such findings were likely to face negative sanctions initiated and enforced by religious leaders and government entities. In response to this religion-centered approach to knowledge, the scientific method of reasoning was developed during the era known as the Enlightenment.

The concept of academic freedom developed during the Enlightenment.[6] Scientific and intellectual developments, such as the discoveries of Isaac Newton, the rationalism of René Descartes, and the empiricism of Francis Bacon and John Locke, encouraged beliefs in natural law and universal order as well as acknowledgments of the value of human reason. These methods of investigation and experimentation took root during the Enlightenment and became pervasive throughout the academy and European society as a whole. More important, it is during the Enlightenment that the scientific method—the rigorous, rational, and replicable manner of analyzing data and establishing hypotheses—became a vital concomitant of academic freedom; the scientific method was invigorated by scholars outside university life, such as Thomas Hobbes, John Locke, and Voltaire.[7]

Accordingly, in the late seventeenth century English philosophers John Locke and Thomas Hobbes led the way to contemporary conceptualizations of academic freedom by showing the need for a general approach to learning that is unfettered by preconceived notions of acceptable forms of knowledge and truth.[8] Contemporaneously, the German universities of Halle and Göttingen, founded in 1694 and 1737, respectively, were among the first European universities to be conceived with strong attachments to academic freedom as the standard for critical teaching and research activities. Acceptance of the principles of academic freedom increased in the eighteenth and nineteenth centuries as universities in Western Europe, Britain, and the United States followed suit. Concomitant to and facilitative of the increased acceptance of academic freedom, religious control of institutions decreased and the experimental methods of the sciences became more widespread.[9]

Consequently, academic freedom arose as a legal concept in Germany circa 1850. Ronald Standler observes that the Prussian Constitution states that "science and its teaching shall be free."[10] This groundbreaking constitutional stance is seen as establishing the foundations of academic freedom as being embedded in the relatively unimpeded communication of knowledge. More important, these early inroads into academic freedom paved the way toward institutionalized standards throughout Western Europe and the United States. Thus the roles of scholars and academic pursuits were established. In addition, we observe the development of a professoriat empowered with the privileges of free expression recognized by tradition, precedent, and, arguably, as a right established by law under the early Prussian Constitution.[11] Thereby the trend toward academic freedom became increasingly entrenched over time. However, during the first half of the twentieth century, infringements into the province of academic freedom increased as totalitarianism emerged in various countries, particularly in Germany, Italy, and the former Soviet Union.[12]

Totalitarian regimes during the early and mid twentieth century (and today) sought to limit access to and to control the dissemination of knowledge. Scholars, in order to remain in their posts, were not free to discuss or represent ideas that were perceived as a threat to the regime. The perceived threat of academic freedom is clearly illustrated by the anti-intellectual crusades of Hitler in Germany, Mussolini in Italy, and Franco in Spain. Books deemed controversial to the state were routinely and publicly burned. Because of their potential influence on the public, in particular, the youth, academics and intellectuals were (and in some cases remain) the early targets of political purges, exile, and execution. Thereby we see the book shut on some of the gains made in support of academic freedom in the West through the mid twentieth century.

Since the events of World War II, there has been a great deal of progress in restoring and securing academic freedom throughout Western Europe. However, such freedoms remain a contemporary concern. Notably, in 1998 the University of Bologna and the Association of European Universities formed the Observatory of Fundamental University Values and Rights in order to monitor academic freedom in Europe. The group, which is based in Bologna, Italy, works to help ensure institutional autonomy and transformations in education related to globalization and commercialization. The Observatory came into being as an outgrowth of the Bologna process that sought recovery from the vagaries of authoritarian regimes, particularly among the Eastern European nations, and it responded to challenges to academic freedom by establishing the Magna Charta of Universities, which was signed by representatives from hundreds of universities in 1988 in Bologna, Italy. The Magna Charta and its supporters sought to ensure that research and teaching were "morally and intellectually independent of political authority and economic power."[13] The Observatory of Fundamental University Values and Rights is joined by the Network for Education and Academic Rights (NEAR), established in June 2001, in its attempts to protect civil liberties in an atmosphere of shifting public opinion and attitudes as they relate to academic freedom in Western Europe as well as fear for public safety and national security (see Chapter 6 for more on NEAR's activities). These organizations signal academic grassroots efforts to expand and protect academic freedom in the wake of post–World War II and post–cold war globalization and the growth of the European Union.

So it is that a brief historical overview uncovers the rise of academic freedom during the Enlightenment and its relative fall during the struggles with authoritarian regimes during World War II and the post–World War II resurgence of academic freedom as an accepted right in terms of the investigation and dissemination of knowledge in Western Europe. And, just as the past has shown a propensity for change on this issue, a look at the present will show that there is no definitive position regarding the rights of academic freedom, particularly within the diverse political contexts of Western Europe.

Next, I argue that among the sociopolitically and economically advanced liberal democracies of Western Europe, the case can be made for academic freedom as a rightful extension of free speech as well as open critiques of political systems and political leaders. Although there has been a great deal of change, many of the observed shifts are related to the developments of burgeoning democratic political cultures. That is, as democratic governments grow and usurp the role of religion as the source of social policies and practices, we observe a shift toward increased academic freedom as it relates to controversial or progressive views and an increased reliance on scientific knowledge.

Likewise, as democratic regimes destabilized as a result of a rise in authoritarian rule, such as that witnessed in Europe shortly before and during World War II, or mass level shifts in the political consciousness, such as the Red Scare that led to the United States's obsession with the presence of communists in their midst, we saw a restriction in academic expression that was perceived as a threat to the relevant sociopolitical norms. As the fears of latent communism subsided, support for academic freedom continued to grow. It seemed that academic freedom would be viewed as an extension of the freedom of expression that is prevalent within contemporary democracies. But does academic freedom exist as an honored privilege or as a basic right? If academic freedom is deemed a privilege, why would freedom of academic endeavors exist as a privileged *exception* rather than a lawful right among the now stable and continually advancing democratic nations where human rights, individual freedoms, and peaceful exchanges of political power are the rule?

Whose Right? Government Involvement Matters

Although European academic standards have influenced and remain related to U.S. systems, the circumstances are often highly variable. More important, the United States has a clear foundation, based on the First Amendment to the U.S. Constitution, for individual freedoms as related to the expression of beliefs that many argue offers support for academic freedom as well.[14] To that end, Justice Brennan writes for the majority opinion in *Keyishian v. Board of Regents* (1967) that academic freedom is "a special concern of the First Amendment."[15] This Supreme Court finding has the force of law in the United States. However, debate regarding the implications of First Amendment rights to the application of academic freedoms continues to occur. In response to the Supreme Court finding, Standler, Byrne, and other legal scholars argue that the First Amendment is more properly applied to individual rights and the protection of political speech.[16] If, as it appears, academic freedom retains some amorphous quality in the United States, which strongly supports free speech and individual rights, it should not be surprising that the principles of academic freedom face even greater challenges throughout Western Europe. The broader political context of Western Europe includes nations (and a supranational structure, the European Union [EU]) that do not have written constitutions; a European Union high court (European Court of Justice [ECJ]) and the European Council on Human Rights (ECHR), which are not fully empowered to address the issue; and individual nation-states that restrict freedom of expression, for instance, as it relates to hate speech. Ultimately, it appears that throughout Western Europe many nations proclaim the values of the quality of speech over unencumbered freedom of speech.

For example, speech that may be harmful to the substantive cohesiveness of perceptions, attitudes, and behaviors within the political culture is viewed by some as undermining diffuse support within and across the alliances of the various European nation-states. Accordingly, we have seen recent attempts to censor Internet interactions that involve hate speech directed at ethnic groups in Germany. Offensive references based on race, gender, and sexuality are subject to negative sanctions based on hate speech laws in the Netherlands. And France (along with Germany and other nations) seeks to limit offensive materials presented on the Internet and other public venues.[17] Therefore, if free speech is qualified throughout the political culture, it comes as little surprise that academic freedom can also be compromised. Combining these points with the tradition of high levels of government involvement in the role and function of universities in Western Europe, there is little wonder that academic freedom is a difficult concept to define and actualize, particularly throughout the European Union.

Just as the political cultures and perceptions of free speech and academic freedom vary, the relationship of European governments to universities is varied. In some cases, such relationships may be fraught with turbulence, making the likelihood of change perhaps the only reliable source of consistency. One key starting point in the examination of Western European university systems in comparison to those in the United States relates to the higher level of state involvement. Governmental entities throughout the European nations are routinely involved in the daily operations, admissions policies, and research agenda of universities. They affect the routines of the administration, student education, and faculty activities and involvements.

For instance, universities such as those in Ireland are not free to decide salary levels, set student fees, construct buildings, or acquire land without government approval.[18] The French and Italian governments are typically involved in hiring practices and the administration of its universities.[19] These governments heavily influence the areas of study in which academics and researchers may be hired as well as the salaries that they may be paid. In addition, the French and Italian governments, among others, determine the buildings and facilities that can be constructed, thereby influencing the quality and types of research that can be pursued. In England, as well as in many other European countries, foreign-born academics and researchers who seek appointments are subject to government approval based on their nations of origin and areas of research.[20]

Furthermore, university education throughout Western Europe typically is made available at a low cost to students who qualify based on various exams that determine their educational track and opportunities. Arguably, such hands-on approaches by government may be justified because of the relative lack of privatization of European universities compared to their U.S. counterparts.[21] Likewise, the limitations on academic freedom by government entities may appear justified by the economic investment that governments have in European university systems. That is, the governments may reasonably perceive a right to monitor and determine academic activities based on the costs that they bear to make the academic experiences possible. However, the devolution of power from government agencies to universities in some European nations is a growing trend, and the results have predictable effects on academic freedom.

Scandinavian countries such as Sweden and Denmark, which have become as well known for their state-centered approaches to education as for their progressive sociopolitical and advanced socioeconomic conditions, have enacted conscious efforts to lessen government involvement in the curriculum and in the number of courses and length of time necessary to graduate from the university level. The decrease in government involvement has been accompanied by increases in academic freedom and productivity in a variety of areas, including medical and social science research.[22]

Throughout Western Europe and beyond, there have been great advances and great ethical debates related to genetics research, the use of embryo-based therapies, and cloning. Putting aside moral positions regarding these forms of research and related medical procedures, in general, these issues and questions are raised and in some instances justified on the basis of necessary freedoms to pursue academic research.[23] Supporters and opponents of such research routinely base their arguments on the need to extend or retract academic freedom as it relates to controversial research. The implications and dilemmas for advocates of academic freedom are clear. How does one balance the need for scientific investigation with the preservation of human dignity and moral concerns? Although I do not seek to resolve such issues here, it is apparent that the consequences of and appropriate limitations to academic freedom deserve due consideration. To address such concerns, the governments of various nations often are asked to intervene and to help define the parameters of academic freedom.

In consideration of ethical issues, security concerns, and academic freedom, Professor Philip Regal concludes that responsibility is key.[24] Regal is particularly concerned with the effects of terrorist threats on sustaining academic freedom as it relates to biotechnological research that can lead to significant social gains in various industries, including agriculture and medicine (see Chapter 5 for more discussion of this topic). At a time when bioterrorism is seen as a significant threat, academics are now called on to balance their interests and potential social and medical advances with the need to manage international borders and threats to their personal and national security. In the cases of both biotechnology and human genetics research, significant advances might depend on the freedom of academics to pursue appropriate studies. However, these cases raise significant issues related to the kinds of research that academics are free to pursue and the consequences of medical and biotechnological advances for human dignity and safety from terrorist threats. Ultimately, discussions of these questions lead to discussions of the proper role of government and the increasing reliance on the private sector, rather than on universities with ties to governments, for research and technological advances. Observing the intermingling of academic research agendas and government involvement in university systems throughout Western Europe draws attention to the role of privatization in the development of academic freedom.

Interestingly, Tony Blair has proposed a more privatized university system in England, similar to that of the United States, which would lessen government involvements and subsidies as well as require students to pay a greater share of educational costs. Blair would also establish government-sponsored loan programs. His stated goals are to increase educational opportunities, lessen government involvement, and decrease the financial burden that the nation faces with regard to university education.[25] Furthermore, Blair notes that this new system could stimulate academic research, presumably because of decreased government involvement in the faculty research agenda.

The case of Ireland also demonstrates the difficulties of defining and operationalizing academic freedom. The 1997 Universities Act declares academic freedom by establishing universities as autonomous institutions. In practice, however, academic freedom in Irish universities is highly restrained. For instance, although professors may discuss their perspectives on subjects included in the curricula, the universities are not free to establish or to terminate academic programs that receive public funds. Academic initiatives are dependent on public funding and thus are subject to the approval of the Higher Education Authority.[26] If the program or scholars do not function in accord with the funding agency, then that academic program could be canceled because of lack of funds. These circumstances have inspired students and faculty members to demonstrate for greater autonomy (although each group also requests lower fees for students). This case illustrates that the intermingling of governmental controls and economic dependence help determine the realities of academic freedom. That is, in the case of Ireland, it is clear that more government involvement means less academic freedom, regardless of policy statements to the contrary.[27]

Furthermore, Italy and Germany, political cultures that rate highly with regard to citizen support for government involvement in social issues and daily life,[28] have been embroiled in debates regarding who will determine the university agenda or, more accurately, what, if any, is the role of government in relation to university education. Since the end of World War II, these nations have been less supportive of academic freedom than many of their European neighbors and more focused on government involvement in the academic activities and research agenda of universities.[29] In part, this approach is affected by benevolent considerations for sustaining diffuse support of the political systems and minimizing opportunities for ostensibly offensive programs of study in nations such as Germany, which remains sensitive regarding its image relative to outgroups and its partners in the European Union.[30] In other words, as Germany and other European nations have negatively sanctioned hate speech, pervasive (and perhaps appropriate) cross-cultural and cross-national sensitivities increasingly and negatively influence the likelihood of unfettered academic freedom in universities that enjoy a great deal of governmental support.[31]

These brief examples illustrate the varying effects of academic freedom present throughout Western Europe, a region that currently seeks harmonization on international social policies. Also, these examples highlight the influence of government involvement on academic freedom in university settings. In regions such as Ireland, Germany, and Italy we see that academic freedom is a matter of debate, the parameters of which are often poorly defined. The high levels of government involvement make the acceptance of academic freedom in these areas less likely to increase.

This perspective is further supported by a recent study of twenty nations to help determine the range of academic freedom, university autonomy, and "who owns the curriculum."[32] The results, based on a survey of experts in government-university relations in the various countries, sustain the observations that I have presented.[33] Authority for government intervention is quite high in France, an outlier among Western nations that experts rate as having a high level of government-university relations, indicating that government has a great deal of power to intervene in matters of academic freedom and university policies and practices. Italy and Germany are in the middle range in relation to government intervention. The governments of Ireland and the United Kingdom are moderately involved in university administration and academic freedom issues. The country rated with the least authority for government intervention is Canada. Notably, U.S. government intervention in the university process averages just above that of Ireland. Although these findings are useful, they are also likely to be influenced by policy at least as much, if not more than, practice. Therefore, for instance, the 1997 Universities Act, which indicates greater autonomy among Irish universities, may have a greater than realized influence as it relates to the overt practices in that region.[34]

In fact, a more detailed look at the data discloses the ratings of governments in which influence is actually exerted. That is, although particular governments may have the authority to influence university activities, the data show which among them is perceived to take the steps to do so on a regular basis. Here we see that out of the twenty nations surveyed, France ranks near the top, the fourth mostly likely to exert government influence.[35] Italy ranks eighth, Germany fifteenth, Ireland seventeenth, and the United Kingdom twentieth in relation to the exertion of government influence on academic freedom and university policies and practices.[36]

The findings indicate that both the potential and the reality of government intervention in academic freedom varies among the European nations. Interestingly, although Ireland scores low on actual government intervention, the lack of academic freedom can be observed in statements made by public officials and in student and faculty protest activities.[37] The key point is that government involvement, even when well intentioned, is linked to decreased academic freedom and independence.

The debate regarding academic freedom, attempts at privatization, and pressures to secure the rights of free expression and self-determination for universities and faculty suggest that there is something to be gained by enhancing independence. In some cases the independent voices enabled by academic freedom inspire government restraint of university autonomy. Containing social movements, sustaining political interests, attempting to preserve security within the nation's borders, and maintaining the status of elected officials may serve as incentives for restricting academic freedom. Next, I review the issues related to academic freedom, political mobilization, and social change as well as the related controversies.

Balancing Freedoms: Facing the Dilemmas of Democracy

Considerations of academic freedom often lend themselves to discussions of the repression of academics themselves. The acts of repression generally are in response to the consequences of the new ideas, concepts, and perspectives associated with the sharing of knowledge and critical analyses of politics, society, and culture. Dissenting scholars throughout the world have faced negative sanctions from their governments. For instance, a cadre of Chinese scholars who were trained and employed in the United States and Western Europe were detained in China throughout 2000 and 2001 because of their outspoken critiques of government entities and their areas of research.[38] Similar examples can be found throughout the Middle East and the former Soviet Union. The consequences for these scholars include imprisonment and severe physical punishments (see Chapter 6). However, governments outside the West are not the only source of repressive actions.

As I have mentioned, there has been a long history of the repression of faculty and students in the midst of political regime changes or cultural panic, such as that experienced during the height of the Red Scare in the United States. Currently, there is a major trend toward vetting the research interests of foreign-born or "ethnic" intellectuals throughout Europe (as well as the United States) in response to the September 11 attacks. Arguably, we are experiencing a contemporary wave of academic repression that is partially related to the terrorist acts that occurred in the United States on September 11, 2001. But, we also can observe fearful actions that precede that pivotal date.

Since 1994 the British Foreign Office has quietly operated the "Voluntary Vetting Scheme."[39] Based on this approach, scholars from targeted nations are likely to be "vetted" before acceptance at a British university if their research can be construed to contribute to the development of chemical or biological weapons.[40] The goal of the scheme is to prevent the infiltration of British laboratories by terrorists.

Universities participating in the vetting process send details about targeted applicants to the British Foreign Office before accepting them as researchers. Vetting activities are observed to have risen significantly since September 11, 2001.[41] Academics and civil liberties groups in Britain and throughout Western Europe have protested the procedure because it compromises academic freedom by curtailing universities' rights to select qualified scholars and undermines basic human rights, as defined by the European Convention on Human Rights, in order to fight potential terrorism.

Although terrorism appears as a linchpin in some activities that may limit academic freedom, terrorists in Western Europe are also responsible for repressing the free expression of academics. Western Europe is typically considered a safe place for professors compared with the tribulations faced by their counterparts in less democratic regions. However, academics in Europe can face dire consequences. Notably, the Euzkaki Ta Askatasuna (Basque Fatherland and Liberty, known as ETA), Spain's militant Basque separatist movement, has been involved in death threats and other fear tactics to silence their critics in the academic community.[42] ETA has taken credit for several attacks on universities and academics in the Basque region of Spain. For instance, ETA admitted to leaving a parcel bomb in an elevator on the Lejona campus of the University of the Basque Country on December 18, 2000. The misfired bomb narrowly missed Professor Edurne Uriarte, an outspoken critic of ETA's tactics. She subsequently stopped teaching out of fear of further assassination attempts. Likewise, Mikel María Azurmendi and José María Portillo also stopped teaching at universities in the Basque region and moved abroad after ETA made attempts to end their lives.[43]

Other academics have narrowly escaped car bombings and other murder attempts related to their positions on ETA terrorist acts or Basque independence. Still others have left their university posts in fear of their lives. However, in one of the most devastating attacks against outspoken academics, economics historian Ernest Lluch of the University of Barcelona, which is outside the Basque territory, was shot dead by members of ETA in November 2000 because of his vocal support for negotiations to end the conflict in the Basque region.[44] ETA continued its campaign of shootings and bombings, killing four people in 2003. ETA participants also continued a campaign of street violence and vandalism in the Basque region in order to influence and intimidate academics and others who have spoken out against them.[45] Although it is clear that ETA does not represent the political mainstream in the region, it is likely that, should there be regime change favoring ETA, academic freedom and the lives and freedom of their opponents would be endangered.

Similarly, the Irish Republic Army (IRA) has posed threats to academics and the social order and has been labeled the greatest internal terrorist threat throughout Britain. Since the 1950s, the IRA has engaged in targeted terrorist attacks to call attention to its nationalistic goals. Bombings, kidnappings, and other attacks have affected the lives of the British public. Violence attributed to or claimed by the IRA has affected people throughout Britain and at various points has been focused on outspoken academics and politicians.

However, since the 1994 cease-fire and the 1998 peace agreement, the overt violent activities of the IRA have subsided. In fact, when granted immunity, some former IRA members have participated in retrieving the remains of victims whose deaths date back to the 1970s. The peace accord between the IRA and the British government is reinforced by the decreased levels of unemployment throughout Ireland, which are related to substantial funding from European Union supranational institutions.[46] Still, the precarious balance continues to face challenges. As recently as May 2003, Sinn Fein (the political arm of the IRA) and its supporters have expressed disappointment with the halted election that would have allowed a vote on a new assembly that would be charged with electing a new government in which Catholics and Protestants are expected to share power. Recent analyses suggest that there are no major threats to academic freedom. The future of IRA-led violent protest remains uncertain. The peace process is somewhat dependent of the continuing role of U.S. envoy Richard Haass.[47]

Balancing academic freedom with a healthy fear of real threats presents a challenging dilemma to democracies and all proponents of civil liberties. The repression of academics by militant entities such as ETA is relatively rare in Western Europe. Nevertheless, these activities raise substantial concerns for continued academic freedom across the nations of Europe. Furthermore, past and present responses to terrorist activities have routinely involved government-sanctioned limitations on academic freedom, as is illustrated by the practices of the British Foreign Office, which continue to raise concerns for human rights and civil liberties in that region.

Inasmuch as free speech is supported as a basic liberty, many argue that academic freedom is a right in a liberal democracy. Constitutional and institutional support for this argument is apparent. However, such support varies by country, and in some cases, such as that of Ireland, the rights of academic freedom exist more as a matter of theory than as actual practice. Government involvement often appears to be connected to a decrease in academic freedom, unless governments, such as those in Scandinavia, actively operate to limit their impact on university autonomy. In any case, whether based on government action, fear of terrorist activity, or, as in the case of Spain, terrorist intimidation, the limits of academic freedom are tested by scholars who seek to influence politics, culture, and society based on their research agenda or access to public forums for the expression of their (educated) perspectives.

Balancing freedoms is a complex matter. It is further complicated in the European Union by the goals of the supranation and the various universities that seek harmonization on social policies, civil liberties, and human rights. However, the challenges are familiar to liberal democracies: addressing the dynamic tension between protecting freedom of expression and protecting a free society from internal and external threats. The greatest tests of a liberal democracy often occur during the time of its greatest threats. Safeguarding democracy from fear-driven attempts to save itself involves sustaining the promises of free speech and the integrity of academic freedom, even during the most challenging times.

Formal Freedoms, Informal Violence: Academic Freedom and Human Rights in Latin America

Enrique Desmond Arias

ON AUGUST 21, 2004, I interviewed the senior police commander in the city of Porto Alegre, a state capital of 2 million in southern Brazil, as part of a research project on persistent crime and violence in urban Latin America. During the interview, which I taped with the interviewee's permission, the police officer made a number of politically compromising statements in which he suggested that the high levels of violence in other metropolitan areas of his country stemmed from "racial miscegenation" and that he thought it was good that police killed suspected criminals before arrest as a way of controlling crime. Immediately after the interview a second police officer seized my recording, and I was detained by officers in the intelligence branch of the state police, who then turned me over to the federal police for three hours while they searched for possible visa violations under which to deport me. After talking extensively with the federal police agent, explaining the nature of my work and assuring him that I was not an official of the United States government, he released me and called the state police intelligence officer to tell him that he should return the tape. He noted that I was okay because I "trained police" as part of my academic appointment.[1] The federal police agent said the tape would be available at the state police headquarters at 5 p.m. that afternoon. I returned later that day, quietly accompanied by a lawyer for the Human Rights Commission of the State Legislative Assembly, but, of course, the tape and the officer who seized it were nowhere to be found. We left a card but the tape has still not turned up.

This experience with police detention in the conduct of scholarly re-search is a pale shadow of the experiences of academics in other parts of Brazil and Latin America. Twenty years after Latin America's au-thoritarian regimes began to fall with the defeat of the Argentine junta in the 1983 Falklands war, many threats to human rights in general and academic freedom in particular remain. As I show later in this chapter, in Haiti, Ecuador, Brazil, and Venezuela faculty have suffered personal threats and, in some cases, actual attacks as a result of their political po-sitions. In Guatemala at least one academic has disappeared. However, as John Akker notes in Chapter 6, Colombia is the standout. In the midst of a forty-year civil war, hundreds of college professors, schoolteachers, and students have been murdered, usually by right-wing paramilitary groups, as a result of alleged sympathies with leftist guerrillas.

Unfortunately, scholars have not widely examined the question of academic freedom in Latin America's new democracies. This is a marked contrast from the previous generation when the rights of students and faculty stood at the epicenter of academic debates about human rights.[2] The principal difference between the threats to academic freedom today and those of the previous generation is that, whereas twenty years ago threats came principally from high-level sources within the state and were systematically carried out across the academy, today violations take place in a capricious manner driven not so much by high-level state officials but by relatively low-level rogue state actors, by elements of society, and, increasingly, by the impact of the global marketplace on the dwindling state structure in which many Latin American academ-ics work.

The September 11 attacks on New York and Washington, D.C., have had little impact on the day-to-day lives of Latin Americans. Neverthe-less, the types of nonstate threats that today affect Latin American aca-demics and that also preoccupy U.S. policymakers reflect a broad shift of concern away from state violence toward social violence. The terror-ists who flew planes into the World Trade Center and the Pentagon did not represent a fixed state that the United States government could tar-get in retaliation. Rather, they reflected a diffuse network of militant, re-ligiously motivated actors. Many of the threats to Latin American aca-demics come from similarly diffuse sources.

On some levels the shift from systematic state abuse of academics to more dispersed violations by individual state officials and social actors has had positive effects. In most of Latin America today academics who criticize their governments do not have to worry about long-term detention, torture, or assassination. In my contacts with Latin American scholars before writing this chapter I had never heard a complaint of abuse. At the same time, however, the persistent violation of academic freedoms in the region raises serious concerns. Although academics do not have to worry as much about criticizing state leadership as they did twenty years ago, today they have to worry about researching subjects that could put them on the wrong side of pernicious social forces. In these difficult situations professors and teachers can expect little help from a cash-strapped state with relatively limited control over a police force and military that may have close ties to social groups that try to intimidate scholars. Furthermore, because threats rarely come from a coherent state body, existing international mechanisms and pressure strategies used by such groups as Amnesty International rarely provide the long-term protection that academics engaged in dangerous work need to complete their research, and they do little to strengthen the overall condition of academic freedom in the region.

In this chapter I examine these issues by looking at the overall problem of human rights in the historical context of academic freedom in Latin America. I then examine representative cases of academic freedom from around the Caribbean and Central and South America. I acquired the information discussed here through a number of interviews conducted in the winter of 2003–2004 with academics and other experts in the region as well as through secondary sources. In the last section of the chapter I examine strategies to more effectively guarantee the rights of university professors and schoolteachers in Latin America.

The History of Academic Freedom in Latin America

On paper, at least, academic freedom in the Americas is stronger than it is in the United States. The watershed moment for university rights in the region were the Córdoba Reforms, which began in Argentina in 1918 and swept through most of the larger countries of Latin America. Developing out of a series of student actions in the early twentieth century that protested elite control of universities, the reform movement demanded places in tertiary education for all secondary school graduates and a notion of shared governance that included professors, administrators, and students.[3] These governance principles go well beyond those of U.S. universities in giving students a significant voice in school policy. In Brazil, for example, student unions participate in campus strike votes.

Academic freedom in Latin America also includes the concept of *libertad de cátedra* ("freedom of the chair"), which in some ways parallels the rights of professors in North American universities to develop their own courses, research freely in their area of expertise, and speak publicly without repercussions from the university. These similarities, however, only go so far. Because one of the goals of the Córdoba Reforms was to decrease some of the privileges of tenured senior faculty, this notion of academic freedom applies as much to students as it does to the professoriat.[4] In Argentina, for example, the reforms led to the elimination of tenure and the principle that two professors must regularly teach every course in order to give students options of how they want to study a given subject, thus granting students a choice of *cátedra*. In other Latin American countries many university professors hold lifetime appointments, although the source of tenure (be it through university or civil service rules) varies from country to country and from university to university.[5] Nevertheless at the heart of *libertad de cátedra* is the idea that professors can research and teach what they choose without outside interference and that students have a free choice of how to study required material.

Perhaps the most distinctive element of academic freedom in Latin America is *autonomía universitaria* ("university autonomy").[6] Although the Córdoba reformers actually called for state intervention to restructure the universities, their intellectual heirs in the 1920s and 1930s began to focus on establishing and strengthening *autonomía universitaria*.[7] This concept, which had developed out of the privileged position of the Spanish university in the Middle Ages, conceives of the university as an almost foreign place within the polity immune from the state where the police cannot enter and where dissident politicians can receive asylum.[8] Many Latin Americans see the university as effectively a self-governing entity, a *"república universitaria."*[9] As one researcher put it, "The police have to ask permission to come into university buildings since the Córdoba Reforms."[10]

Unfortunately many of these principles do not hold up well in practice. One analyst from the early 1970s wrote: "More often, governments have closed universities as a result of statements obnoxious to the regime, have fired professors at such critical times as a sudden change of government, and have even arrested and shot university faculty and students if matters became too far out of hand. . . . In short, autonomy has been honored more in the breach than in the practice."[11]

An article on student violence in the early 1970s notes that the existence of university autonomy and the reluctance of police to enter campuses created an environment that heightened the likelihood of a confrontation between the university and the state and made it more likely that the state would eventually violently intervene in the university.[12] As one former Panamanian academic notes of the 1968 coup d'état in his country, "Torrijos [Panama's left-populist dictator] invaded the university because he was a dictator and the students were carousing. [After that] they got rid of the students opposing Torrijos and closed the University for a couple of months."[13]

Panama was not the only country to suffer attacks on academic freedoms during the period of bureaucratic authoritarian dictatorships that began with Brazil's 1964 military coup and ended when Augusto Pinochet stepped down from the presidency of Chile in 1990. As in other dictatorial periods during the twentieth century, universities and their faculty came under extended assault in many countries. In Brazil the dictatorship, which hardened under the administrations of Generals Costa e Silva and Medici between 1966 and 1974, dismissed large numbers of professors from federal universities in Rio de Janeiro, São Paulo, and Rio Grande do Sul. The state run Conselho Nacional de Pesquisas (CNPq, National Research Council) had to approve all research by local and foreign academics.[14] The Ford Foundation provided aid and support to newly unemployed Brazilian academics by funding private research centers to provide temporary employment to those forced from the public universities.[15]

One of the most dramatic violations of university autonomy occurred in Mexico City in 1968 when the government invaded a set of dormitories and the Universidad Nacional Autónoma de México (UNAM) to break up student protests. The police action resulted in the death of numerous students and undermined a significant amount of support that the Mexican revolutionary regime drew from academics.[16] The two worst cases of violence and repression within universities occurred in Chile and Argentina. Under the Pinochet regime many Chilean professors lost their positions as a result of their politics, and politically appointed university rectors gained the ability to name new faculty. All told, the government forced 2,000 professors and 20,000 students from the universities.[17] Under political pressure many universities cut political science and sociology departments and redirected resources into such areas as business administration and engineering, which the regime felt lent themselves to political complacency and economic growth.[18]

Conditions in Argentina were also quite bad. With the 1966 coup that brought General Juan Carlos Onganía to power, the National University became a center of protest, although the university administration quickly distanced itself from these activities so as not to antagonize the government and remain open for scholarly activities and teaching. The government then issued decrees subordinating the university to the Ministry of Education, which led to mass faculty resignations and violent student protests. The government ordered police onto campus to reestablish order and, as one observer put it, "The Metropolitan Police, permitted for once to penetrate the sanctuary of the university Halls in order to dislodge the students, carried out the assignment with great enthusiasm, settling in the process many long standing accounts."[19] During a second period of dictatorship that began in 1976, universities, which remained hotbeds of dissent, again drew military repression. Many of the more than 30,000 Argentines arrested and disappeared during this period had affiliations with universities.[20]

The preceding discussion provides only a few examples of the types of challenges that faced academics during this period. What holds these disparate cases together is that, uniformly, threats to academic freedom emanated from the state apparatus itself. The government would send troops into schools, order the arrests of students, fire professors, close departments, and order the imprisonment or assassination of academics. This threatening environment posed serious challenges to university education and the academic project in general, because many social scientists and humanities scholars either had to leave their positions or choose scholarly projects that the government did not object to.

The story of Latin America's late twentieth century dictatorships, however, ends happily. After years of repression and popular struggle against abusive regimes, almost all of the dictatorships eventually fell, and civilian popularly elected governments took their places. The constitutions that came into existence in the late 1980s and 1990s legally enshrined basic rights to freedom of association and expression. These new governments established independent judiciaries to help make the state and its representatives accountable to the citizens. All of this effectively paved the way for a much greater respect for individual rights than had existed at any time in Latin America since the immediate postwar period.

Academic Freedom in the Transition to Democracy

The establishment of new, more open regimes in much of Latin America happened under severe constraints as pro-authoritarian and pro-democracy forces jockeyed for political advantage in the twilight of the dictatorships. Many analysts of politics in Latin America called for a moderate transition to formal liberal democracy (a system defined by basic civil and political rights with a rule of law and regular free fair and open elections) rather than a broader transition to a fuller social democracy (a system defined by the basic rights that characterize formal democracy but with certain economic guarantees necessary to ensure the full participation of all segments of the populace in the democratic process) for fear that too radical a push could result in an authoritarian backlash.[21] This system would guarantee free, open, fair, and competitive elections as well as the basic civil and political rights needed to make those elections meaningful. Having watched the torture, imprisonment, murder, and exile of their colleagues and friends who opposed the dictatorship, many academics favored these moderate transitions in order to prevent further unlawful detentions and bloodshed. Eminent political scientist Adam Przeworski noted that the purpose of democracy was "that people shall not be killed!"[22] Ultimately, Latin America, with the exception of Cuba, made its transition to liberal democracy, and the entire population of Latin American countries now enjoys at least nominal rights.

Beyond regular elections and basic guarantees, the story of Latin America's new democracies is much cloudier. Human rights abuse and social violence persist in much of Latin America, and in Brazil human rights abuse has actually increased since the end of the dictatorship.[23] In general, those with enough resources to hire lawyers to protect their rights in court and to live in gated communities have little to worry about. The problem lies in the lives of the remainder of the citizenry. Most violence and human rights abuses suffered in Latin America today do not stem from systematic decisions made by state leaders but rather takes place at the hands of criminals, paramilitary groups, guerrillas, and rogue state actors operating outside the law but often with the tacit approval of some higher ranking state officials. Those who are too poor to effectively protest police violence, use courts to their advantage, or relocate to more secure surroundings bear much of the abuse that occurs in the Americas today.

In this transition academics have generally fared well. Whereas before abuse resulted from the political positions that one took, today human rights violations correlate to social class and race. Poor people have many more problems than the well-off do. Despite not receiving large salaries, Latin America's academics are firmly part of the middle and upper classes. Most make enough money to hire legal representation when the government threatens their rights and can move to safer neighborhoods if crime increases. The basic protections available to the middle class through lawyers and other social connections do insulate most academics in their day-to-day lives from concrete threats to their lives and livelihoods. As we will see later in the chapter, one academic who lost her job as a result of political statements has actually retained lawyers in civil and administrative actions to demand redress for her loss. As a result of these types of connections, persecution of academics today often has little to do with their political stances, and most academics can work within the university and conduct their research with little worry of the state acting against them. Indeed, Latin American academics today regularly criticize the politicians and political systems that govern their countries. One Argentine wrote, "Political pressure has not been a major reason to lose your *cátedra* [academic chair] since the democratic transition in 1983."[24] An American academic currently working in Brazil noted, "I will say one thing, as profs we have a lot more autonomy. No one checked my syllabus or what I was planning to teach and the department sides with profs in professor-student conflict[s]."[25] A Brazilian academic working in the United States noted, "I would say the following. It is more open in Brazil than here in the United States. I say your ability to place yourself as a professor is a little easier [there]."[26] Referring to life in Ecuador's three major public universities, an otherwise more pessimistic academic noted, "Professors cannot be repressed for [their] ideas. You cannot lose your job for public thought."[27] These comments reflect the general tenor of discussion on academic freedom in Latin America. There exists no generalized fear of repression today, and most professors comfortably go about the business of teaching and research. Coming from comfortable positions in society, academics in much of Latin America today have security in their positions and little fear of violence.

Academic Freedom in Latin America Now

Although not generally targeted as a class, many Latin American academics today face considerable threats to their lives and livelihoods. If we dig below the surface, we find that a small number of academics and researchers work under constant threat by nonstate and rogue state actors whom Latin American governments seem to have little ability or, at times, desire to control. Challenges to academic freedom in the region can be divided into two groups: threats of violence against academics and nonviolent threats against positions or access to scholarly resources.

Because of a lack of recent writing on this issue, especially outside the Colombian context, most of the data in this section were drawn from interviews with academic freedom activists and Latin American academics in both the United States and Latin America. Most of these interviews were conducted between December 2003 and January 2004 in person, by phone, or by e-mail. I conducted all the interviews in a semistructured format that I have used for ethnographic research on other projects. Throughout this chapter I use pseudonyms to protect the identity of the respondents.

Threats of Violence Against Academics.   Across Latin America today extensive evidence suggests that some academics suffer from threats of violence as a result of the positions they hold, the research they undertake, and their political activities associated with campus governance. More often than not, violence comes from nonstate actors with the tacit approval of some state officials. A variety of cases support this contention.

The greatest violations of academic freedom in Latin America take place in Colombia, where violence from the nation's forty-year civil war has spilled over from armed combatants into the educational system. Without a doubt the most threatened academic group in the Americas today is Colombia's rurally based primary and secondary school teachers, who serve as representatives of the government in remote villages and towns in this hilly country. According to the leadership of the Federación Colombiana de Educadores (FECODI, Federation of Colombian Educators), a union representing primary and secondary school faculty, since 1980 more than 650 teachers have been murdered. Nearly one-third of these murders have taken place in the last five years.[28] Ninety-five percent of the attacks happened at the hands of right-wing paramilitary groups that maintain alliances and receive training from elements of the state's security apparatus. Left-wing guerrillas and government forces account for the remaining 5 percent. Nearly all the murders occurred in isolated rural areas. Many teachers have left their posts in the countryside under threat and have relocated to urban areas. The government has failed to offer these state employees new positions. FECODI reports that all cases of violence against educators that the union has denounced to the government remain unpunished.[29] One union official stated that paramilitary groups target teachers for four reasons: (1) union activities, (2) their role as one of the few state representatives in many towns and villages, (3) their refusal to allow combatants to use school facilities for meetings and housing, and (4) their objection to the forced recruitment of children into armed groups.[30] The reasons for killing school faculty combined with paramilitary groups' prohibition on teaching certain subjects in some towns raise grave questions about the condition of academic freedom in Colombia.

Violence in Colombia, however, does not limit itself to precollege educators. Universities in some cities have become the sites of contention among paramilitary groups and guerrilla supporters. Following the reports of Oscar, an exiled faculty member from the Universidad de Antioquia in Medellín, one of Colombia's most important universities, paramilitary groups informally organized students on that campus in opposition to a left-wing student movement. To stem tensions, a working group was organized within the university's collective governance structure. In response, paramilitaries assassinated a leftist student involved in the working group who had accused members of the university administration of connections to paramilitary groups. Paramilitaries labeled academics who took positions contrary to theirs as subversives and collaborators. These right-wing groups would go on to murder an academic colleague of Oscar's in another part of the country and a university union representative while he was off university property. All told, between 1987 and 1999, Oscar believed that thirty-three professors had been killed around the country. During the 1990s paramilitary groups murdered seven professors at the Universidad de Antioquia alone.[31] In some cases militant groups kidnapped and brutally tortured professors. These groups eventually directed threats against Oscar as a result of his political organizing on campus and the fact that in the late 1980s he had participated as a candidate in municipal elections for a demobilized guerrilla group. In none of these cases did government forces take action against faculty. Rather, threats came from paramilitary groups. On a number of occasions, however, university professors denounced these acts of violence to police, who then failed to take any action.[32]

The American Association for the Advancement of Science has also reported on the murders of Colombian university faculty. In 1999 paramilitary groups murdered Professors Dario Betancourt Etchverry and Hernán Henao Delgado, prominent researchers on violence and human rights based in Bogotá, Colombia. That same year paramilitary groups attempted to murder a law professor.[33] Oscar, the exiled professor from Medellín, noted that researching social justice issues, working with the poor, and raising questions about violence can create difficulties for academics. He aptly concluded, "To offer a critical perspective is dangerous."[34]

Other countries in the region also experience similar types of violence. Juan, an exiled professor from Venezuela, related a harrowing story of his own experiences during the 2002–2003 general strike that his country's conservative opposition launched against the neopopulist government of President Hugo Chávez. As a business professor working on tourism policy, Juan had raised some questions about the focus on tourism in the government's long-term economic plan. A student auditing one of his classes, with Juan's permission, reported his criticisms of the government to members of the campus *Circulos Bolivarianos* (Bolivarian Circles), pro-Chávez civic organizations that occasionally operate as mobs in defense of the government. Although this did not lead to a direct confrontation, Juan's position in the university worsened considerably after faculty became divided over whether to adhere to the national antigovernment strike. Some faculty members advocated walking out, but supporters of the government thought it was important to go on with classes. Juan says he emerged as a prominent voice of moderation by advocating, along with many others, a third position that called for keeping the university open but not teaching classes. Eventually the faculty as a whole voted in favor of this position over objections from both extreme groups. The next day Juan received a call from a relative in another city saying that the government television channel had broadcast a report by the university vice-rector (the equivalent of the provost in a U.S. university) and pro-Chávez students that "denounced" him and his collaborators as "terrorists and the *golpistas* [coup plotters] who are assassinating the population in the university." This report played several times on the television that day and the next. After the reports Juan started to receive phone calls and notes with specific threats against him from pro-Chávez groups. He reports that on at least one occasion a motorcycle drove at him with the intent to kill him. Juan eventually sought the support of a human rights organization, which recommended that he not go to the courts for redress of these grievances against his suspected attackers. The human rights advocates he worked with told him that the government controlled the courts and that the courts might "have called the Circulos Chavistas and say that 'Look, here is this guy that is scared giving a denunciation that you are threatening him so come here and get him.'" Juan decided to finish out the semester despite these threats. On the day he went to turn in his grades, he said he "had to go secretly to campus." He went on to say that he "parked the car eight or ten blocks away and when I returned from submitting the grades my car had a paper on the windshield that I thought was an advertisement until I saw it was handwritten and it said that you took your car here and we [found it and] could [have] put a bomb under the car. If they had done it I would have blown up." After this incident, he decided to leave Venezuela. He sold his property and moved to the United States, where he lives with his son while he waits for political conditions to improve in his country.[35]

Academics also find themselves under pressure in Ecuador.[36] In 2000 the government arrested the president of the national teachers union and police raided union offices. In a more sinister development, over the past few years a secretive proto-fascist paramilitary group known as the *Legión Blanca* (White Legion) that is believed to have ties to the state has emerged. This group has repeatedly issued statements accusing *"sociólogos vagos"* ("empty sociologists") of working with Colombian guerrillas and terrorists. They have issued lists of people that they intend to kill and on at least one occasion have murdered an academic.[37]

The concerns seen in Ecuador have close links to the unique political preoccupations facing a country that has undergone at least five political transitions in the last seven years. The sitting government has taken action against indigenous peoples and other groups aligned against it to prevent further activism. In addition, Ecuador's government is under pressure to provide some services to the U.S. military in its operations against the insurgency in neighboring Colombia.[38] This creates a tense environment that leads to more actions on the part of the state and sympathetic social actors to undermine activism and academic freedom.

Brazil also suffers from a similar set of problems emanating from state and nonstate agents. In addition to the minor case of harassment detailed in the introduction, two cases of violence or threats of violence against researchers have prompted international attention. The first case involved Professor Mariana Ferreira, an anthropologist of Brazilian origin who teaches at a university in the United States. While studying landholding rights and mapping property boundaries on an Indian reservation in Mato Grosso in central western Brazil, Ferreira and her collaborators received threats and, on at least one occasion, were directly attacked by unknown assailants. The center of the issue facing Ferreira was her work with the residents of an indigenous village who had decided to press the government for an expansion of their landholding rights in accordance with the 1989 Brazilian constitution. The efforts of the indigenous residents had already led to severe tensions with local representatives of the Fundação Nacional do Índio (FUNAI, National Indian Foundation), the organization within the federal government responsible for the affairs of indigenous people, and with the local landholders whom they had made claims against. This led to severe threats against the indigenous group before Ferreira's involvement in the dispute. Ferreira and her team used advanced mapping techniques to help improve the indigenous groups' claims in court.

Upon her arrival at the research site, Ferreira met with the head FUNAI official for the area and encountered immediate hostility and harassment. Ferreira reports that the local FUNAI director made partially veiled threats to her and said that it might be "dangerous for a pretty woman" like her to be out in the countryside. As her group made progress with their mapping efforts, they came under further harassment and, eventually, attack. At one point armed men attempted to stop them from crossing a bridge on their way to a research site. On another occasion a truck from the Fundação Nacional de Saúde (FUNASA, National Health Foundation) attempted to violently force a truck carrying Ferreira and her collaborators off the road. Eventually Ferreira received a note saying that if she did not stop her research, she would be killed. Since June 2003, after an indigenous leader was murdered by the relative of a landowner, Ferreira and her collaborators have not returned to their field site for fear of their safety.[39]

In a similar case, Dominique Gallois, a Belgian anthropologist who teaches at the Universidade de São Paulo, encountered difficulties researching indigenous peoples in Amapá, a state in northern Brazil. According to records maintained by the American Anthropological Association and the American Association for the Advancement of Science, Gallois was working with a group of indigenous people involved in a land dispute with miners associated with a Brazilian congressman. A federal prosecutor filed actions against Gallois in court and initiated a series of petty criminal investigations to derail her activities.[40] In another case a researcher from the United States has received some threats related to her research on certain types of black market trades in Brazil.[41]

In a slightly different case, Luis Eduardo Soares, a highly respected sociologist at the Instituto Universitário de Pesquisas do Rio de Janeiro (IUPERJ), was forced into exile while serving in a government post coordinating policing and public security in the Rio de Janeiro state government. As part of the governing coalition's platform, Soares undertook wide-ranging reforms of the state's public security apparatus that involved dismantling corrupt groups within state police agencies. His efforts eventually led to a series of frequent and specific threats against his and his family's lives. In 2000 he fled Brazil and lived briefly in the United States.[42]

These Brazilian cases are consistent with the observations of a senior Canadian researcher who has worked intermittently over the past thirty years in academic institutions in São Paulo and northeastern Brazil. In setting up programs to assist the less well-off in dealing with flooding in the impoverished northeast, he noted, "Oligarchs would get upset if you were empowering poor people by giving information about drought and flooding. So professors that were indigenous watched what they did publicly. I didn't have to and I must say that I never felt threatened by any of it." This academic thought, however, that within the university a general respect for academic freedom existed. The problems started when a researcher went outside the university and dealt in the complex politics of wealth and social inequality in Brazil. In this case, as in the Ferreira and Gallois cases, the powerful did not take well to outsiders researching and giving aid to the disadvantaged.[43] This difference between freedom to teach within the university and freedom to research or engage in other scholarly activities outside the university clearly played a role in the violations of academic freedom described here.

Guatemala also has a troubling history of violence against academics. In recent years researchers at two Guatemalan institutes have received threats or have been murdered by death squads left over from that county's long civil war that ended in the 1990s.[44] The researchers were involved in historical or archeological work related to human rights abuse during the civil war, which left between 50,000 and 75,000 indigenous people dead.[45] At the AVANSCO, a think tank in Guatemala City, a number of researchers have received death threats and two have been killed as a result of ongoing studies of the effects of the war on the indigenous population. In the most famous case, a death squad murdered Myrna Mack, one of the leaders of AVANSCO.[46] In a separate instance, researchers involved in forensic archeology teams studying war victims' remains have received threats and have left the country.[47] The American Association for the Advancement of Science has reported a similar case in which unknown foes harassed an Argentine forensic archeologist who was studying victims of that country's dictatorship.[48]

The abuse of academics also occurs in other parts of Latin America. Perhaps the most troubling violation of academic freedom in recent months was the invasion of the Université de Haiti by a mob of government supporters that led to armed attacks on members of the university administration and faculty. Assailants directed these attacks against the human sciences and humanities faculties, areas of the university known to harbor opponents of the government of Jean Bertrand Aristide.[49] The unstable nature of the regime transition in Haiti coupled with concerns about the commitment of many in the opposition to civil and political rights suggests that conditions for academics may not improve markedly in the near future. In Mexico, researchers in Chiapas have experienced threats and harassment from police.[50] Also teachers union leaders have been involved in intense conflicts that have led to some shootings.[51]

In most of the cases presented here, threats against academics have come from nonstate actors or from state actors operating outside normal state law and regulations. In Colombia, Ecuador, Guatemala, Venezuela, and Haiti violence against academics has come at the hands of members of paramilitary organizations that often have ties to state officials. In Brazil, academics suffer threats from some social actors but also from certain low-level state actors either operating outside the law or manipulating the law to their own advantage. Nevertheless, high-level government actors only rarely involve themselves in attacks against academics.

The violence affecting academics in Latin America today shares two broad similarities with the types of concerns that have emerged in the United States since the September 11 attacks. First, threats to academics, as well as most threats to human rights in Latin America today, emerge not from state entities but rather from violent social actors who thrive on violating national and international norms. By mounting attacks, these groups play to core supporters while creating greater degrees of chaos and conflict in society that they can then further exploit to build support for their activities. Second, evidence from Venezuela, Colombia, and Ecuador suggests that violent actors have picked up on the language used by powerful Western governments to describe terrorists and have labeled their opponents with those terms to justify their violent acts. The frequent use of the label "terrorist" has become a major challenge in efforts to guarantee the rights of academics. Irresponsible statements, such as the one made by former education secretary Rod Paige referring to the National Education Association as a "terrorist organization," can only reinforce this problem. As one academic freedom activist I interviewed stated:

We [the United States] have been using the same rhetoric that oppressors have used throughout time to justify repression. This [charge of terrorism] undermines efforts here to help people. It increases the credibility of a dictator or a repressive state when they make that allegation. Twenty years ago it was the Soviet Union and people didn't take it seriously. Now when a repressive state accuses someone of being a terrorist it affects efforts here. People who might help become jittery when the person they try to help is accused of being a terrorist.[52]

The exception to all these cases, of course, is Cuba, the one remaining dictatorship in the region. Unlike all the other cases discussed here (with the limited exception of Ecuador), Cuba arrests, tries, and jails dissident academics much like the former Soviet Union and right-wing dictatorships did in recent Latin American history.[53] This exception, of course, proves the rule. Cuba is a throwback to an earlier period of Latin American politics, and its violations of academic freedom follow the same general state-centered pattern of that era. Eventually the country will experience a transfer of power and most of these problems will likely end. Until that time it is essential that human rights groups maintain pressure on the Cuban government to treat its academics with respect. Cuba, nevertheless, is an isolated and declining case.

The rest of Latin America, however, lives in a different time and under different conditions. Participation in international organizations and ongoing democratic elections mean that states cannot actively engage in the types of human rights violations described here. As a result, threats to academic freedom come from social actors or from state actors operating outside the law. These types of violations present serious long-term challenges to academics and the human rights community.

Other Threats to Academic Freedom in Latin America. Conversations and correspondence with academics active in these issues make apparent two other important threats that face faculty in the region. The first emerged from the neoliberal economic turn of the past ten years and the concomitant decrease in government funding to state universities. The second stemmed from the rigid immigration restrictions that the U.S. government adopted in the wake of the September 11 attacks and the ways that these restrictions prevent academics from fully participating in conferences and academic life in the United States.

Some academics fear the effects that the process of economic globalization and structural adjustment will have on the Latin American university system. Since its inception centuries ago, the public sector has dominated academic life in Latin America. The region's best faculty generally holds permanent or semipermanent positions at public universities that provide them, effectively, with tenure and protection for their academic work.

As I discussed earlier in this chapter, however, university autonomy and independence have always been contentious issues that governments have frequently overlooked during times of crisis. A corollary to this is the idea that dissent may not be truly possible in an institution funded by the state itself. The more critical universities become of the government, the more likely it is that the government will reduce the university's funding.

In an important recent work on academic freedom and autonomy in the Americas, Maria de Figueiredo-Cowen takes up this argument and looks at it in the context of the political and budgetary changes affecting Latin American universities in the last decade. She notes that "the development of higher education in some countries, as it does in Argentina, depends heavily on the World bank programmes with their large loans. The extent to which these policies are to be successful is yet to be checked."[54] Although she notes that the main issue facing Latin American universities is not privatization, de Figueiredo-Cowen states a clear concern about how decreasing state financial sovereignty and changing domestic political relationships will affect academic freedom and autonomy.

A number of academics that I talked to expressed some concerns about the pressures that decreasing state funding could put on universities. As an Ecuadoran academic put it:

The advent of the neoliberal period has produced a form of more subtle repression that consists of the changes in the systems of hiring and promotion in the universities, a process of tailorization of higher education. A strategy that consists of mechanisms of pay based on incentives in which competence between professors is rewarded, that induce privatized academic work to break the esprit de corps and the organizations of professors. The incentives also encourage functionalist lines of investigation and they destroy counter-hegemonic lines of investigation.[55]

Other academics share these feelings. A Colombian living in the United States said, "McCarthyism never died [because] the corporations took control of public education (they already had in their hands the private) . . . here in the U.S. and in many other countries around the world."[56]

On some level these statements about the impact of the economy on education may seem overblown in light of the violence reported in the previous section. In the Latin American context, however, the concern about the threat that global market forces pose to academic freedom has a special resonance. The vast majority of opportunities for tenure in Latin America emanate from public institutions.[57] As one Brazilian academic noted, "[In private universities] you don't have a link with the . . . university and you are not contracted to do research. In PUC [a Catholic university] you teach and depending on how you are contracted you give classes and you give research also. In PUC or in other universities that pay you, in the majority of them, you just give classes."[58] Another Brazilian academic who teaches at a Catholic university in southern Brazil and who is involved in a lawsuit on academic freedom noted that when you are contracted at her university, you "have to sign [a] paper saying [you] will not talk about a variety of things [such as] homosexuality, abortion, family planning. You cannot speak against Catholic doctrine." She went on to note that these universities only hire on a term basis.[59] Finally, an Ecuadoran academic noted that "private universities are degree factories" and that private universities operated like businesses because they could cancel an academic's employment at any time and, as a result, exerted strong control on thinking. He went on to note that in some Catholic universities a "mixed" situation existed in which some deans and university rectors would protect the rights of some of their contracted faculty while they held power. When they were replaced, however, there was no guarantee that the new administrator would protect faculty rights.[60]

One case casts these concerns in a stark light. Several years ago Debora Diniz, a highly respected bioethicist at the Universidade Católica de Brasília, agreed to give a lecture on abortion rights at the central offices of Brazil's federal public prosecution service. At some point the meeting was rescheduled as a debate among Professor Diniz, a pro-life Catholic priest, and a prosecutor. Following Diniz's account, she so handily defeated the other panelists that a major city newspaper carried a story mocking the other panelists as if they had lost a prizefight. Although Diniz had asked that her affiliation with the Universidade Católica not be used in public communications about the debate, the newspaper reported that she worked there as a professor. Within a few days Professor Diniz found herself under pressure from university administrators, who threatened to fire her. She was allowed to stay, but the administration reassigned her from teaching bioethics at the graduate level to less prestigious duties teaching methodology. Later, after she published a book on abortion, the administration fired her without notice.[61]

Professor Diniz has initiated a lawsuit to demand that the Brazilian government elaborate and define a brief reference to academic freedom in the 1989 constitution. Although a constitutional right to academic freedom exists in Brazil, until now there has been no legal reasoning that defines the protections received by professors contracted to work in private universities. Professors in public universities have their rights protected by tenure regulations that affect government employees who have won open civil service competitions. Academics who teach in private institutions have a constitutional right to academic freedom, but there is no operational definition of this freedom or way to enforce it.[62]

Until now the conditions of academic work have not been a major concern of those thinking about academic freedom in the Americas because most students and most of the productive faculty taught in public universities where they often had the protection of civil service rules. As Diniz observes, however, today the trend is away from public financing for higher education, and more students rely on private universities for their degrees. As a result, every day more faculty work in private universities with almost no guarantee of academic freedom or long-term employment.[63] Increasing globalizing pressures will only worsen this situation unless governments and faculty take concrete action to define the rights of professors working in nonpublic institutions.

A final source of threats to the Latin American academy comes not from concerns within their own countries but from access to the United States after the September 11 terrorist attacks. For the purposes of this chapter it is worth mentioning that academics have had difficulty traveling to conferences in the United States. Some academics that have visas are fearful of traveling to the United States for political reasons. Last year, when I chaired a panel at the Latin American Studies Association conference in Dallas, two of the five panelists dropped out for fear of traveling to the United States or as a result of visa troubles. The U.S. government also delayed the visas of numerous Cuban professors, although these academics eventually obtained the visas in time to travel to the conference. A Cuban exile living in Colombia claimed that he nevertheless did not receive a visa. Given the importance of U.S. universities and professional associations to the activities of Latin American academics, the ongoing reluctance of the U.S. government to facilitate access of legitimate professionals in the field poses a major challenge to academic freedom not just in Latin America but also in the United States, where academics will have less and less access to conversations with their foreign colleagues.

Possible Solutions to the Problems Facing Latin American Academics Today

The challenges to academic freedom in Latin America today parallel the broader challenges facing human rights throughout the region. Although massive, systematic, and direct threats to academic freedom and human rights are not as common in the region as they were in the 1970s and 1980s, today numerous persistent and diffuse threats continue to exist. No longer does the state attack its citizens as part of a wide-ranging policy to recreate society, but elements of state and society engage in long-term yet often incoherent assaults on human rights and academic freedom.

This situation has its positive and negative implications. On the positive side governments no longer round up dissidents with impunity and torture or kill them. In general, most academics seem happy with their ability to practice their profession, and active research goes on in all fields. On the negative side the new challenges facing academic freedom in Latin America come from much more diffuse, difficult to control sources. Although a change in government or simply a change in policy can end systematic forms of persecution, violence emanating from varied social and state actors can be eliminated only through the establishment of a coherent and effective set of government policies to address these problems. Cash-strapped governments, subject to significant international spending constraints, will undertake these difficult policies only under substantial and ongoing social pressure.

The problems facing those concerned with academic freedom in Latin America, then, are the same problems facing the human rights community more generally. In the dictatorships of the late twentieth century those concerned with human rights knew where to lay blame and how to demand redress. In the 1970s an international human rights network emerged that brought together domestic human rights organizations, international nongovernmental organizations such as Amnesty International and Human Rights Watch, international governmental organizations, and some powerful states to put pressure on dictatorial governments to observe international human rights norms. The ability to focus pressure on a single state institution and, within that institution, on a few high-level policymakers helped network members to succeed not only in eliminating most human rights abuse on the part of state but also in changing the structure of government in the region. Ultimately in these efforts to promote human rights and democratic rule, academics benefited greatly.[64]

Today human rights abuse comes from all directions. Governments even allow some violence by social actors as a way of punishing opponents without taking actions for which courts or human rights organizations could hold them accountable. To make matters worse, some social actors, especially paramilitary groups appealing to an extreme base of support, may actually benefit from taking radical actions that violate basic freedoms. Human rights organizations have had trouble responding to these new endemic forms of abuse.[65] How do those concerned with human rights and academic freedom effectively counter the diffuse and pervasive causes of these problems in Latin America? The human rights community as a whole has yet to find an effective answer to this question.

Viewed from the outside this would seem to pose an immense challenge to those concerned with academic freedom. How can a small and generally underfunded professional group hope to protect its members in the face of reprisals from a broad base of social actors sometimes supported by state officials? Moreover, with all the rights violations occurring in guerrilla conflict and as a result of crime and police violence, how can academics get their issues on the agenda? Indeed, these challenges seem daunting.

Of all the groups that continue to suffer abuse under Latin America's democratic regimes, academics may be uniquely positioned to help address these questions and, perhaps, to develop a more comprehensive framework through which to resolve the human rights issues of other social and professional groups. Unlike many of the other groups suffering endemic human rights abuse today, academics have the resources, skills, and connections to make demands of the state and international actors. Furthermore, if they do suffer serious threats, most academics can relocate to other institutions or countries more readily than indigenous populations or the poor.

Unfortunately, despite excellent efforts by many organizations, the problem of academic freedom in Latin America is dealt with in an ad hoc way by a variety of concerned organizations located, for the most part, outside Latin America. Professional associations such as the Canadian Association of University Teachers (CAUT), Education International, the American Association for the Advancement of Science, and the American Anthropological Association maintain ongoing efforts to work with Latin American academics, pressure governments to control violence against academics, and maintain a minimum level of academic freedom. In addition, groups such as the Scholars at Risk Network and the Network on Education and Academic Rights (NEAR) engage in important efforts to promote academic freedom, although these organizations have not developed the types of extensive contacts in Latin America that they have developed in other regions of the world that are facing more traditional violations of academic freedom. Indeed, not only does no single organization appear to have a definitive list of cases of violations of academic freedom in the Americas, but also many violations never come to the attention of these international organizations. This problem is reinforced by the fact that professional interest groups such as the American Association of University Professors (AAUP) and the CAUT do not exist in Latin America in the way they do in North America. Rather, unions, concerned more with negotiating faculty contracts with the state than with protecting faculty rights against the state and other actors, represent professors. These unions maintain only limited cross-national ties and are likely to be poorly organized internally as a result of a history of efforts on the part of Latin American states to co-opt labor organizations and the need of these unions to maintain strong relations with state officials with whom they must negotiate. No informant in this study suggested that any organization operated to represent the interests of faculty at private universities. Finally, occasionally ad hoc groups of academics focused on a particular country or issue spring up to address egregious violations of academic freedom. For example, a group has formed to address the concerns of one Guatemalan institution, and a small international professional organization working on bioethics has picked up the Diniz case. Despite this disorganization, Latin American academics have much greater support for their concerns than poor shantytown dwellers in the region.

All of this suggests that academic freedom could provide a testing ground for effective strategies to control the types of diffuse threats that define human rights problems in Latin America today. Existing groups focused on academic freedom, such as the Scholars at Risk Network and NEAR, could reinforce current efforts to develop stronger networks in the region to track violations of academic freedom and provide assistance to academics by developing contacts with local groups and by working with existing professional associations and ad hoc groups concerned with human rights and academic freedom. Advocacy of academic freedom issues must go beyond the case-by-case letter writing strategy used by such groups as Amnesty International to address the concerns of specific professors. Rather, groups working on academic freedom in the region need to develop sets of principles associated with academic freedom that make sense in Latin America's specific political and historical context and work with academics and professional organizations active in Latin America to establish them as working norms. These organizations could pick up on such issues as the Diniz case, which seeks to establish a standard for academic freedom, and use those types of court rulings to advance efforts to secure academic freedom in the region. Finally, an open and active dialogue between international actors, Latin American academics, and policymakers needs to be established that will allow academics to fully express their concerns on these issues and find collaborative ways to work to resolve these questions.

Conclusion

Despite marked improvements over the last fifteen years, considerable challenges remain for Latin America's academics. With a handful of exceptions faculty have little trouble working within the university system. Those who hold jobs in the region's prestigious public universities are not likely to lose their jobs for political reasons, and, outside Colombia, those professors who pursue research that does not bring them directly into contact with violent actors are extremely unlikely to suffer threats of bodily harm. Nevertheless, a few serious challenges remain. First, academics conducting research on controversial issues in many countries face the possibility of threats and violence. Second, academics in Colombia face serious concerns stemming from the extension of that country's forty-year civil conflict into primary and secondary schools and the university system. Third, increasing pressure to restrict the growth of the public sector results in a larger percentage of the region's academics working in private institutions that provide little if any guarantee of academic freedom. Professors at nonpublic institutions who disagree with the administration can lose their jobs with little or no notice. The absence of broad professional organizations native to Latin America that represent professors' concerns about academic freedom in the region only worsens this situation.

With the exception of some new restrictions of visa access, recent restrictions on the publication of materials produced by Cuban academics, and the increasing use of the war on terror to justify certain types of repression, none of the threats facing academics in Latin America today come directly out of the September 11 attacks. Nevertheless, the sources of threats to academic freedom in the region have a disturbing similarity to the threats facing the United States today. Actors from society who have an interest in intimidating those who might speak out against them and who would like to create a general climate of fear pose the greatest threats to academics in Latin America. Like terrorists in the Middle East or Al-Qaeda terrorists who took refuge in Florida, violent actors in Latin American society have proven difficult to control. The existing mechanisms used by governments and the human rights community to deal with threats to national security or basic rights posed historically by states do little to control the diffuse threats emanating from society.

With the exception of the case of Cuba, the serious threats to academic freedom emerge either from outside the state apparatus or from rogue actors within the state. Any solution to these problems must focus on the fact that high-level state actors often have little interest in violating basic principles of academic freedom but at the same time often have difficulty controlling violent social actors. Simply demanding that states protect academics more effectively will do little to solve these problems because even the most powerful state officials may have little control over these issues. Instead, groups concerned with academic freedom must find ways to adequately catalog and document cases of violations of academic freedom, offer some protection to those faculty suffering the most serious threats, and find ways to work with academics and government officials to build a better environment to protect faculty in Latin America.[66]

PART FOUR

*Conclusions, Reflections, and Remarks
on Academic Freedom*

CHAPTER 9

Two Theories of Self-Censorship

Paul M. Sniderman

ONE MERIT OF THIS BOOK, odd as it may seem to say, is that it is self-contradictory. A number of the chapters tell an optimistic story about academic freedom in our times. It is not a story of unblemished optimism: Violations are acknowledged and the risk of further ones is noted. But it is an optimistic story even if the optimism is guarded. On the other hand, other chapters tell a story about academic freedom in our times that is anything but optimistic: Violation after violation is recorded but only the occasional reversal is noted. It is a pessimistic story notwithstanding the occasional note of optimism.

There is good reason to believe *both* the optimistic and the pessimistic stories of academic freedom in contemporary America. They complement rather than contradict one another, because they are stories about the protection of academic freedom in different policy domains.

The optimistic story, related by Robert O'Neil but seconded by Donald Downs, is about responses of university authorities to post-9/11 challenges to academic freedom. O'Neil's chapter provides an excellent guide. He is clear-eyed, not starry-eyed. Of the ten incidents following 9/11 that he reviews, three concern reactions to remarks made in class and three relate to academic conferences. In O'Neil's judgment, the responses of university authorities in all six incidents represent responsible—effective—defenses of academic freedom; in the seventh case, he points out important procedural failings. A good record it would seem, all in all.[1] O'Neil also points to a trio of hostile public reactions to commencement speeches. Three out of 10,000 or so graduation speeches, he observes, is not a large number. Downs, although concerned about threats to academic freedom from another direction, seconds O'Neil's evaluation of the staunchness of university defenses to post-9/11 threats to academic freedom.[2]

The pessimistic story is about political correctness, to borrow the popular phrase. Downs presents an account of professors and students being punished for saying what university authorities judge to be objectionable and of their declining to say what they fear university authorities may judge to be objectionable. But freedom of expression is the heart of the matter. For Downs the core problem is the trade-off between certain administrative policies and practices intended to promote racial and ethnic tolerance and political tolerance—that is, freedom of expression and inquiry. The trade-off is unavoidable in his view, and the threat to academic freedom is a broad one. It is not just a matter of speech codes. As Downs observes, there also are "very broad anti-harassment codes, orientation programs dedicated to promoting an ideology of sensitivity, and new procedures and pressures in the adjudication of student and faculty misconduct."[3] Finally, Downs observes that the problem of censorship and self-censorship is to be found at universities and colleges of quite various sizes, status (public or private), and missions (the relative balance between teaching and research).

Just as with the optimistic story, a number of evaluative standards can and should be applied to the pessimistic stories. Is the evidence that Downs offers in support of his hypothesis of censorship confined to a small number of highly publicized and endlessly recycled cases—indeed, possibly heavily publicized and endlessly recycled just because they are exceptional? How consistent is the pattern of findings across different incidents? Where contrary interpretations are offered for common cases, how compelling is their account?[4]

O'Neil's and Downs's accounts of post-9/11 cases reinforce each other, reinforcing my confidence that each is describing correctly the domains of speech on which they focus. And although I do not have professional expertise, I do have personal experience. I see no way to avoid taking seriously the hypothesis of a double standard: on the one side, an impressive (although obviously imperfect) readiness of university leadership to defend academic freedom in the context of post-9/11 threats; on the other side, a practice of university authorities initiating policies or acquiescing in institutions to monitor and punish speech and conduct.

To bring out what is distinctive about the contemporary dilemma of academic freedom in the United States, I want to examine two hypotheses: the conformity hypothesis and the authority hypothesis. I argue that the heart of the contemporary problem of academic freedom is political, not social psychological.

The Standard Theory: Conformity

Why do some censor what they say on some campuses on some issues? There is an on-the-shelf answer, a quite general answer in fact: the conformity hypothesis. Roughly, pressure to conform drives censorship and self-censorship on a number of issues—affirmative action, hate speech codes, and harassment policies, not to mention a number of others that fall under the umbrella of embracing diversity, which I shall dub, for convenience, the civil rights agenda. Pressure to conformity, in this view, drives censorship and self-censorship of positions on this agenda.

The conformity hypothesis has a distinguished lineage. In the first volume of *Democracy in America*, Tocqueville declares that there is "less independence of mind and genuine freedom of discussion" in America than in any other country.[5] Why is this so? Because, he famously answers, of "the tyranny of the majority."

How is this tyranny exercised? Speaking specifically of politics, Tocqueville writes:

In America the majority draws a formidable circle around thought. Inside those limits, the writer is free; but unhappiness awaits him if he dares to leave them. . . . Everything is refused him, even glory. Before publishing his opinions, he believed he had partisans; it seems to him that he no longer has any now that he has uncovered himself to all; for those who blame him express themselves openly, and those who think like him, without having his courage, keep silent and move away. He yields, he finally bends under the effort of each day and returns to silence as if he felt remorse for having spoken the truth.[6]

Here are two core elements of a theory of conformity, telegraphically expressed: a desire for social approval and the germ of an idea about the importance of beliefs about others' beliefs. The first is a matter of common observation. There is a general desire to be valued, approved, esteemed by others, or at least to avoid their disapproval, censure, ostracism. The second element, beliefs about others' beliefs, is less obvious.

What happens, Tocqueville asks, when an individual breaches accepted social limits? Those who disagree with him "express themselves

openly," whereas "those who think like him, without having his courage, keep silent and move away." This asymmetry—open expression
on one side of an issue, withdrawal into silence on the other—is at the
heart of Tocqueville's account. The problem is not merely that the minority view is in the minority. Discussion and argument are the ways in
which today's minority can become tomorrow's majority. But that is just
the problem. The tyranny of the majority can become a tyranny if a minority, by virtue of being a minority, is led to shrink from discussions
and argument.

Contemporary theories of politics and conformity have accepted
Tocqueville's insight. People are less likely to take the unpopular side
of an issue publicly to the extent that others around them are unwilling
to do so openly. But all they—we—can observe are the opinions that
people express publicly. Yet they have emphasized the dynamics of the
conformity process. Insofar as those on one side do not express their
views openly, then everyone's sampling of opinions is biased: Those
who hold the majority opinion think that even more of their fellows
agree with them than do; those who hold the minority position think
that even fewer agree with them than do. And insofar as still more in
the minority are persuaded not to express their views publicly because
they perceive themselves to be in an even smaller minority than they
are, there is a "spiral of silence" in Elisabeth Noelle Neumann's evoca-
tive phrase.[7] One unvoiced belief increases the likelihood of another. So
a plurality can grow into a commanding majority.

A cascade is the modern metaphor for the self-reinforcing character
of conformity processes. Contemporary theories distinguish between
two types of cascades: informational and reputational.[8] Both lead to
self-censorship of dissenting beliefs, but by two rather different mechanisms. It would be irrational not to take the account of what some
believe as a guide to the way things are; and often there are particular
reasons to treat the beliefs of others as especially valuable information—they are experts on a particular problem, for example, or they
have proven themselves reliable guides in the past. The result is a
cascade.

The beliefs of others matter for a second reason. Nearly everyone has
some need for the approval of others. This need for approval motivates
people to develop a reputation as a person whose views are reliable and
as a person who respects the views of others. The incentives are thus
asymmetric: On the side of the majority, the incentive is to express one's
true views; on the side of the minority, it is to censor them. The result,

whether informationally or reputationally driven, is the same: biased estimates of what others believe.

Pluralistic ignorance is the term of art for biased estimates about the frequency of others' beliefs.[9] Consider beliefs about racial tolerance. A series of studies have shown that people who are racially intolerant tend to overestimate the number of other people who are racially intolerant. Conversely, people who are racially tolerant tend to underestimate the number of other people who are racially tolerant. The result, ironically, is the opposite of the standard story of social desirability pressures. The racially tolerant are the majority but believe they are the minority; the racially intolerant are the minority but believe they are the majority. Perversely, it is the majority that is under pressure to be silent because it believes it is the minority; the minority is licensed to speak because it believes it is the majority.

The extreme example of conformity to an illusory consensus illustrates, by its extremity, the potential power of pressures to conformity. We seem to have on hand a quite satisfactory theory of self-censorship. People on university campuses, like people everywhere, determine what others think by a sampling process. They observe what most others around them say they believe, perhaps still more closely, what they actually do. Over time those who are critical, say, of affirmative action are increasingly likely to infer that the majority opinion is otherwise, hence making them increasingly less likely to express their dissenting view. It does not matter whether the mechanism is informationally driven or reputationally driven. Either way the result is the same—to increase the estimate of the proportion who support the civil rights agenda and hence to increase the pressures on people *not* to express a dissenting view—to censor what they say publicly.

Social science has a jousting mentality. Alternative hypotheses are treated as though the truth of one entails the falsity of the other. Testing their validity becomes a form of intellectual combat, the proponents of one view arrayed against their opponents, the proponents of the other view. I have no adversarial intention here. The conformity hypothesis represents a powerful insight. The question is not whether the hypothesis is true. It is what are the conditions under which it holds.

The Asch Studies of Conformity. The seminal studies of conformity were done by Solomon Asch.[10] Here, in brief, is the layout of Asch's most famous experiment on conformity. Experimental subjects were presented with a line of a certain length and three other lines of differing length for comparison. They were then asked which of the three comparison lines was the same length as the first. All but one of the subjects were confederates of the experimenter. These confederates were under instructions to pick, on prearranged trials, one of the comparison lines that obviously differed in length from the test line. One by one, each gave the same (false) answer. By design, the experimental subject was last, or near last, to answer. An impressive number of times, approximately one in three, the experimental subject yielded under pressure of the group, giving an answer that manifestly was at odds with the facts of the matter.

Asch's experiment demonstrates the extraordinary power of group pressures to conformity. Substantial numbers, the experiment shows, can be induced to conform to the judgment of a group even when doing so requires them to deny the plain evidence of their senses. The extrapolation from judgments of physical objects to judgments of social and political issues seems obvious. Surely, group pressure is more effective still where the question of what is right and what is wrong is not easily verifiable with evidence immediately before one's eyes. Surely, people can more easily be induced to conform to standards of the group where the judgment of what is right and wrong is less definite and more open to interpretation.

And what is the takeaway lesson? Threefold: (1) Individuals are exceedingly susceptible to group pressure; (2) indeed, under pressure they may even say that what is false is true, even when it plainly is false; and (3) they will say that what is false is true because of the strength of the desire to obtain social approval, or at any rate, the intensity of their need to avoid social disapproval.

The second lesson is straightforwardly true; the first and third are not. Here is a different way to view the choice situation in the Asch experiment—indeed, a point of view that turns things on its head. Rather than the story being that it is remarkable that people will say that something they know to be false is true, it is instead that it is remarkable that, given what they have good reason to believe is true, people can avoid saying something that they know to be false is true. Think of the situation from the perspective of an experimental subject, Lee Ross and his colleagues (and indeed, Asch himself) urge.[11] On one of the critical trials, the subject's peers unanimously give an answer that is obviously wrong. The people around the subject are much like himself. They have been taking the task seriously. They have shown themselves to be competent: Their previous judgments have matched the judgments that the experimental subject had reached on his own. What, then, could possibly account for the clash between the peers' judgments and his own?

This "attributional crisis," to use the phrase of Ross and his colleagues, is the heart of the matter. The experimental subject is in a predicament, not because of his diffuse need for social approval but because of his quite specific need to make sense out of a genuinely baffling situation. The answer may have something to do with his peers. Alternatively, it may have something to do with himself. The subject's peers have shown themselves competent. They are credible. They have no reason to engage in deception; and even if they had, how could they possibly agree to collude on the spot. So, many experimental subjects reason, the problem must lie not with their peers' judgment but with their own. Perhaps they did not hear the instructions correctly on this trial; or perhaps they actually do have things wrong; or perhaps some other factor that they can't put their finger on is at work. Whatever occurs to them by way of explanation, the point is that it is precisely because the situation is extraordinary that the experimental subject has a reason to take the judgments of his peers as the best estimate of the correct response.

This view of conformity, as a rational response in the face of uncertainty, casts a different light on the phenomenon and points, among other things, to crucial factors that limit conformity per se in the laboratory and on academic campuses.

Limits on Group Pressure.   In the standard Asch setup, unanimity is the rule. All the experimental confederates give, one by one, the false answer. The experimental subject has no footing to support his own view of the matter. To explore the conditions under which the conformity process is strengthened or weakened, Asch systematically altered the unanimity condition. The number of "defectors" was systematically varied: In one condition one confederate gave the correct answer; in another, two; and so on. The result was a dramatic finding. The power of small groups to extract conformity in the classic Asch experiment was sharply cut if just one member of the group dissented.

Doesn't the problem of conformity disappear then? If it takes only one other person who shares your view to break the power of a group over you, how much power does the group have? This seems too sanguine a conclusion. The difficulty is that the strength of the Asch experiment is a weakness. The power of the manipulation, as Asch suggested, follows from the absence of any reasonable explanation for the disparity between the group's judgment and the subject's judgment, apart from misjudgment of some kind on the subject's part. Imagine that you are the experimental subject. The first two or three of your fellow "judges" are giving an obviously wrong answer. What, you ask yourself, could possibly be the reason? Then a judge gives exactly the answer you can see is the right answer. Just because the conformity in the Asch situation requires experimental subjects to deny the evidence of their own senses, it takes only one other person who sees the situation as they do to largely dissolve their concern about entirely misunderstanding the situation.

In circumstances more akin to real life, it takes more than one other person to break the power of a group. But what is the likelihood of dissent within the groups we belong to? A long string of studies have shown that each of us tends to surround ourselves with, or be surrounded by, others who are politically like-minded.[12] The outcome is homophily: convergence of beliefs within groups, divergence between them. But dissent within groups as well between them is a fact of life. How is this possible?

In a path-breaking study, Robert Huckfeldt and his colleagues worked through the social ecology of political acquaintanceship.[13] This is the underlying intuition: Members of a common group tend to similarity of belief. But in addition they belong to other groups. A husband and wife living entirely on their own would be exceedingly likely to wind up agreeing with each other. But they do not live entirely on their own. Each belongs to other groups: He has his associates at work and elsewhere; she has her associates at work and elsewhere. The ties between husband and wife are stronger, one would hope, than those between either one and, say, associates at work. But their ties to others, although weaker than their ties to each other, expose them to different beliefs and to that degree provide a built-in limit on pressures to conformity. As Mark Granovetter has remarked, "It is unlikely that we will be close to people with views widely or wildly divergent from our own, but we could be their acquaintances, and by being so, we are connected to ideas and folks who would otherwise be much more distant in network terms." The result, thanks to, in Granovetter's marvelously epigrammatic phrase, "the strength of weak ties," is social support for minority views.[14]

None of this is a denial that there are social pressures to conform. Some people censor their views on controversial issues to avoid the disapproval of others; also, it is worth adding, some people censor their views out of courtesy and respect for colleagues, who might take them to be personally insulting.[15] The social ecology of preferences ensures only that a minority will persist. It, all the same, is a minority. The issue, for academic freedom, is not whether a minority can persist in its views but under what conditions it feels free to express them.

In the standard story of conformity, a minority is unlikely to feel free to express its views on a particular issue to the extent that it recognizes its views to be in a minority and perceives that its views are morally offensive to the majority. Notice the two elements: knowledge that most have a different view of the matter and risk of punishment for differing publicly with their view of the matter. This formulation thus combines both informational and normative conceptions of conformity.[16] Is it, even so, strong enough to account for self-censorship on controversial issues on campus?

It is not obvious that any formulation of the conformity hypothesis is strong enough to account for self-censorship on campus. Consider informational cascades. They depend on two conditions. First, there must be a disparity between publicly expressed and privately held beliefs. Second, community members must be ignorant of the disparity. But how likely are faculty to be unaware of the disparity between publicly expressed and privately held beliefs on an issue such as affirmative action? Not very. Universities are communities. There are high rates of interaction, if not across the community, then segment by segment. A university community is composed disproportionately of people who are articulate, who are practiced at distinguishing between what people say and what they mean. All these factors work the same way. They increase the chances that any given person who dissents knows that there are a number of others who agree with him or her. Moreover, the absolute size of the dissenting minority in the academic community on some elements of the civil rights agenda—say, affirmative action—is impressive. Here are the results of a survey, conducted by the Roper Center for Public Opinion Research, of the University of California Academic Senate ($n = 1,000$), taken in December 1996 after the university regents' decision to end affirmative action.[17] Asked "Do you favor or oppose using race, religion, sex, color, ethnicity, or national origin as a criterion for admission to the University of California?" 52 percent of senate members were in favor and 34 percent opposed. Asked which of two statements "best describes" the policy that UC should pursue— granting preferences to women and certain racial and ethnic groups in admissions, hiring and promotions, or promoting "equal opportunities

in these areas without regard to an individual's race, sex or ethnicity"—
48 percent of the UC faculty polled chose "equal opportunities,"
whereas only 31 percent chose "preferences." The specific numbers in
surveys will vary from one campus to another; indeed, from one particular characterization of affirmative action to another. But for the
forms of affirmative action that are controversial, at a minimum a substantial minority of faculty—and sometimes an absolute majority—
express opposition when they can express their opinion anonymously.

But the opinions expressed in opposition, one might reply, are private opinions. They are the views people feel comfortable expressing
because they can express them anonymously. They are safe to say whatever they want to say. No one whose opinion is of importance to them
in their real lives can possibly find out what they have said. And insofar as minority views are expressed anonymously, it is possible to
square the sharp division over affirmative action among faculty shown
in polls with a widespread presumption of consensus in its favor.

As a general proposition, the probability of faculty members being
unaware of a division of opinion is inversely proportional to the divi-
siveness of the issue, and the issues on which conformity pressures
now are said to operate are the very definition of divisive issues. Moreover, the world of the university is a world of argument and counter-
argument, of discussion and exchange. Accordingly it is unlikely that
faculty members are unaware that there is a difference of opinion over
an issue such as affirmative action. I am not contending that there is no
disparity in some situations on campus between publicly expressed
and privately held beliefs. Just the reverse. I assume that the disparity
is a matter of common knowledge. And insofar as it is common knowledge, it is hard to see how there can be an informational cascade, with
the minority perceiving itself to be an ever shrinking minority.

If informational effects are not responsible for the disparity between
publicly expressed and privately held beliefs, then what is? The other
possibility, under the standard account of conformity, is reputational.
In this interpretation, a minority in a group self-censor their opinions
out of a need for social approval.

My intuitive sense is that this hypothesis is more nearly on the right
track, with one important modification. I do not believe that people on
campus censor what they say on some controversial issues out of a
need for social approval. I believe that instead they do it out of a desire
to avoid social disapproval. The two are not two sides of the same coin.
The first centers on obtaining a reward; the second on avoiding a pun-

ishment. Fear of punishments has more power in this domain than hope for rewards.

My hypothesis is that merely social punishments are not sufficient to account for the level of self-censorship on many academic campuses. The disapproval of one's colleagues on campus is not a goal many seek. But most of one's colleagues on campus are distant colleagues—people one sees rarely, if at all. Distance tempers the sting of their disapproval. To be sure, the disapproval of one's immediate colleagues can be a potent punishment. But there are constraints on the expression of their disapproval. The need to directly interact on a continuing collegial basis is one. Conflict is costly for majorities as well as minorities, especially when tenure removes a majority's option to compel exit. Weak bonds of familiarity and respect, the kinds of bonds that tie academic colleagues together, combined with the indefinite time horizon of collegiality impose sharp limits on social sanctions.

My experience at my university has left me with a respect for the restraint my colleagues exercise. But I do not doubt that on some campuses some colleagues act without restraint. What interests me, however, are the conditions under which social disapproval is most likely to be expressed. I believe reconsideration of the most infamous modern example of self-censorship will be helpful.

McCarthy and McCarthyism

Nearly all histories of the time paint the same picture: "a kind of American national nervous breakdown."[18] It began, in 1950, with a speech by Senator Joseph McCarthy in Wheeling, West Virginia. He had, he announced, "a list of 205—a list of names that were made known to the Secretary of State as being members of the Communist Party and who, nevertheless, are still working and shaping policy in the State Department."[19] McCarthy's charge was riveting. The national press picked it up, launching him on an oceanic wave of national publicity, which he rode recklessly but skillfully until the Army-McCarthy hearings.

A few actors in the drama remain alive in the memory of onlookers, most notably perhaps, Joseph Welch, counsel for the army who, in response to McCarthy's attack on a young colleague of his, famously responded, "Let us not assassinate this lad further, senator. You have done enough. Have you no sense of decency, sir, at long last. Have you left no sense of decency?"[20] By and large, though, it is the dramatic line of the times that is remembered: McCarthy rocketing to prominence; his theatrical command of the national stage; the wreckage of lives before his committee; his sudden flame-out. And the dominant motif, running through all the parts of drama, is a political witch hunt fueled by the fears and anxieties of ordinary Americans. McCarthy played on those fears, heightening them, directing them, orchestrating them.

The standard story of McCarthyism fits the conformity theory of self-censorship—in particular, the hypothesis of reputational cascades. Enormous social pressures were generated. Fear of the disapproval of others—primarily at work, to a lesser extent in friendship circles—was grounded in reality. Many who were caught up in the process, either by virtue of being accused or by virtue of refusing to accuse, literally lost their reputations.

Without question, many who disagreed with McCarthy chose not to disagree publicly.[21] But the standard story of social conformity as the mechanism misses two key points. First, the accepted view of McCarthyism supposes that public hysteria over Communist subversion was the motivating force behind popular support for McCarthy. This component of the accepted view, however, is false. In a study conducted at the height of McCarthyism, Samuel Stouffer asked representative samples of ordinary citizens what kinds of things they worry about most. In his words, "The number of people who said that they were worried . . . about the threat of Communists in the United States was, even by the most generous interpretation of occasionally ambiguous responses, *less than 1%* (emphasis in original)."[22] Hardly evidence of public hysteria.

The second point is still more important. The standard story of McCarthy, as Nelson Polsby has remarked in a classic study, is a story of a politician who "was . . . uniquely powerful at the grass roots; [who] . . . had a vast following which cross-cut party lines and loyalties, which he could call upon to defeat his enemies."[23] In fact, as Polsby and others have shown, McCarthy's electoral support was largely confined to Republicans; he himself did not run ahead of the Republican ticket; indeed, he ran behind it."[24]

What, then, was the basis of McCarthy's power? Not popularity, but the perception of popularity. Believing that McCarthy was immensely popular, the politically influential believed he was immensely powerful. Accordingly, many deferred to him, including many who despised him.

So far this is a standard story of pluralistic ignorance—an erroneous belief that a towering majority was on McCarthy's side when, in fact, only a minority were. But what allowed McCarthy to exercise power was different. It was his institutional position. In the Senate he could make any accusation without risk of libel suits. As chair of a subcommittee, he had a staff, power to issue subpoenas, and, for an extended period, the authority to hold hearings at will, by himself if he wished, without authorization of the subcommittee itself. Without the resources of his position, McCarthy would have been powerless, however popular he was. But to exploit his institutional powers, McCarthy had to have the support of the Republican leadership in the Senate. When Republican leaders turned against him, he lost power almost immediately. It was acquiescence of leadership and institutions that allowed McCarthy to wreak damage.

This revisionist version of McCarthyism points to a pair of potentially critical considerations: the role of institutions and the role of punishment. Focusing on the two, I want to sketch an alternative theory of conformity.

Authority and Conformity

My starting point is a theory of self-censorship developed by Glen Loury.[25] In Loury's theory, there are two actors: a "speaker" and a "listener."[26] The speaker is attempting to persuade the listener. The listener knows the speaker is attempting to persuade her. The strategic problem is thus, How does a speaker persuade a listener, given that the listener knows that persuasion is the speaker's goal and that he may resort to manipulation to accomplish it?

An especially effective way is to persuade the listener that the speaker and the listener share the same values. Here is the reasoning. Believe that a speaker "has goals similar to our own [and] we are confident that any effort on his part to manipulate us is undertaken to advance ends similar to those we would pursue ourselves."[27] Conversely, believe that a speaker is committed to values at odds with our own, and we are much less likely to take him at his word.

How, then, do we decide if a speaker shares our values? According to Loury's theory, the key mechanism is establishment of a practice of punishment. If a practice of punishing, of ostracizing, those who offend the values of a community has been well established, members of the community will be more likely to assume that a person who speaks in a way that challenges a community's values does not share the values of the community. They will make this assumption because *"the only ones who [will] risk ostracism by speaking recklessly are those who place so little value on sharing our community that they must be presumed not to share our dearest values"* (emphasis in original).[28]

There is much to recommend Loury's theory of self-censorship: its effort at generality, for one; its conception of persuasive communication as strategic behavior, for another. Its most important contribution, however, is to bring the role of punishment to the fore.

I believe punishment is the hinge of a theory of self-censorship, although not primarily for the reason Loury suggests. Social ostracism is a cost, but both the likelihood and the magnitude of it are a function of formal authority. The expression "the process is the penalty" is dead-on.[29] Mounting a defense is a time sink. Being caught up in a formal hearing comes at the cost of all the other activities one would prefer to be doing. The costs are also economic. Mounting a legal defense, even turning for advice to a lawyer, is expensive. What is more, the stigma of being charged sticks even if the charge itself does not. And of course there are the formal sanctions that a university can impose. There is reason to fear punishment by university authorities. And, of course, a necessary condition for establishment of a practice of punishment of "offensive" speech or "harassment" on a campus was the acquiescence of university leadership.

A Simple Model of Academic Politics

Why did university leaders acquiesce, indeed, sometimes take the initiative? An account of motives is required at two levels: individual and institutional.

At the individual level there is an obvious hypothesis. A consensus has been reached, in the most educated and influential sectors of American society, that the reality of slavery, segregation, discrimination, and so on is the defining evil in the American experience. For a generation, the effort to right this wrong has formed the moral high ground in American politics. An integral part of this effort has been acceptance of a fundamental obligation of American institutions, very much including the university, to try to put things more nearly right. Only an issue that appeals so profoundly to the American conscience could have persuaded university leadership to acquiesce—indeed, sometimes to take the lead—in establishing a practice of punishment for offensive speech.

According to this hypothesis, then, only an issue that appeals so profoundly to the American conscience could have persuaded university leadership to acquiesce in establishing a practice of punishment for "offensive" speech. True, official sanctions have been generalized through a cascade of similarity judgments. If speech and antiharassment codes are appropriate for race, surely they are appropriate for issues of women's status, or gays', and so on. The rules for punishment have accordingly been generalized. But, according to this hypothesis, the underlying dynamic of official sanctions and academic self-censorship is rooted in the unique status of the issue of race in the American experience.

This conjecture is not self-evidently correct. There is a rival hypothesis. Protests over the Vietnam War breached the commitment to free speech before speech or conduct codes became an issue. Supporters of the war were prevented from speaking on campus. University leadership yielded to political bans on speech not out of a commitment of their own to opposition to the war. Rather, their decision was the product of a practical calculus: It was a way to bring peace to a campus so the regular business of a university—teaching and research—could go on; indeed, it seemed that efforts to resist resistance to the war inevitably boomeranged, alienating the faculty and thus strengthening still more the hands of the protestors.

Here, then, we have two hypotheses. If the civil rights hypothesis is correct, the key mechanism is the commitment of university authorities to core liberal values. If the Vietnam hypothesis is right, the key mechanism is the acquiescence of universities in the interests of university governance. The two hypotheses are not mutually exclusive. Both may hold, although the first is a better fit than the second with the specific regimes of punishment that have been developed.

But there are also institutional incentives for universities to establish punishment practices.[30] I want to draw them out by examining a simple model of academic politics. There are three players: university authorities and two groups of faculty.[31] Let me characterize them briefly.

Group 1 comprises university authorities, roughly from the level immediately above department chair all the way up. These authorities are drawn from the faculty and typically hold pivotal offices for relatively brief periods of time; then, with exceptions at the highest level, they return to the faculty. Group 2 comprises the portion of the faculty active in promoting a civil rights agenda. Group 3 comprises faculty primarily or exclusively concerned with their university work. They do the lion's share of research, fund-raising, graduate student training, and under-graduate teaching. Members of Group 3 are to be found in all parts of the university, but their relative numbers are highest in the sciences and lowest in the humanities.

Group 2 and the university authorities need Group 3, the balance of the faculty. Group 3 is both the largest in number and the largest con-tributor to the standing of the university. But if it is professionally the most important, it is politically the least important—and both for the same reason: its focus on work and, in consequence, its inattention to internal university politics. This is not to say that Group 3 need be disengaged completely from university involvement. It is to say that they have no systematic incentive to counterbalance Group 2, faculty activists. Narrowly, the most prestigious component of Group 3 is the scientists; and they bear the least costs in implementing the civil rights agenda. More broadly, everyone in Group 3 knows that they risk be-ing stigmatized as racially insensitive if they disagree with Group 2. What is more, Group 2 knows that Group 3 knows that the risk of stig-matization is real because of the natural alliance between Group 2 and Group 1.

There is a natural alliance between university authorities and activist faculty for a number of reasons. The first is shared beliefs. It would go too far to say that university authorities are picked because they have a particular political point of view; it is only necessary to suppose that they are markedly less likely to be picked if they have objected openly to already established university practices on the civil rights agenda. Minimally, then, they start with sympathy for the concerns of Group 2; more often, perhaps, they bring with them their own commitment to a civil rights agenda. In any case, Group 1 is vulnerable to Group 3. The politically engaged faculty, on their own and in collaboration with in-ternal university constituencies (students especially) and, sometimes, external ones, can make life difficult for Group 1. What university au-thority wants to have tents outside his office and sit-ins inside it? At a minimum, Vietnam protests taught a lesson about Group 2's success in institutional intimidation; and the recruitment into the faculty of a number who had protested the war and had become broadly disaf-fected from American government has provided a constituency within the university sympathetic to ideas and movements critical of Ameri-can society. And if university leaders are to make a contribution in the relatively brief time they are in office, they must focus their energies. For that matter, university authorities also have a civil rights agenda budget, with professional university administrators already in place, including administrative units formally charged with implementing and monitoring policies on diversity and the like. It follows that Group 1 characteristically has strong incentives to implement and weak incentives to challenge the agenda of Group 2.

How does all of this bear on a possible connection between the two stories of academic freedom in America in this book, the optimistic and the pessimistic? Downs points to one possibility in his chapter.[32] September 11 threats to academic freedom, he points out, fit the accepted framework of defenses of academic freedom—attempts at censorship by external agents of dissent on campus on expressly political issues. In this framework legitimacy of dissent is easier to appreciate. This is not to minimize the problems that 9/11 raises. To say that dissent on these issues is easier is not to say that it is easy. But to the extent that 9/11 threats to academic freedom raise threats similar to those raised in, say, the McCarthy era, the chances are better that university leaders—and the academic community—will respond to the former as they learned to respond to the latter. On this view, the pressure to give similar answers to similar problems may yet lead to a wider opening of speech and inquiry on academic campuses.

This is a reasonable conjecture, and Downs may well be proven right. Here, however, is an alternative hypothesis. September 11 and its sequelae are political in much the sense that the Vietnam War was political: inviting objection from those critical of the larger American society and indignant to its continuing imperfections and inequalities. I do not mean at all to suggest that criticism of the war in Iraq or of the Patriot Act, for example, is confined to the political left, still less that criticism of the Vietnam War was confined to it. But activist faculty members are a natural constituency to protest threats to academic freedom following 9/11. And university authorities, by virtue of both their own convictions and their alliance with Group 2, have reason to defend against these external threats to academic freedom. But this is to say that, for just the reasons that university authorities defend against 9/11 threats to academic freedom, they acquiesce in civil rights agenda threats to academic freedom. And to the extent that this is so, the two stories, optimistic and pessimistic, are in fact one and the same story.

Caveats and Conclusions

Let me mention some obvious caveats. First, I do not assume sincere actors. University authorities and faculty members act for a variety of reasons—sometimes, even, for reasons that are the opposite of their announced reasons for action. It is my conjecture, however, that the problem of authority is more severe when university authorities are more sincere. The more confidence they have in their probity, the more confidently they will not use the new rules in an arbitrary or restrictive fashion; hence the risk in the new rules is minimal. In any case, motives run over a continuum, from high-minded commitment to make universities and colleges genuinely inclusive to bureaucratic needs to satisfy formal legal and informal political requirements.

I have also neglected external actors, most important, the federal government. As part and parcel of receiving federal aid, colleges and universities sign on to a special set of affirmative responsibilities to monitor and spur progress on the civil rights agenda, broadly understood. I also take it for granted that universities and colleges are distributed over a continuum in administrative practice. Some are exemplary in their concern for due process; others are egregiously irresponsible; most fall somewhere in between. The final caveat is the most important. My stock-in-trade is statistical tables and figures. In this case I not only lack what I standardly define as evidence, but I also rely, at some points, on personal experience. What I rely on for evidence is therefore subject to the idiosyncrasies of my life and the hazards of memory. It is, all the same, as close to the truth as I can manage.

The issue of academic freedom and self-censorship is an important issue in its own right. But it is also an aspect of a broader issue in democratic societies—protecting diversity in belief. I have set out two theories of self-censorship. The first, the standard one, posits that the source of danger is social pressures to conform. Tocqueville, among many others, was right to be concerned about social conformity. Ostracism is a potent punishment. But I have become persuaded, perhaps because politics is my field, that a social psychological account is insufficient. A political one is necessary, hence the need for a second theory centered on institutional authorities' powers of punishment. Regrettably, the two theories of punishment reinforce each other.

The Century Ahead: A Brief Survey of Potential Threats to Freedom of Speech, Thought, and Inquiry at American Universities

Evan Gerstmann

ON THE WHOLE, THE contributors to this volume express a wary optimism about the state of academic freedom in post-9/11 America. Robert O'Neil concludes that the First Amendment, both as a legal and a cultural force, has helped shield university faculty from government pressure to sanction unpopular or unpatriotic speech. Although Donald Downs is far more critical of universities, he sees the opportunity, albeit not yet taken advantage of, for universities to augment their protections for free speech in response to post-9/11 pressures. Furthermore, Downs argues that the institutionalization of political mobilization in response to "progressive censorship" in the 1980s and 1990s can help ward off other forms of attempted censorship. Paul Sniderman argues that lack of institutional support for freedom of speech can lead to self-censorship at universities and that such support has been lacking with regard to the campus debates about affirmative action and speech codes. Nonetheless, Sniderman is considerably more optimistic about free speech for dissenters in the war against terrorism, because institutional support for such dissent has been greater.

Nevertheless, there is still much reason to be cautious. John Akker reminds us that academic freedom is a fragile thing, still absent in much of the world. Antonio Brown, writing about Western Europe, also reminds us that threats to academic freedom are not limited to dictatorial regimes in developing nations; even governments with the kindest of intentions can seriously jeopardize academic freedom. Further, Enrique Desmond Arias, writing about Latin America, shows that academic freedom can be just as imperiled by weak governments, unable to control violent private actors, as by powerful, tyrannical governments.

These global scholars remind us that academic freedom cannot be taken for granted. What, then, of the future of academic freedom in the United States? For the reasons cited by O'Neil and Downs, the most visible and dramatic threats to such freedom, such as government pressure to fire or punish faculty for anti-American speech, are likely to be successfully resisted by American universities. But as Susan Lindee demonstrates, subtler, yet even greater threats to free inquiry and speech are less likely to be effectively resisted by university administrators, especially if there is another major terrorist attack on the United States. Lindee warns that "in 2004, threats to academic freedom and scientific integrity continue from more than one direction. University ties to private industry shape tenure decisions; many believe that the Bush administration chooses scientific appointees based on their sympathy to administration positions; and the 'war on terror' justifies new kinds of scientific witch hunts. . . . In the post-9/11 world, scientists face new challenges and new threats to academic freedom."

Thus the optimism expressed by some contributors must be a wary optimism. Therefore I conclude this volume with a review of some of these less overt but potentially potent threats to academic freedom in the United States.

The Issue of Corporate Funding

Threats to freedom of inquiry at American universities do not all come from the government. Ever-increasing university dependence on corporate funding is a serious potential threat to academic freedom. One prominent critic of modern universities' reliance on funding by corporations, right-leaning foundations, and wealthy individuals is Lawrence C. Soley. Soley charges that

corporate, foundation, and tycoon money has had a major, deleterious impact on universities. Financial considerations have altered academic priorities, reduced the importance of teaching, degraded the integrity of academic journals, and determined what research is conducted at universities. The social costs of this influence have been lower quality education, a reduction in academic freedom, and a covert transfer of resources from the public to the private sector.[1]

Soley charges that professors have allowed stock options and pressures from corporate sponsors of their research to alter their research methods and even to distort their results. Less dramatically, but perhaps just as important, Soley argues that many academics have allowed corporate funding to drive their research agenda.[2] He also charges that this influence is as pernicious in the social sciences as it is in the natural sciences and that the influence is often hidden because most social science journals do not require disclosure of corporate funding of research, as is the usual practice in the natural sciences.[3]

The Persistence of Mandatory Loyalty Oaths for Faculty

Other threats to academic freedom are lurking in the background but have received little public attention so far. For example, in many states, teachers, including university professors, are legally required to take "loyalty oaths" in order to teach. As of 2003, fourteen states required loyalty oaths from at least some professors and teachers, including seven states that "explicitly or arguably" apply the requirement to private schools and universities.[4] The U.S. Supreme Court upheld the mandatory oath even for professors at private universities in *Knight v. Board of Regents*.[5] In that case, twenty-seven faculty members at Adelphi University, a private university in New York state, refused to swear or affirm loyalty to the U.S. and New York state constitutions, arguing that the requirement violated their rights of freedom of speech and religion. Their arguments were rejected by the courts.

Other states, such as Indiana, have mandatory oath statutes that require the individual to "promote respect for the flag and institutions of the United States and Indiana, reverence for law and order and undivided allegiance to the government of the United States."[6] Nebraska has a statute that requires oath takers to forswear advocacy of the forceful overthrow of the government.[7] Although still on the books, these two oaths are doubtless unconstitutional.[8] Yet even the more general oaths, such as the one upheld by the Supreme Court in *Knight*, could seriously jeopardize academic freedom should the political climate make enforcement of the oaths more likely. It is not difficult to imagine a state legislator, prosecutor, or university administrator arguing that the oath to support the Constitution[9] was violated by a professor who was advocating civil disobedience to protest a war or by a faculty member who was averring that the Constitution was nothing but an economic pact between white male elites.

The Withering of Tenure

Another snake in the grass that is threatening academic freedom is the steady erosion of tenure protection. Tenure is, of course, widely regarded as a cornerstone of academic freedom, but fewer and fewer university faculty members have tenure. As Gwendolyn Bradley reported in 2004:

Over the past few decades, the increase in contingent appointments—part- and full-time positions off the tenure track—has been dramatic. As of 2001, the most recent year for which U.S. Department of Education data are available, 44.5 percent of faculty appointments were part time. According to 'Assessing the Silent Revolution: How Changing Demographics Are Reshaping the Academic Profession' published in the October 2001 issue of the *AAHE Bulletin* by higher education researchers Martin Finkelstein and Jack Schuster, only 3.3 percent of faculty appointments were off the tenure track in 1969, *but by the 1990s, over half of new full-time appointments were off the tenure track. Only one in four faculty appointments was to a full-time, tenure-track position.* (emphasis added)[10]

It is difficult to measure or even estimate the actual impact on academic freedom of this situation. Nevertheless, it seems likely that having so many university and college faculty members teaching and conducting research without the protection of tenure has already had a significant chilling effect on controversial ideas. As Bradley notes:

That there have been few well-publicized violations of academic freedom involving contingent faculty members may not be so much a sign of hope as the symptom of a silent crisis. The greatest threats to academic freedom today may not be the kinds of blatant attacks that make headlines, but rather the silent self-censorship of thousands of professors holding temporary, insecure appointments. . . . Largely unprotected against sudden termination of their employment, contingent faculty have every incentive to avoid taking risks in the classroom or tackling controversial subjects. Vulnerable to student complaints, contingent faculty members may not feel free to teach rigorously, discuss controversial topics, make heavy reading assignments, or award low grades to those who earn them. To the extent that prepackaged courses—or courses that are designed by one person to be delivered identically by others—do not allow professors and students freely to discuss subject matter, they also threaten academic freedom.[11]

Although the threat to academic freedom is obvious, as with heavy dependence on corporate funding, there are powerful market forces that prevent universities from rectifying the situation. Should pressures to support government policies, including future military activities, increase, then the large and growing number of faculty members without tenure or the hope of tenure would surely be most vulnerable to such pressures.

The Expansion of Institutional Review Boards

Furthermore, even tenured professors are vulnerable to coercion and pressure, especially when their research is partly funded by the government, as a great deal of research is. One significant source of such pressure is the growing number and ever-expanding jurisdictional scope of institutional review boards (IRBs). IRBs began modestly in the 1960s at the order of the U.S. surgeon general to monitor and evaluate the ethics of human subject research. They were endorsed by Congress and expanded in number in the 1970s partly in response to the revelation of the infamous "Tuskegee experiments," which purposely withheld treatment from a group of African American men who suffered from syphilis.[12]

Although originally limited in scope, IRBs have greatly expanded: About 4,000 IRBs now operate at public and private research centers such as universities and hospitals, all seeking to enforce the presumably laudable principle of "respect for persons."[13] More significantly, over time the IRBs have expanded their mission to evaluate the ethics of research having nothing to do with medicine or even any physical contact with people. This expansion has led to concerns that IRBs are becoming serious constraints on academic freedom. Cary Nelson, a vice president of the American Association of University Professors, has warned:

When "respect for persons" is inflected with a heightened sensitivity to the risks inherent in biomedical research, the concept may be adopted with particular fervor. Then an IRB can effectively become a virtual police force—enforcing across campus a philosophy of liberal humanism and its "respect for persons." As IRBs review more and more sorts of research—contributing to what C. K. Gunsalus, special counsel at the University of Illinois, aptly described last November in the *Chronicle of Higher Education* as "mission creep"—physical risk is conceptually leveraged to restrain a much wider range of scholarly inquiry. In some cases, one encounters a kangaroo court ironically enforcing "respect for persons."[14]

Although the Tuskegee experiments clearly violated the concept of "respect for persons," this concept is full of ambiguities when applied to the social sciences and humanities, especially when the subjects of research are morally complex. As Nelson argues:

Of course, "respect for persons" can hardly entail respect for every human action, but IRBs are ill equipped to negotiate the difference. Instead, they often give unquestioned allegiance to a concept that might be given more nuanced application to, say, Ku Klux Klan or Nazi Party members, who might merit humanity qualified with disapproval and who might on occasion appropriately be challenged aggressively in an interview. A historian might well wish to investigate the self-understanding of a Ku Klux Klan member and might choose to present a neutral account of the organization, but academic freedom means that the decision to do so needs to be the historian's, not that of an IRB. One consequence of an unreflective commitment to "respect for persons" is that IRBs have great difficulty accepting research destined to be critical of its "human subjects" and to cause them pain, even though interviewers may treat them with cordiality during the research phase.[15]

IRBs are not monoliths, of course, and some doubtless are capable of negotiating these issues better than others. Nevertheless, if interviews with the Ku Klux Klan are likely to run afoul of some IRBs, then similar problems are likely to arise for any scholar seeking to conduct interviews with those who support terrorism or anti-American extremism. Furthermore, there is little doubt that many IRBs would consider such interviews within their jurisdiction, as many have been interpreting their jurisdiction quite broadly. Writing of the IRB at the University of Illinois, Nelson says:

As recently as 2003, our IRB insisted that a student needed approval before interviewing his or her mother. But not to worry. Provided the course instructor has filed the twelve-page IRB form, and as long as the mother is mentally competent to make her decision (there's a place to confirm that), university approval for the family conversation should be forthcoming in a matter of weeks. Better safe than sorry. Back in 1964, I was daring enough to call home without a bureaucrat's okay. . . . In 2002, it was worse still for University of Illinois anthropologists. Undergraduate students assigned to write papers about body language at the university gym were asked to get consent forms from everyone they watched. Although all the students were members of the facility, the IRB contended that the Intramural Physical Education Building was a private club and could not be treated as a public space. Students interviewing their friends and roommates about their reactions to magazine ads were also required to get signed forms.[16]

None of this means that IRBs are not important protectors against the type of abuse uncovered in Tuskegee. Nonetheless, the expansion of their jurisdiction into the social sciences and humanities and the prevention of emotional discomfort in interview subjects have created a potential infrastructure for academic censorship.

Academic Freedom and Government Surveillance

Other, more subtle threats to academic freedom also lurk in the background, should the political climate move in certain directions. The famed philosopher and social critic Michel Foucault argued that the most powerful form of social control is the ability to create among citizens a sense of constant surveillance.[17] Most academic research is conducted or put into written form on computers that are owned by the university, not by faculty members. The significance of this was discovered in 2003 by Martha McCaughey, director of the women's studies program at Appalachian State University, when the police became interested in an e-mail sent to her by alleged campus vandals, which she had forwarded to some colleagues:

In forwarding the e-mail to my colleagues, I attracted the attention of the campus police, who wanted the message to trace its origin and catch the senders/vandals. They called to ask me for it, and I offered to forward it to them. . . . Some days later, a campus detective called, asking for my entire computer to perform an e-mail recovery operation. I said he did not have my permission to take my entire computer and that I was about to leave town to see my father, who'd become critically ill. The day I returned, I found two police officers at my campus office to confiscate my computer. The request had become a demand. I asked them for a warrant. One officer said that they did not have or need a warrant, because the computer was university property. He said I must touch nothing, print out nothing (not even the paper I was writing under a publisher's deadline), and shut down the computer. My files for which I hold the copyright and in which I have intellectual property rights were not "university property," I protested. They conveniently ignored any distinction between the machine and the electronic files.[18]

After the computer was returned to her, McCaughey discovered that police had opened various files without her permission, none of which had any connection to the apparent vandalism:

When I got my copy of the hard drive back (police kept another), I used technology to do my own form of surveillance of my hard drive. I found that some of my files had been opened, including, for example, those saved as Pervert Evol Narr-Conf Version, WS Pictures, and Sex Toy Parties McCaughey. The documents were all part of bona fide research projects, most of them published already. The article on women's sex-toy parties was published in the academic journal *Sexuality and Culture*. WS Pictures was a backup file of online images of illustrious women—in their clothes. I couldn't help being shocked that my academically legitimate files looked like obscenity. After all, it's not as if my computer contained files with titles like WSNakedPictures or Pervert under 18. . . . Other documents on my computer—and on yours, too, I'm betting—might look suspicious to prying eyes.[19]

As McCaughey notes, the lack of protection for the privacy of professors' files contained in university-owned computers threatens academic freedom both at home and abroad:

Allowing the police unfettered access to files stored on university-provided computers at state schools compromises free speech and academic freedom more generally. It threatens our international colleagues, both professors and students, even more than it threatens me, a U.S. citizen of European descent. What if several professors of Iraqi descent received an anonymous e-mail message containing political arguments critical of U.S. foreign policy or claiming responsibility for anti-U.S. graffiti?[20]

Although government surveillance of what academics do is not as likely to make newspaper headlines, as, for example, the firing of a professor for an unpopular statement, it can be an equally insidious form of intellectual oppression. Fear and a constant sense of potential surveillance can be an even more effective form of control than punishment.

Restrictions on Access to Information

Another important issue regarding the issue of academic freedom in the United States is access to information, without which, freedom of inquiry is of little value. Robert O'Neil correctly argues that First Amendment protections are greater today than they were during the McCarthy period, but it is also true that the First Amendment apparently gives no special weight to the academic freedom of university professors. In the case *Urofsky v. Gilmore*, the United States Court of Appeals for the Fourth Circuit ruled against a group of public university professors who challenged a Virginia law limiting access to sexually explicit materials on state-owned computers. The court, ruling *en banc*, held that "to the extent that the Constitution recognizes any right of 'academic freedom' above and beyond the First Amendment rights to which every citizen is entitled, the right inheres in the University, not in the individual professors, and is not violated by the terms of the act."[21]

This lack of any special right of access to information could become a major academic freedom issue because the government, since the September 11 terrorist attacks, has moved to restrict more and more information. The authority to designate information as classified, previously the prerogative of such executive officials as the secretaries of state and defense and the director of the CIA, has been expanded by the Bush administration to include the secretaries of health and human services and agriculture as well as the head of the Environmental Protection Agency.[22]

Even more significantly, the Bush administration has made aggressive use of the category "sensitive but unclassified":

Soon after September 11, federal agencies cut off public access to thousands of documents on the Internet, ordered information in government-deposit libraries to be withheld or destroyed, and stopped providing information that had been routinely made available to the public. In March 2002, the White House instructed the heads of federal agencies and departments to undertake "an immediate reexamination" of current measures for identifying and protecting information concerning weapons of mass destruction "as well as other information that could be misused to harm the security of our nation and the safety of our people." Forty federal agencies, given ninety days to conduct this review and report to the newly established Office of Homeland Security, moved quickly into compliance. The Homeland Security Act of 2002 followed suit by requiring federal agencies to "identify and safeguard homeland security information that is sensitive but unclassified."[23]

Unfortunately, "sensitive but unclassified" is a poorly defined, ambiguous category. Nonetheless, the Bush administration has been asserting the right to review government-funded university research before publication for the disclosure of such sensitive but unclassified information. According to a faculty committee at the Massachusetts Institute of Technology:

Increasingly of late, MIT has seen the attempt by government contracting officials to include a requirement that research results be reviewed, prior to publication, for the potential disclosure of "sensitive" information. Such a request implies potential restrictions on the manner in which research results are handled and disseminated, and may also restrict the personnel who have access to this material. The difficulty with this approach is that the term "sensitive" has not been defined, and the obligations of the Institute and the obligations of the individuals involved have not been clarified and bounded. This situation opens the Institute and its faculty, students, and staff to potential arbitrary dictates from individual government contracting agents—however well intended. We are aware that many universities have had similar experiences.[24]

Barriers to Foreign Students

Several of the contributors to this volume discussed the post-9/11 difficulties that foreign professors have had in attempting to travel to the United States. These difficulties have affected foreign students as well. Robert M. Gates, former director of the Central Intelligence Agency and the current president of Texas A & M University has written:

After 9/11, for perfectly understandable reasons, the federal government made it much tougher to get a visa to come to the United States. Sadly, the unpredictability and delays that characterize the new system—and, too often, the indifference or hostility of those doing the processing—have resulted over the last year or so in a growing number of the world's brightest young people deciding to remain at home or go to other countries for their college or graduate education. Thousands of legitimate international students are being denied entry into the United States or are giving up in frustration and anger.[25]

The results of the government's post-9/11 policies have been dramatic. Ninety percent of American colleges and universities report a decline in applications from foreign students, and applications to research universities from international students are down 25 percent overall.[26] Ironically, not only do these figures represent a threat to the free flow of ideas at American universities, but they also undermine the very security that they are designed to protect. As Gates warns:

> More troubling is the impact that declining foreign enrollments could have in the war on terrorism. To defeat terrorism, our global military, law enforcement and intelligence capacities must be complemented with positive initiatives and programs aimed at the young people in developing nations who will guide their countries in the future. No policy has proved more successful in making friends for the United States, during the cold war and since, than educating students from abroad at our colleges and universities.[27]

Should there be another major terrorist attack or should the political environment become increasingly xenophobic, this situation could become far worse. After the September 11 attacks, some drastic measures came close to becoming the law of the land. Senator Diane Feinstein proposed a complete moratorium on student visas for six months, and the House of Representatives passed a total ban, contained in its version of the Patriot Act, which would have banned *all* foreign students from working in American research laboratories.[28] This raises obvious concerns for the free movement of scholars and students should the political climate worsen.

Conclusion

Of course, all this is only a thumbnail sketch of the potential threats to academic freedom in the years ahead. It is intended merely to point out the many subtle but significant potential tools of censorship at a time when the professoriat has grown more dependent on university-owned computers, government and corporate funding, and the cooperation of organizations such as IRBs and the Immigration and Naturalization Service, even as traditional protections such as tenure have eroded.

As noted at the beginning of this chapter, there is reason for a wary optimism about academic freedom here in the United States, even in the wake of the September 11, 2001, terrorist attacks. Our Constitution and Bill of Rights are strong, and we have many judges, university officials, faculty members and students, and independent organizations such as those discussed by Donald Downs that would likely resist government efforts to threaten academic freedom. But we have also seen that academic freedom is threatened in much of the world and that it is by no means assured at home. The potential threats to academic freedom are many, and complacency is far from warranted. Thomas Jefferson's admonition of "eternal vigilance" remains as true as ever and even more so in our nervous age.

Notes

CHAPTER ONE

1. O'Connor, "You're Being Watched," p. E1.
2. Murphy, "Academic Freedom," p. 448.
3. Simmons, "Students Fight Alleged Political Prejudice," p. 1B.
4. Simmons, "Students Fight Alleged Political Prejudice," p. 1B.
5. Glenn, "The War on Campus," p. 13.
6. 342 U.S. 485, 493 (1952).
7. Murphy, "Academic Freedom," p. 453.
8. Quoted in Murphy, "Academic Freedom," p. 454.
9. 354 U.S. 234 (1957).
10. Moshman, "Intellectual Freedom for Intellectual Development," p. 30.
11. O'Neil, "Academic Freedom and National Security," p. 21.
12. American Association of University Professors, "Academic Freedom and National Security in a Time of Crisis."
13. Lichtblau, "House Votes for a Permanent Patriot Act."
14. Gaouette, "Senate Republicans Announce Deal for Renewal of Patriot Act," p. A7.
15. American Association of University Professors, "Academic Freedom and National Security."
16. American Association of University Professors, "Academic Freedom and National Security."
17. Reid, "Professor Under Fire for 9/11 Comments."
18. Gray, "Bill Could Limit Open Debate at Colleges," p. 1C.
19. Siegel, "Ohio's Public Universities Keep Politics Out of Class," p. 4C.
20. Pinker, "Sex Ed."
21. See, for example, the discussion in the American Association of University Professors report, "Academic Freedom and National Security."

22. American Association of University Professors, "Academic Freedom and National Security."

23. American Association of University Professors, "Academic Freedom and National Security."

24. Wallach Scott, "Higher Education and Middle Eastern Studies."

25. Golden, "Colleges Object."

CHAPTER TWO

I would like to thank Joseph James Braun, Donald Downs, W. Lee Hansen, Jerry Kapus, and Robert O'Neil for their insightful suggestions regarding this paper.

1. Professor Ely supported city-run electric companies, gasworks, waterworks, and street railways; federally run telegraph and telephone companies, railroads, canals, forest and mineral lands; the inheritance tax; greater protections for female and child labor; civil service reforms; better legal outcomes for labor unions; slum clearances and the creation of urban parks; savings banks; restriction of immigration; and tax relief for lower classes. See Schlabach, "An Aristocrat on Trial," p. 43.

2. Published in *Madison Democrat*, September 19, 1894. Reprinted in Herfurth, "Sifting and Winnowing," pp. 66–67.

3. To read seven excellent essays about the Ely case, see Hansen, *Academic Freedom on Trial*, pt. 1.

4. *Abrams v. United States*, 250 U.S. 616, 630 (1919).

5. See, for example, the American Association of University Professors 1940 Statement of Principles on Academic Freedom and Tenure:

   a. Teachers are entitled to full freedom in research and in the publication of the results, subject to the adequate performance of their other academic duties; but research for pecuniary return should be based upon an understanding with the authorities of the institution.

   b. Teachers are entitled to freedom in the classroom in discussing their subject, but they should be careful not to introduce into their teaching controversial matter which has no relation to their subject. Limitations of academic freedom because of religious or other aims of the institution should be clearly stated in writing at the time of the appointment.

   c. College and university teachers are citizens, members of a learned profession, and officers of an educational institution. When they speak or write as citizens, they should be free from institutional censorship or discipline, but their special position in the community imposes special obligations. As scholars and educational officers, they should remember that the public may judge their profession and their institution by their utterances. Hence they should at all times be accurate, should exercise appropriate restraint, should show respect for the opinions of others, and should make every effort to indicate that they are not speaking for the institution.

6. The mission of the University of Wisconsin system, for example, is set out in statute 36.01(2):

The mission of the system is to develop human resources, to discover and disseminate knowledge, to extend knowledge and its application beyond the boundaries of its campuses and to serve and stimulate society by developing in students heightened intellectual, cultural and humane sensitivities, scientific, professional and technological expertise and a sense of purpose. Inherent in this broad mission are methods of instruction, research, extended training and public service designed to educate people and improve the human condition. Basic to every purpose of the system is the search for truth.

7. Ely did not appeal to academic freedom or freedom of speech in his public defense, instead denying the charges and admitting that if he were guilty, he would be unworthy of the honor of being a professor in a great university. Yet in private he commented, "If I am slaughtered, others in different Universities will perish, and what will become of freedom of speech, I do not know"; and he encouraged Amos Wilder at the *Wisconsin State Journal* to appeal to academic freedom, for if the university "should yield to popular clamor and discharge me for my views, it would be an injury to the University from which it would not soon recover. . . . Freedom is the glory of a State University and intolerance is its shame." Yet again, during World War I, Ely advocated the dismissal of any professor who opposed, criticized, or in any other way undermined the U.S. war effort. See http://faculty.uwstout.edu/shiellt/freespeech1/academic/ely.htm

8. I borrow most items in this list from Sunstein, *Democracy and the Problem of Free Speech*, pp. 149 and 199.

9. Doughty, "Academic Freedom."

10. Schmitt, "Academic Freedom," p. 120.

11. See, for example, Fish, *There's No Such Thing as Free Speech*, p. 115; and Katz, "The First Amendment's Protection of Expressive Activity in the University Classroom," p. 857. J. Peter Byrne notes, "Attempts to understand the scope and foundation of a constitutional guarantee of academic freedom . . . generally result in paradox or confusion. . . . Lacking definition or guiding principle, the doctrine floats in law, picking up decisions as a hull does barnacles" (Byrne, "Academic Freedom," p. 251). See also Harrub and Thompson, "The Illusion of Academic Freedom"; and Schneider, "To Many Adjunct Professors."

12. American Association of University Professors, "Report of Committee A, 2003–04."

13. Commission on Academic Freedom and Pre-College Education, *Liberty and Learning in the Schools*, p. 1.

14. It is for rhetorical and pedagogical purposes that I single out only three conceptions. There are of course many points along the spectrum that one might identify and discuss. Moreover, I do not specifically address the views or circumstances of private schools, which are exempt from constitutional requirements.

15. For example, *Hazelwood v. Kuhlmeier*, 484 U.S. 260 (1988), and *Ward v. Hickey*, 996 F.2d 448 (1st Cir. 1993), allow restrictions to avoid exposing material

inappropriate for the maturity of the student. *Mabey v. Reagan,* 537 F.2d 1036, 1046–1048 (9th Cir. 1976), distinguishes the *Pickering* and *Tinker* high school cases as not applying to a university. For a recent legal analysis, see Martin, "Demoted to High School."

Hazelwood was a K–12 case, but it has been applied to universities in a student newspaper case, *Hosty v. Carter,* No. 01-4155 (7th Cir., June 20, 2005), and to the curricular speech of university professors in *Axson-Flynn v. Johnson,* 151 F. Supp. 2d 1326 (D. Utah 2001), *rev. and remanded,* 356 F.3d 1277 (10th Cir. 2004), and *Bishop v. Aranov,* 926 F.2d 1066 (11th Cir. 1991).

Some commentators argue that only college teachers have genuine academic freedom because K–12 educators are conveyers of knowledge, not creators of knowledge, and only creators of knowledge deserve academic freedom. See, for example, Standler, "Academic Freedom in the USA."

16. Examples of student academic freedom issues include the creation of so-called free-speech zones (see, e.g., "'Free-Speech Zones' at Texas, Wis. Universities Challenged," at the Student Press Law Center website, http://www.splc .org), student speech codes (see, e.g., "Student Speech Code of the Month" on the FIRE website, http://www.thefire.org), and student performances (see, e.g., "Washington State University Bankrolls Vigilante Censorship," available at http://www.thefire.org/index.php/article/6106.html).

One example of an institutional academic freedom petition for court deference to institutional policy making is the Bakke case. The *Bakke* court said, for example, that a university may determine for itself on academic grounds (1) who may teach, (2) what may be taught, (3) how it will be taught, and (4) who may be admitted to study. See *Regents of the University of California v. Bakke,* 438 U.S. 265, 312 (1978). See also *Megill v. Board of Regents of Florida,* 541 F.2d 1073, 1077 (5th Cir. 1976): "This court does not sit as a reviewing body of the correctness or incorrectness of the Board of Regents' decision in granting or withholding tenure. This is founded on the policy that federal courts should be loathe to intrude into internal school affairs." See also *DiBona v. Matthews,* No. 016032, Supreme Court of California, 1990 Cal. LEXIS 3309 (July 25, 1990), *cert. denied,* 498 U.S. 998 (1990); and *Clark v. Holmes,* 474 F.2d 928 (7th Cir. 1972), *cert. denied,* 411 U.S. 972.

17. See, for example, 1940 AAUP Statement. Donald Kennedy stresses faculty obligations in *Academic Duty.* Robert O'Neil explains, "Not all words, even those uttered by professors, are fully protected. First Amendment freedoms have limits, especially for government employees. The Supreme Court has recognized that government, as an employer, has certain special needs that may warrant restricting public workers' speech more than the speech of citizens at large. People who take government jobs are expected, for example, not to speak in ways that disrupt an agency's operations or destroy the confidence of an agency's clients. They often may be required to pursue established grievance channels and can be disciplined for advocacy that takes substantial time away from their assigned tasks. To be protected, public employees' speech must also address matters of public concern and not be mere personal vendettas" (O'Neil, "First Amendment Rights When Discourse Offends or Demeans," pp. B6–B7).

18. I use the term *civil libertarian* as a term of convenience because civil liberty strictly construed would conflict with academic freedom in some cases, for example, an instructor endorsing astrology in an astronomy class.

19. *Sweezy v. New Hampshire*, 354 U.S. 234 (1957), was the first U.S. Supreme Court decision to recognize academic freedom. Important later cases include *Shelton v. Tucker*, 364 U.S. 479 (1960); *Keyishian v. Board of Regents*, 385 U.S. 589 (1967), which held that academic freedom is a special concern of the First Amendment; *Pickering v. Board of Education*, 391 U.S. 563 (1968); and *Tinker v. Des Moines School District*, 393 U.S. 503 (1969).

20. Schmitt, "Academic Freedom," p. 112.

21. Kennedy, *Academic Duty*, p. 1.

22. Pincoffs, "Introduction," p. viii.

23. Many disputes over academic freedom or free speech are moral, not legal, disputes, and both existed as moral ideals before being recognized in the law.

24. *Wilson v. Chancellor*, 418 F. Supp. 1358 (D. Ore. 1976).

25. *Cohen v. San Bernardino Community College*, 92 F.3d 968 (9th Cir. 1996), cert. denied, 117 S. Ct. 1290 (1996).

26. Based on an incident at the University of Wisconsin, River Falls, in 1991.

27. See "What Exactly Is the Bible?" in *Stoutonia*. My colleague's reply appeared in the next week's issue.

28. *Keefe v. Geanakos*, 418 F.2d 359 (1st Cir. 1969).

29. Hence the civil libertarian can accept judgments by colleagues about the content of a teacher's or a professor's claims in hiring, promotion, tenure, and dismissal decisions. For example, a geography teacher who teaches that the world is flat will not last long in a geography department.

30. Searle, "Two Concepts of Academic Freedom," pp. 89 and 93. Searle describes claims 1 through 4 as the "special theory of academic freedom" and claim 5 as the general theory of academic freedom. For the present purposes, I ignore the controversy over whether claim 5 is genuinely "academic" in nature. See Van Alstyne, "The Specific Theory of Academic Freedom," reprinted in Pincoffs, *The Concept of Academic Freedom*, pp. 59–85; and "Reply to Comments," in Pincoffs, *The Concept of Academic Freedom*, pp. 125–130.

31. Emerson, *Toward a General Theory of the First Amendment*, pp. 6–8.

32. See Mill, *On Liberty*, ch. 2.

33. Curtis, *Free Speech*, pp. 136–137.

34. Stone, "Academic Freedom and Responsibility." Not to be outdone, abolitionists forced out the president of Franklin College and had a federal judge who enforced the Fugitive Slave Act dismissed from his lectureship at Harvard. Opposite politics—identical impulses to censor.

35. USF/UFF, "Why Freedom for Academics?"

36. See Lipstadt, *Denying the Holocaust* and Lipstadt, *History on Trial*.

37. See Graff, "To Debate or Not to Debate Intelligent Design?" Graff cites numerous others who argue the same point.

38. For a philosophical and legal analysis of harm and offense, see Feinberg, *Harm to Others*.

39. For example, truthful expression that harms is protected from libel actions. See, for example, the Wisconsin Constitution: "In all criminal prosecutions or indictments for libel, the truth may be given in evidence, and if it shall appear to the jury that the matter charged as libelous be true, and was published with good motives and for justifiable ends, the party shall be acquitted; and the jury shall have the right to determine the law and the fact." Yet truth is not always exculpatory; for example, truthful but unlicensed medical or legal advice might be successfully prosecuted.

40. Rockwell visited Lawrence University, Wisconsin State College, Eau Claire (now the University of Wisconsin, Eau Claire), and Wisconsin State College, River Falls (now the University of Wisconsin, River Falls). That winter Rockwell also appeared at schools such as Hamilton College and Hunter College in New York, Brown University, Wake Forest University, and the University of Northern Iowa.

41. For example, in the midst of the Churchill controversy, when the Republican-controlled Wisconsin Assembly discovered he was scheduled to give a speech at the University of Wisconsin, Whitewater, they passed a resolution recommending that the university withdraw its invitation. The controversy began when a Hamilton College student discovered Churchill's comments in Reid, "Professor Under Fire for 9/11 Comments." Churchill's essay became a book, *On the Justice of Roosting Chickens: Reflections on the Consequences of U.S. Imperial Arrogance and Criminality*. For a provocative defense of Churchill, see Jensen, "Ward Churchill Has Rights." Although the University of Colorado defended his right to his opinion, it went on to investigate further charges against Churchill.

42. *Dambrot v. Central Michigan University*, 55 F.3d 1177 (6th Cir. 1995). Unfortunately for Dambrot, the court ruled that his speech was private rather than public and thus that the university was within its rights to fire him.

43. Jenkinson, "Child Abuse in the Hate Factory," p. 15 ff.

44. See, for example, *Cohen v. California*, 403 U.S. 15 (1971).

45. Compare, for example, *Silva v. University of New Hampshire*, 888 F. Supp. 293 (D. N.H. 1994), and *Rubin v. Ikenberry*, 933 F. Supp. 1425 (C.D. Ill. 1996).

46. See, for example, Hajdin, *The Law of Sexual Harassment*, and Browne, "Title VII as Censorship."

47. See, for example, *Broadrick v. Oklahoma*, 413 U.S. 601, 611 (1973), and *Texas v. Johnson*, 491 U.S. 397 (1989). For an early academic case, see *Papish v. University of Missouri*, 410 U.S. 667 (1973).

48. See, for example, *Broadrick*, at 607.

49. *Doe v. University of Michigan*, 721 F. Supp. 852 (E.D. Mich. 1989).

50. Examples of facial overbreadth cited by the court included class discussion, jokes, and decisions to exclude individuals from dorm parties or a study group. The three examples of applied overbreadth included a graduate student in social work punished for expressing his belief that homosexuality is a disease and that he intended to develop a counseling plan to change gay clients into

straight ones; an undergraduate student punished for reading an alleged homophobic limerick during a public-speaking exercise in a scheduled class for an entrepreneurship course; and a dentistry student punished for expressing concerns about a professor's alleged unfairness to minorities in an informal class discussion about problems anticipated in a course.

51. *Doe v. University of Michigan*, 721 F. Supp. 852 (E.D. Mich. 1989), at 867.

52. For example, time, place, and manner restrictions on expression generally are accepted when they are within the constitutional powers of the government, further an important or substantial government interest, are content-neutral, and are no greater than necessary to the furtherance of the legitimate government interest.

53. For example, Mill's consequentialist defense of free inquiry is driven by his utilitarianism. Ronald Dworkin, on the other hand, rejects consequentialist defenses of academic freedom. See Dworkin, *Freedom's Law*, ch. 11.

54. Categorical approaches attempt to classify speech into categories of protected speech (e.g., political debate) and unprotected speech (e.g., obscenity). Balancing approaches disdain categories in order to balance competing rights in particular cases. For an illuminating discussion of these approaches, see the debate between the majority, minority, and dissenting opinions in *R.A.V. v. City of St. Paul*, 505 U.S. 377 (1992).

55. Brainerd, "The Notion of Academic Freedom."

56. See, for example, three pamphlets in the collection of the Wisconsin Historical Society published in 1890: J. J. Blaisdell, "The Edgerton Bible Case: The Decision of the Supreme Court of Wisconsin"; W. A. McAtee, "Must the Bible Go? A Review of the Decision of the Supreme Court of Wisconsin, in the Edgerton Bible Case"; and W. F. Brown, "An Official Deliverance in Regard to the Late Decision of the Supreme Court of Wisconsin, Concerning the Bible and Our Public Schools." For a summary of their arguments, see http://faculty.uwstout .edu/shiellt/freespeech1/edgerton/against.htm

57. *Donahoe v. Richards*, 38 Maine 376 (1854), held that Bible reading can be required. *Spiller v. Inhabitants of Woburn*, 94 Mass. 127 (1866), held that Bible reading did not violate a student's right of conscience or interfere with his religious professions or sentiments. *Board of Education v. Minor*, 23 Ohio 211 (1872), found that Bible reading and the singing of hymns is constitutional so long as it is optional. *McCormick v. Burt*, 95 Ill. 263 (1880), rejected a pupil's complaint against his teacher and school board for suspending him when he refused to discontinue his studies during reading of the Bible. *Moore v. Monroe*, 64 Iowa 367 (1884), held that Bible reading does not make the public school into a place of worship.

58. *Weiss v. Edgerton School District*, 76 Wis. 177 (1890). The *Minor* decision upheld a Cincinnati School Board resolution repealing Bible reading in public schools but did not mandate an outright ban: "The only fair and impartial method, *where serious objection is made*, is to let each sect give its own instructions, elsewhere than in the State schools" (emphasis added). Quoted in Blakely, *American State Papers Bearing on Sunday Legislation*, pp. 194–195. Of

course the Bible may be used for nonreligious instruction in public schools. See, for example, *Stone v. Graham*, 449 U.S. 39, 42 (1980): "The Bible may constitutionally be used in an appropriate study of history, civilization, ethics, comparative religion, or the like." See also *Abington School District v. Schempp*, 374 U.S. 203, 1225 (1963).

59. *John Doe, Mary Roe, and Freedom from Religion Foundation v. Porter and the Rhea County Board of Education*, U.S. District Court, Eastern District of Tennessee at Chattanooga, Case No. 1:01-cv-115 (February 8, 2002).

60. http://faculty.uwstout.edu/shiellt/freespeech1/edgerton/schoolboard .htm

61. For example, the American Civil Liberties Union, a leading civil libertarian organization, actively argues for a strict separation of church and state.

62. *Roberts v. Madigan*, 921 F.2d 1047 (10th Cir. 1990), *cert. denied*, 112 S. Ct. 3025 (1992).

63. *Axson-Flynn v. Johnson*, 151 F. Supp. 2d 1326 (D. Utah 2001).

64. See, for example, Harrub and Thompson, "The Illusion of Academic Freedom." This suggestion has received increased attention since President George W. Bush endorsed it in a public interview on August 2, 2005. John G. West, who advocates for the inclusion of intelligent design through the auspices of the Discovery Institute said, "President Bush is to be commended for defending free speech on evolution, and supporting the right of students to hear about different scientific views about evolution" (quoted in Baker and Slevin, "Bush Remarks on 'Intelligent Design' Theory Fuel Debate," p. A1).

65. Haynes, "Darwin Under Fire (Again)."

66. Foundation for Individual Rights in Education, "Letter to UW-EC Chancellor Donald Mash," and American Center for Law and Justice, "Staff Counsel Letter to Kent Syverson."

67. See, for example, David Horowitz's Center for the Study of Popular Culture (http://cspc.org) and "Students for Academic Freedom Host the Academic Bill of Rights" (available at http://www.studentsforacademicfreedom.org/abor .html).

68. *Craig v. Harney*, 331 U.S. 367, 376 (1947).

69. Hentoff, *Free Speech for Me, But Not for Thee*.

70. Broadly conceived, viewpoint neutrality says that open public forum speech should not be regulated with regard to the point of view of the speaker (as opposed to a limited public forum, which may be limited according to the purposes of the forum). See, for example, *Board of Regents v. Southworth*, 529 U.S. 217 (2000), and *ACLU v. Mote*, No. 04-1890 (4th Cir., September 12, 2005). For a legal analysis of viewpoint neutrality in secondary education, see Tobin, "Divining *Hazelwood*."

71. See, for example, *Levin v. Harleston*, 966 F.2d 85 (2nd Cir. 1992).

72. Littlefield, "Effort to Punish UNLV Professor Gains Exposure."

73. Schurz, *Speeches, Correspondence, and Political Papers of Carl Schurz*, pp. 58–59.

74. See, for example, American Civil Liberties Union of Wisconsin, "ACLU and American Conservative Union Launch New Ads."

75. See FIRE Board of Directors and Board of Advisors, at http://www
.thefire.org

76. Matsuda, "Public Response to Racist Speech"; Lawrence, "If He Hollers
Let Him Go"; and Delgado, "Campus Antiracism Rules."

77. Following a survey of 355 institutions, the Carnegie Fund for the Advancement of Teaching estimated that 60 percent of colleges and universities
had a hate speech code and another 11 percent were considering such a policy.
See Carnegie Fund for the Advancement of Teaching, *Campus Life.*

78. See, for example, Delgado, "Words That Wound," note 32, and pp. 136–
149; and Matsuda, "Public Response to Racist Speech," pp. 2331–2341.

79. *Chaplinsky v. New Hampshire,* 315 U.S. 568 (1942).

80. For an early verbal racial harassment case, see *Rogers v. EEOC,* 454 F.2d
234 (5th Cir. 1971), *cert. denied,* 406 U.S. 957 (1972). For an early verbal sexual harassment case, see *Bundy v. Jackson,* 641 F.2d 934 (1981). U.S. Supreme Court decisions on verbal sexual harassment include *Meritor Savings Bank FSB v. Vinson,*
477 U.S. 57 (1986), and *Harris v. Forklift Systems Inc.,* 510 U.S. 17 (1993).

81. Often these two arguments were combined. For early statements of the
fighting words argument, see Lawrence, "If He Hollers Let Him Go," and Grey
(author of the Stanford speech code), "Civil Rights vs. Civil Liberties," pp. 81–
107, and "Discriminatory Harassment and Free Speech." For early statements of
the hostile environment harassment argument, see Lange, "Racist Speech on
Campus"; Shapiro, "The Call for Campus Conduct Policies"; and Gale, "Reimagining the First Amendment."

82. See, for example, Sunstein, *Democracy and the Problem of Free Speech,*
p. 196; Delgado, "Campus Antiracism Rules"; and Wilson, *The Myth of Political
Correctness,* p. 96.

83. See, for example, Sunstein, *Democracy and the Problem of Free Speech*;
Greenawalt, *Fighting Words*; Smolla, *Free Speech in an Open Society*; and Haiman,
Speech Acts and the First Amendment.

84. American Association of University Professors, "On Freedom of Expression and Campus Speech Codes."

85. *UWM Post Inc. et al. v. Board of Regents,* 774 F. Supp. 1163, 1171 (E.D. Wis.
1991). Cf. *Clarke v. Board of Education,* 215 Neb. 250 (1983), in which a tenured
teacher lost his job for using racial epithets in the classroom.

86. See, for example, Will, "Academic Liberal's Brand of Censorship" and
"In Praise of Censure."

87. *R.A.V. v. St. Paul,* 505 U.S. 377, 392 (1992). Marquis of Queensbury Rules
refers to the rules of modern boxing formulated ca. 1867 under the supervision
of the eighth Marquis of Queensbury (1844–1900).

88. Foundation for Individual Rights in Education, "Washington State University Bankrolls Vigilante Censorship."

89. Beito et al., "Consulting All Sides on 'Speech Codes,'" p. 11.

90. Gould, "The Precedent That Wasn't," p. 345.

91. I have argued elsewhere that restrictions should be: (a) content-neutral
and regulate only speech that is (b) targeted at a captive audience, (c) intended

to cause harm, (d) repeated or egregious or conjoined with illegal conduct, and (e) lacking academic justification. See Shiell, *Campus Hate Speech on Trial.*

92. When the progressive newspaper *The Flipside* sought student-fee funding and no good basis existed to exclude it, the Student Senate voted for the ban on March 14, 2005.

93. Foundation for Individual Rights in Education, "University of Wisconsin-Eau Claire Wages Campaign Against Student Viewpoints."

94. Schurz, *Speeches Correspondence, and Political Papers of Carl Schurz*, excerpts from pp. 222–239. Schurz had planned to speak on "American Civilization," but when he learned that an excited crowd led by prominent businessmen had broken up a meeting of abolitionists a few days earlier, he seized the opportunity to address a favorite topic, renaming his talk, "Freedom of Speech."

95. Nelson, "The Significance of and Rationale for Academic Freedom," p. 21.

96. Commission on Academic Freedom and Pre-College Instruction, *Liberty and Learning in the Schools*, p. 12.

97. Jennifer Elrod writes, "Many public university professors subscribe to an overly broad vision of what free speech means. They often believe that their expression, both professional and personal, approaches the level of nearly complete protection under the First Amendment; this, however, is not the current legal reality" (Elrod, "Academics, Public Employee Speech, and the Public University," p. 1).

98. See John S. and James L. Knight Foundation, available at http://www.knightfdn.org

99. Chaltain, "Does the First Amendment Have a Future?" p. 126.

100. See John S. and James L. Knight Foundation, available at http://www.knightfdn.org

101. See First Amendment Center, available at http://www.fac.org

102. Franklin et al. "The State of the First Amendment in Wisconsin." Survey posted with permission at http://faculty.uwstout.edu/shiellt/freespeech1/survey/index.html

103. Foundation for Individual Rights in Education, "Religious Liberty in Peril on Campus, National Surveys Reveal."

104. Paulsen, "Keeping Government Out of Religion—and Vice Versa."

105. Chaltain, "Does the First Amendment Have a Future?" pp. 127–128.

106. During the Ward Churchill controversy at the University of Colorado, faculty worried that the affair might have a chilling effect on academic freedom and free speech at the university. A newspaper columnist opined, "Good. It's about time," and expressed his belief that the affair presented an opportunity for the university to become a "bastion of conservativism" (Rosen, "CU Is Worth Fighting For," p. 43A).

107. The Wisconsin survey found that nearly 70 percent opposed government monitoring of public library records as part of the war on terrorism. See Franklin et al., "The State of the First Amendment in Wisconsin," p. 31.

108. Excerpts from Eldredge's speech, *The Congressional Globe* (1863), pp. 1577–1578. In his original speech Long pointed out that the views he was expressing were shared by several newspapers, including the *Cincinnati Commercial*, the *New York Tribune*, the *Indianapolis Journal*, the *Chicago Tribune*, the *New Haven Palladium*, and the *Columbus Journal*, and by some Republican politicians, including Salmon P. Chase, Lincoln's secretary of the treasury (*Congressional Globe* [1864], April 18, p. 1501).

109. Available at http://www.senate.gov/artandhistory/history/resources/pdf/FreeSpeechWartime.pdf

110. Jenkinson, "Child Abuse in the Hate Factory," pp. 14–15.

111. La Haye, *The Battle for the Public School*, p. 13.

112. Jenkinson, "Child Abuse in the Hate Factory," pp. 12–13.

113. Four university cases illustrate this point: (1) Eastern Kentucky University successfully dismissed a professor for her teaching style, *Hetrick v. Martin*, 48 F.2d 705 (6th Cir. 1973), *cert. denied*, 414 U.S. 1075 (1973); (2) Central Washington University successfully dismissed a professor for missing class while presenting a research paper at a seminar in Israel, *Stastny v. CWU*, 647 P.2d 496 (Wash. Ct. App. 1982), *cert. denied*, 460 U.S. 1071 (1983); (3) the University of Colorado, Boulder, disciplined a professor for refusing on academic grounds to distribute standardized student evaluation forms, *Wirsing v. University of Colorado*, 739 F. Supp. 551 (D. Colo. 1990), *aff'd without opinion*, 945 F.2d 412 (10th Cir. 1991), *cert. denied*, 503 U.S. 906 (1992); and (4) the City College of New York stripped Leonard Jeffries of his chairmanship of the Black Studies Department because of his controversial off-campus speech, *Jeffries v. Harleston*, 21 F.3d 1238 (2d Cir. 1994), *cert. denied*, 516 U.S. 862 (1995). See Elrod, "Academics, Public Employee Speech, and the Public University," for an analysis of the university setting. Two recent analyses of the high school setting are Wernicke, "Teachers' Speech Rights in the Classroom," and Daly, "Balancing Act."

114. *Hillis v. Austin State University*, 665 F.2d 547, 553 (5th Cir. 1982), *cert. denied*, 457 U.S. 1106 (1982). See also *Mahoney v. Hankin*, 593 F. Supp. 1171, 1174 (S. D. N.Y. 1984).

115. *Cohen v. San Bernardino Community College*, 92 F.3d 968 (9th Cir. 1996), *cert. denied*, 117 S. Ct. 1290 (1996).

116. Here are two examples. A Michigan teacher was awarded compensatory and punitive damages when his school board wrongfully fired him after receiving parent complaints about his life science course [*Stachura v. Truskowski, et al.*, 763 F.2d 211 (6th Cir. 1985)]. The court commented, "Substantial as are the jury awards, it is clear to us that the damages suffered by [Mr.] Stachura will affect his professional career for his entire lifetime." A University of Wisconsin, Madison, physics professor, Henry Barschall, was legally vindicated after winning a series of U.S., German, Swiss, and French lawsuits filed by a publisher over his articles on the costs of physics journals (see, e.g., Barschall and Arrington, "Cost of Physics Journals"), but his legal ordeal lasted even beyond his death (his estate was sued) and legal fees exceeded $6 million.

117. Franklin et al. "The State of the First Amendment in Wisconsin," p. 26.

118. Nelson, "The Significance of and Rationale for Academic Freedom," p. 22.

119. Gary Pavela writes, "Constitutionally protected academic freedom is a fragile concept. It's not clear that courts will continue to see it as a 'special concern' of the First Amendment. . . . Now more than ever, professors' claims to academic freedom can't be based on blanket assertions of unquestioned 'rights' or prerogatives; they must be grounded instead on carefully crafted, widely respected, and consistently practiced professional and ethical standards" (Pavela, "A Balancing Act," p. 25).

120. USF/UFF, "Why Freedom for Academics?"

121. *Sweezy v. New Hampshire*, 354 U.S. 234 (1957). To be sure, Justice Frankfurter wrote this in the context of institutional academic freedom. *Keyishian v. Board of Regents*, 385 U.S. 589 (1967), introduced academic freedom for professors, and *Rosenberger v. Rector*, 515 U.S. 819 (1995), makes clear that university students also have a right to academic freedom.

CHAPTER THREE

1. National Public Radio, *All Things Considered*.
2. Schrecker, *No Ivory Tower*.
3. Wilson and Smallwood, "One Professor Cleared," p. A12.
4. Wilson and Smallwood, "One Professor Cleared," p. A12.
5. Nidiry, "CUNY Trustees," p. A50.
6. Greenwell, "Bollinger," p. 1.
7. Fox News, *The O'Reilly Factor*.
8. Walsh, "The Drake Affair," p. 8.
9. See American Association of University Professors, "Academic Freedom and Tenure."
10. Nicholson, "At CU, Arab Activist Urges Free Palestine," p. B5.
11. See Cranford and Rooney, "Speechless."
12. For a general discussion of these and other post–September 11 events, see American Association of University Professors, "Academic Freedom and National Security."
13. American Association of University Professors, "Academic Freedom and National Security," p. 36.
14. Jayson, "UT System Revises Employee Policy," p. B6.
15. Van Alstyne, *Freedom and Tenure in the Academy*.
16. *Wieman v. Updegraff*, 344 U.S. 183, 191 (1952) (Frankfurter, J., concurring).
17. *Sweezy v. New Hampshire*, 354 U.S. 234 (1957).
18. *Sweezy v. New Hampshire*, 354 U.S. 234 (1957), p. 262.
19. *Regents of the University of California v. Bakke*, 438 U.S. 265 (1978).
20. *Board of Regents v. Southworth*, 529 U.S. 217 (2000).
21. *Keyishian v. Board of Regents*, 385 U.S. 589 (1967).
22. *Keyishian v. Board of Regents*, 385 U.S. 589 (1967), p. 603.
23. *Speiser v. Randall*, 357 U.S. 513 (1958).

24. *NAACP v. Alabama ex rel. Patterson*, 357 U.S. 449 (1958).

25. *Gibson v. Florida Legislative Investigation Committee*, 372 U.S. 539 (1963).

26. *Watkins v. United States*, 354 U.S. 178 (1957).

27. *Gibson v. Florida Legislative Investigation Committee*, 372 U.S. 539 (1963).

28. *McAuliffe v. Mayor of New Bedford*, 29 N.E. 517, 518 (Mass. 1892).

29. *Pickering v. Board of Education*, 391 U.S. 563 (1968).

30. *Yellin v. United States*, 374 U.S. 109 (1963).

CHAPTER FOUR

I am dismayed that Alan Charles Kors's essay for this volume had to be dropped in order to satisfy reviewers. Kors is the single leading defender of academic freedom in the country, and he has taken difficult stands in pressure-packed cases that no one else has matched, to my knowledge. Previous reviewers of this volume were wrong to take this stand. Accordingly, I would like to dedicate this chapter to Kors.

1. Madison, "Federalist No. 51," p. 322.

2. See, for example, Lewis, "Kastenmeier Lecture," p. 257.

3. See, for example, Hamilton, *Zealotry and Academic Freedom*, ch. 1; and Schrecker, *No Ivory Tower*.

4. See, for example, Carter, "The Independent Counsel Mess," p. 105.

5. Unger (*Law in Modern Society*, ch. 3) writes that social contract theory (based on this logic) is the essence of liberalism.

6. Lowi, *The End of Liberalism*.

7. See, for example, Meiklejohn, *Political Freedom*; Justice Brandeis's concurring opinion in *Whitney v. California*, 274 U.S. 357 (1927); and Lahav, "Holmes and Brandeis."

8. Kors's speech (delivered at the Academic Freedom Conference, Loyola Marymount University, February 2004) in possession of author.

9. Many philosophers have discussed these two faces of rights. See, in general, Melden, *Rights and Persons*; and Downs, "Human Rights/Civil Liberties."

10. Rauch, *Kindly Inquisitors*, p. 86. See also Pelikan, *The Idea of the University*, especially p. 48.

11. Primus, *The American Language of Rights*, p. 7.

12. Weinstein, *Hate Speech, Pornography, and the Radical Attack on Free Speech Doctrine*, p. 181. See also Kalven, *The Negro and the First Amendment*.

13. See Rabban, *Free Speech in Its Forgotten Years*, chs. 5–7.

14. Tocqueville, *Democracy in America* (1961), v. 2, bk. 2, chs. 8 and 9. See also John Rawl's portrayal of "reflective equilibrium" in *A Theory of Justice*, pp. 48–50. Liberalism's practice of equal rights is like an insurance policy.

15. See Eidelberg, *The Philosophy of the American Constitution*, p. 153. On undue moral consensus and orthodoxy as detrimental to the Socratic virtues and democratic citizenship, see Villa, *Socratic Citizenship*.

16. See, for example, Canon and Johnson, *Judicial Policies*.

17. See, for example, Stouffer, *Communism, Conformity, and Civil Liberties*.

18. Hentoff, *Free Speech for Me, But Not for Thee.*

19. Tocqueville, *Democracy in America* (1961), v. 1, especially ch. 15.

20. Tocqueville, *Democracy in America* (1961), v. 2, bk. 2, ch. 4.

21. See, for example, Pelikan, *The Idea of the University*, especially p. 48.

22. Marcuse, "Repressive Tolerance."

23. Downs, *Restoring Free Speech and Liberty on Campus.*

24. E-mail to Thor Halvorssen, July 2001. Interview with Thor Halvorssen, July 2001.

25. *Doe v. University of Michigan*, 721 F. Supp. 852 (E.D. Mich. 1989); *UWM Post Inc. et al. v. Board of Regents of the University of Wisconsin*, 774 F. Supp. 1163 (E.D. Wis. 1991); *Robert Corry et al. v. Stanford University*, County of Santa Clara Superior Court, No. 740309 (February 27, 1995).

26. *R.A.V. v. City of St. Paul*, 505 U.S. 377 (1992).

27. Gould, "The Precedent That Wasn't."

28. See Shiell, *Campus Hate Speech on Trial*; and Golding, *Free Speech on Campus.*

29. On Massachusetts, see Kors and Silverglate, *The Shadow University*, p. 321. A colleague at Edinboro recently told me about the new code there, which was ultimately abandoned.

30. See the discussion of these cases on FIRE's web page (http://www.thefire.org/wsu). See also Peters, "Battle over Students Rights Comes to Head."

31. On the "six waves of zealotry" in American history that witnessed powerful attacks on academic freedom, see Hamilton, *Zealotry and Academic Freedom*, ch. 1.

32. See, for example, Zinsmeister, "The Shame of America's One-Party Campuses."

33. See O'Neil, Chapter 3 of this book.

34. Hall, quoted in Young, "Free Speech Dilemmas," p. 1.

35. Foundation for Individual Rights in Education, http://www.thefire.org

36. See Downs, *Restoring Free Speech and Liberty on Campus*, especially ch. 2.

37. See the discussion of the case on the FIRE web page (http://www.thefire.org).

38. See French, *FIRE's Guide to Religious Liberty on Campus*; and Bernstein, *You Can't Say That.*

39. See a discussion of the case on FIRE's web page (http://www.thefire.org). See also Price, "Jesuit College Bars Pro-Life Group for 'Bias'"; and *Boy Scouts of America v. Dale*, 120 S. Ct. 2446 (2000).

40. American Association of University Professors, "Academic Freedom and National Security in a Time of Crisis," p. 20.

41. See Williams, "Student."

42. Leo, "Campus Censors in Retreat," p. 64.

43. Gould, "The Precedent That Wasn't."

44. See, for example, Rosenberg, *The Hollow Hope*; and McCann, *Rights at Work*. McCann and Rosenberg are often seen as antagonists, but in many ways they represent two sides of the same coin. Both agree that political mobilization is an important part of meaningful legal change.

45. Shiell, *Campus Hate Speech on Trial*, p. 55. See Walker, *Hate Speech*, p. 2. On the contrary, the speech code movement at Duke was stopped by the intervention of noted constitutional law professor William van Alstyne. See Redlawsk, "'We Don't Need No Thought Control,'" p. 217.

46. See FIRE's extensive archive of cases on its web page (http://www.thefire.org).

47. The faculty member who brought this issue up is a friend of mine. I am not presently authorized to divulge his name.

48. The court decision is on FIRE's web page. See also, Foundation for Individual Rights in Education, "FIRE Declares War on Speech Codes."

49. See Epp, *The Rights Revolution*.

50. Kors and Silverglate, *The Shadow University*, chs. 1 and 13; Downs, *Restoring Free Speech and Liberty on Campus*, ch. 5.

51. I am presently the president of CAFR, replacing the original president, historian Stanley Payne. Art historian Jane Hutchison is the treasurer.

52. See Downs, *Restoring Free Speech and Liberty on Campus*, chs. 1, 6–8. Articles and editorials appeared in the *Wall Street Journal*, the *New York Times*, the *Boston Globe*, the *National Journal*, the Associated Press, National Public Radio, the *Village Voice*, *Reason*, *Liberty*, and the *Chronicle of Higher Education* (the latter published a cover story and several follow-up articles), to name a few.

53. See Jonathan Rauch's depiction of the political importance of the Wisconsin free speech/civil liberty movement in "A College Newspaper Messes Up."

54. See, for example, Hansen, *Academic Freedom on Trial*, pp. 58–89; Downs, *Restoring Free Speech and Liberty on Campus*, chs. 6 and 7.

55. American Association of University Professors, "Academic Freedom and National Security in a Time of Crisis," p. 20.

56. See, for example, Cole and Dempsey, *Terrorism and the Constitution*.

57. American Association of University Professors, "Academic Freedom and National Security in a Time of Crisis," p. 22. See also Jayson, "UT System Revises Employee Policy," p. B6.

58. American Association of University Professors, "Academic Freedom and National Security in a Time of Crisis," p. 22.

59. See Foundation for Individual Rights in Education, "Writing Instructor Loses Job."

60. American Association of University Professors, "Academic Freedom and National Security in a Time of Crisis," p. 22.

61. On all these cases, see American Association of University Professors, "Academic Freedom and National Security in a Time of Crisis," p. 22.

62. American Association of University Professors, "Academic Freedom and National Security in a Time of Crisis," pp. 22–23.

63. American Association of University Professors, "Academic Freedom and National Security in a Time of Crisis," p. 20. The other cases discussed here are from this report.

64. On Schmidt's role as a prominent speech code critic in higher administration, see Shiell, *Campus Hate Speech on Trial*, pp. 53–66.

65. American Association of University Professors, "Academic Freedom and National Security in a Time of Crisis," pp. 20–21.

66. See Rauch, *Kindly Inquisitors*.

67. American Association of University Professors, "Academic Freedom and National Security in a Time of Crisis," p. 19. The "grave" case is the University of South Florida case (affecting Sami Al-Arian). On past transgressions against academic freedom resulting from national security concerns, see Lewis, "Kastenmeier Lecture." For a more specific focus on academic freedom, see Hamilton, *Zealotry and Academic Freedom*.

68. Epp, *The Rights Revolution*, pp. 2–3.

69. Randall, *Freedom and Taboo*, pp. 5–6.

70. Yardley, "Politically Corrected."

71. These were Meiklejohn's words when Harry Kalven Jr. informed him of the Supreme Court's famous decision on the libel of public figures, *New York Times v. Sullivan*, 376 U.S. 254 (1964). This decision was premised on Meiklejohn's theory of self-governance. See Meiklejohn, *Political Freedom*.

CHAPTER FIVE

1. DuBridge, "The State, Industry, and the University," p. 369.

2. DuBridge, "The State, Industry, and the University," p. 369.

3. See Heilbron, *The Dilemmas of an Upright Man*.

4. See Beyerchen, *Scientists Under Hitler*.

5. See Proctor, *The Nazi War on Cancer*; and Proctor, *Racial Hygiene*.

6. Soyfer, *Lysenko and the Tragedy of Russian Science*.

7. Badash, *Scientists and the Development of Nuclear Weapons*.

8. See Hollinger, *Science, Jews, and Secular Culture*, p. 157.

9. Leslie, *The Cold War and American Science*, p. 256.

10. Radosh and Milton, *The Rosenberg File*.

11. See Wang, *American Science in an Age of Anxiety*.

12. Wang, *American Science in an Age of Anxiety*, pp. 135–138.

13. Badash, *Scientists and the Development of Nuclear Weapons*.

14. Schweber, *In the Shadow of the Bomb*; Herken, *Brotherhood of the Bomb*.

15. Miller, "Butler Gets Two Years in Prison."

16. Miller, "Butler Gets Two Years in Prison."

17. Miller, "Smallpox Expert Decries Treatment of Two Scientists."

18. The Federation of American Scientists has a website with links to all these letters of support (available at http://www.fas.org/butler).

19. Endicott and Hagerman, *The United States and Biological Warfare*.

20. A key source on this question is Harris, *Factories of Death*.

21. See Union of Concerned Scientists, "Scientific Integrity in Policy Making." This report, which is fully reproduced on the Union's website with all relevant links, chronicles numerous specific incidents when the Bush administration "misused science to support its political agenda." See the website for a full report and extensive data; the URL is http://www.ucsusa.org/scientific_integrity/interference/reports-scientific-integrity-in-policy-making.html

22. Greco, "Political Censorship of Science."
23. Union of Concerned Scientists, "Scientific Integrity in Policy Making."
24. Environmental Protection Agency, "Report on the Environment."
25. Revkin and Seelye, "Report by EPA Leaves Out Data on Climate Change," p. A1.
26. Environmental Protection Agency, "Internal Memo."
27. Revkin and Seelye, "Report by EPA Leaves Out Data on Climate Change." The discredited study was Soon and Baliunas, "Proxy Climatic and Environmental Changes of the Past 1,000 Years." The American Petroleum Institute study discrediting Soon and Baliunas's paper was Mann et al., "On Past Temperatures and Anomalous Late 20th Century Warmth."
28. Environmental Protection Agency, "Internal Memo."
29. Environmental Protection Agency, "Internal Memo."
30. Proctor, *Cancer Wars.*
31. This description is drawn from Robinson, "Ignacio Chapela."
32. See Lee and Zia, *My Country Versus Me*; and Stober and Hoffman, *A Convenient Spy.*
33. Nelkin, *The Military and the University*, p. 24.

CHAPTER SIX

I would like to thank Natalie Nicora of the NEAR Secretariat for the assistance she has given in the preparation of this chapter.
1. *Regents of the University of California v. Bakke*, 438 U.S. 265 (1978).
2. See http://www.legislation/hmso.gov.uk
3. Robbins, "Of Academic Freedom."
4. Robbins, "Of Academic Freedom."
5. See http://www.nearinternational.org
6. Network for Education and Academic Rights, "Egypt Tortures Students."
7. Kapuya, "I Will Face the Gun to Fight for Academic Freedom," p. 14.
8. Kapuya, "I Will Face the Gun to Fight for Academic Freedom," p. 14.
9. Kapuya, "I Will Face the Gun to Fight for Academic Freedom," p. 14.
10. See http://www.nearinternational.org
11. Network for Education and Academic Rights, "Biology Professor Sentenced."
12. Network for Education and Academic Rights, "Biology Professor Sentenced."
13. Network for Education and Academic Rights, "Former President of University Released."
14. Network for Education and Academic Rights, "Ethnical Mass Arrest of Students Condemned."
15. Amnesty International, "PUBLIC AI Index."
16. "Writer and Academic Lesley McCulloch Detained."
17. U.S. Agency for International Development, *Foreign Aid in the National Interest.*

18. United Nations Economic Commission for Africa, "Report of the Regional Conference on Brain Drain and Capacity Building in Africa."

19. Barka, "Statement."

20. See Palombini, "Stories of Italian Researchers Fled Abroad."

21. Boyd, "A Task as Large as Africa Itself."

22. "Brain Drain or Gain?" *South Africa News*, p. 1.

23. Addis Ababa University Alumni Network Discussion Forum, "Reverse Brain Drain Model for Ethiopia."

24. Addis Ababa University Alumni Network Discussion Forum, "Reverse Brain Drain Model for Ethiopia."

25. Addis Ababa University Alumni Network Discussion Forum, "Reverse Brain Drain Model for Ethiopia."

26. Macmillan, "Near Research Paper for UNESCO."

27. Amnesty International, "Cuba."

28. Matsuura, "The Unfulfilled Promise."

29. Human Rights Watch, "Scared at School."

30. Sall, *Women in Academia*.

31. Tamale and Oloka-Onyango, "'Bitches' at the Academy," p. 1.

32. Tamale and Oloka-Onyango, "'Bitches' at the Academy," p. 1.

33. U.K. Government Foreign and Commonwealth Office, "Colombia."

34. Amnesty International, "Trade Unionists Subjected to Death Threats in the Department of Arauca."

35. American Association of University Professors, "Academic Freedom and National Security in a Time of Crisis."

CHAPTER SEVEN

1. See Hyman, *Political Socialization*; Dawson and Prewitt, *Political Socialization*; Jennings, "Pre-Adult Orientations to Multiple Systems of Government"; and Inglehart, *Culture Shift*.

2. Gazlay, "Bombings Target London Minorities"; Geary, "Who's Bombing London?"

3. "World Watch," *Time*.

4. Staten, "Carlos Captured."

5. Anderson and Johnson, *University Autonomy in Twenty Countries*; Hofstadter and Metzger, *The Development of Academic Freedom in the United States*.

6. Hofstadter and Metzger, *Development of Academic Freedom*.

7. Hofstadter and Metzger, *Development of Academic Freedom*; Caplan and Schrecker, *Regulating the Intellectuals*; MacIver, *Academic Freedom in Our Time*.

8. Hofstadter and Metzger, *Development of Academic Freedom*; Caplan and Schrecker, *Regulating the Intellectuals*.

9. Anderson and Johnson, *University Autonomy in Twenty Countries*.

10. Standler, "Academic Freedom in the USA," p. 2.

11. Notably, the German academic design, which emphasizes scholarly research, has had a profound effect on the foundation of the U.S. university system, the conceptions of academic freedom and the professoriat, and the goals

of the American Association of University Professors (AAUP) (see Standler, "Academic Freedom in the USA").

12. This regressive trend in academic freedom is also noted in the United States as the threat of communism absorbs the national consciousness and as many academics, their ideas, and critiques come into question (see Chapters 3 and 4).

13. "New Group to Monitor Academic Freedom," *Academe*, p. 6.

14. Poch, "Academic Freedom in American Higher Education"; MacIver, *Academic Freedom in Our Time*.

15. *Keyishian v. Board of Regents*, 385 U.S. 589, 603 (1967).

16. Standler, "Academic Freedom in the USA"; Byrne, "Academic Freedom."

17. Douglas-Scott, "The Hatefulness of Protected Speech"; Mattijssen and Smith, "Dutch Treats"; Allen, "Tolerance Fuels Social Experiment."

18. Kelly, "Lesson One."

19. Anderson and Johnson, *University Autonomy in Twenty Countries*.

20. Adams, "Call to Vet Scientists Who Work on Biological Agents"; Suroor, "Indian Scholars on U.K.'s Vetting List."

21. Anderson and Johnson, *University Autonomy in Twenty Countries*.

22. Auberbach et al., *Generational Accounting Around the World*; Anderson and Johnson, *University Autonomy in Twenty Countries*. Notably, these countries have traditionally supported academic freedom and have produced a great deal of influential research in the natural and social sciences, ranging from medical studies to research in peace and international politics. Furthermore, these educational systems feature strong support for the equitable and egalitarian participation of students and encourage professional relationships between students and faculty.

23. See United Nations Ad Hoc Committee on International Convention Against Reproductive Cloning of Human Beings, "Meeting Minutes."

24. Regal, "Bioterror."

25. Basham, *Public Policy Sources*.

26. See Kelly, "Lesson One"; and Higher Education Authority, "Financial Management of Irish Institutions of Higher Education."

27. Students and faculty members continue to debate the restrictions on academic freedom that they experience and seek more academic independence through privatization (Kelly, "Lesson One").

28. See Inglehart, *Human Values and Social Change*; Inglehart, *Modernization and Postmodernization*; and Inglehart, *Culture Shift*.

29. Anderson and Johnson, *University Autonomy in Twenty Countries*.

30. See Douglas-Scott, "The Hatefulness of Protected Speech"; and Sacerdoti, "The European Charter of Fundamental Rights."

31. I do not offer this as a critique of attempts to enhance social capital by negatively sanctioning hate speech. However, I offer for consideration the possibility that benevolent attempts to enhance sociopolitical relations may affect academic freedom or hold unintended consequences. Notably, Ronald J. Krotoszynski Jr. ("The Chrysanthemum, the Sword, and the First Amendment") offers another viewpoint that suggests that notions of academic freedom and free

speech must be viewed through an appropriate cultural lens. That is the American perspective on free speech, and traditionally strong support for First Amendment rights may not be the most useful in response to the norms and needs of differing political cultures.

32. Anderson and Johnson, *University Autonomy in Twenty Countries.*

33. For details regarding methodology and sampling frame, see Anderson and Johnson, *University Autonomy in Twenty Countries.*

34. Sweden is also ranked relatively high; however, this was before the explicit efforts to devolve power from the government to the universities. To place the results in clearer perspective, the nations that routinely are rated with high levels of intervention are those outside the West and those that share high levels of religious intervention in institutional norms, such as Malaysia and Indonesia.

35. Only Singapore, China, and Indonesia are more likely to influence university activities than the French government.

36. Canada actually ties with Ireland, and the United States is sixteenth.

37. Kelly, "Lesson One."

38. Human Rights Watch, "Academic Freedom."

39. Suroor, "Indian Scholars on U.K.'s Vetting List."

40. The target nations include India, Pakistan, Iran, Iraq, Syria, Israel, Egypt, Cuba, Libya, and North Korea. Areas of research that trigger the vetting of a researcher include but are not limited to aeronautical engineering, computing science, mechanical engineering, microbiology, and mathematics as well as ceramics and glass.

41. Adams, "Call to Vet Scientists Who Work on Biological Agents"; Burns, "Academics Warn Against Stricter Anti-Terror Vetting of Bioscience"; Suroor, "Indian Scholars on U.K.'s Vetting List."

42. Human Rights Watch, "Academic Freedom."

43. Human Rights Watch, "Academic Freedom."

44. Bollag, "Separatist Movement Seeks to Eliminate Any Who Criticize Its Views."

45. Bureau of Democracy, Human Rights, and Labor, "Country Reports on Human Rights Practices."

46. Bureau of Democracy, Human Rights, and Labor, "Country Reports on Human Rights Practices."

47. Cadwallader, "Halted N. Irish Election Dents Power-Sharing Process."

CHAPTER EIGHT

1. I am an assistant professor at John Jay College of Criminal Justice, City University of New York.

2. Readers will notice throughout the next section a large number of pieces on academic freedom written in the Americas from the 1960s through the 1980s. The only significant paper that even attempted a region-wide analysis of the problem since the transition is de Figueiredo-Cowen, "Latin American Universities, Academic Freedom, and Autonomy."

3. Arnove, "A Survey of Literature and Research on Latin American Universities," pp. 45–46; Goodman, "The Political Role of the University in Latin America," pp. 284–285. The demands of the Córdoba reform movement were (1) representation of students on university councils, (2) selection of professors through competition with student input and that professors hold limited terms subject to student review, (3) complete elimination of regular attendance requirements, (4) adding certain courses to the curriculum, (5) improvement of teaching, (6) extension courses for workers, (7) social assistance for enrollees, and (8) no fees for students. For an analysis of the Córdoba and earlier reforms, see Van Aken, "University Reform Before Córdoba," pp. 459–460; on the impact of the Córdoba Reforms in Cuban politics, see Benjamin, "The Machadato and Cuban Nationalism, 1928–1932," pp. 72–74; on the impact of the Córdoba Reforms in Peru, see Klaiber, "Popular Universities and the Origins of Aprismo, 1921–1924," pp. 693–700; also see Walter, "The Intellectual Background of the 1918 University Reform in Argentina."

4. Jaksic, "Philosophy and University Reform at the University of Chile," p. 80.

5. For a discussion of *cátedra*, see de Figueiredo-Cowen, "Latin American Universities, Academic Freedom, and Autonomy," p. 473.

6. For an analysis of the history of university autonomy and the tensions between autonomy and the demands of the Córdoba Reforms movement, see Cowart, "The Development of the Idea of University Autonomy," pp. 261–262.

7. Van Aken, "University Reform Before Córdoba," p. 461.

8. Suchlicki, "Sources of Student Violence in Latin America," pp. 34–35; Goodman, "The Political Role of the University," pp. 287–288; conversation with an Ecuadoran academic working in the sciences, February 19, 2004; personal correspondence with a former Panamanian academic specializing in social science, November 19, 2003.

9. Newton, "Students and the Political System of the University of Buenos Aires," p. 636.

10. Conversation with an Ecuadoran academic working in the sciences, February 19, 2004.

11. Goodman, "The Political Role of the University," p. 288.

12. Suchlicki, "Sources of Student Violence in Latin America," pp. 40–41.

13. Conversation with Martín, former Panamanian academic specializing in social science, November 19, 2003.

14. Schmitter, "The Persecution of Political and Social Scientists in Brazil," pp. 124–128; on violations of academic freedom in Minas Gerais during the 1964–1967 period, see Pimenta, *Universidade*; for a discussion of federal intervention in Universidade Federal de Minas Gerais during the Vargas dictatorship in the 1930s, see de Moraes, *História da Universidade Federal de Minas Gerais*; on violations of academic freedom in the Pontifício Universidade Católica do Rio de Janeiro, see Ferreira Paim, *Liberadade Acadêmica e Opção Totalitário*.

15. Keck and Sikkink, *Activists Beyond Borders*, pp. 98–103; Bell, "The Ford Foundation as a Transnational Actor," p. 477.

16. A summary of the effects of this on academics' perceptions of Mexico

can be found in Levy, "University Autonomy in Mexico," p. 130. Levy goes on in this article to show that despite brutal repression of students in 1968, the UNAM retained a high degree of autonomy; Franco, "South of Your Border," p. 325; for a look at the impact of this attack on the political system in Mexico, see Davis and Brachet-Marquez, "Rethinking Democracy in Historical Perspective," pp. 99–100.

17. de Figueiredo-Cowen, "Latin American Universities, Academic Freedom, and Autonomy," p. 477.

18. Levy, "Chilean Universities Under the Junta," pp. 104–106, 110, and 119; also see Huneeus, *La Reforma en la Universidad de Chile*, pp. 37– 42; for an argument against academic freedom during the Pinochet regime, see Rodriguez Grez, *Contrarreforma Universitária*.

19. Newton, "Students and the Political System," pp. 633–634.

20. Merret and Gravil, "Comparing Human Rights," pp. 258–259; for an example of this, see Rosenberg, *Children of Cain*, pp. 83–84.

21. O'Donnell and Schmitter, *Transitions from Authoritarian Rule*, pp. 13–14.

22. Quoted in Wanderley Reis, "The State, the Market, and Democratic Citizenship," p. 121.

23. Pereira, "An Ugly Democracy?" p. 217.

24. To provide some more detail here, *cátedra*, or academic chair, is effectively a tenure line within a university. Although in some countries these lines operate as lifetime appointments similar to tenure in the United States, in other countries, such as Argentina, these lines are permanent within the university but those holding the lines must regularly stand for reappointment. However, in Argentina, as in the United Kingdom, those holding these lines and who effectively and seriously pursue teaching and research are almost always reappointed to their positions. My research shows no indication that the reappointment process in Argentina is used for political purposes. An important point in the Argentine case, however, is that following the Córdoba Reforms all *cátedras* within a university must be taught by two professors to ensure that students can choose between different perspectives and methodologies in studying a subject. Having several faculty members hold a chair allows for the freedom of the *cátedra* from the control of one professor. Questionnaire response from Rolando, Argentine social scientist working in the United States, November 19, 2003.

25. Personal correspondence with Sarah, American academic holding a junior faculty position at the Brazilian Federal University, November 12, 2003.

26. Conversation with Tomás, senior Brazilian academic conducting research in the United States, December 4, 2003.

27. Conversation with Miguel, Ecuadoran science faculty member, February 19, 2004.

28. Report of FECODI to Katarina Tomasevski, Special Reporter of the United Nations for Education, received through personal communication with FECODI directorate, pp. 6–7.

29. Report of FECODI to Katarina Tomasevski, p. 7.

30. Conversation with a member of the FECODI executive committee, January 22, 2004.

31. Conversation with a member of the FECODI executive committee, January 22, 2004. Also, conversation with Oscar, anthropologist and exiled academic, January 28, 2004.

32. Conversation with Oscar, anthropologist and exiled academic, January 28, 2004.

33. Conversation with Oscar, anthropologist and exiled academic, January 28, 2004.

34. Conversation with Oscar, anthropologist and exiled academic, January 28, 2004.

35. Interview with Juan, exiled Venezuelan business professor, January 23, 2004.

36. Conversation with Miguel, Ecuadoran science faculty member, February 19, 2004.

37. Conversation with Miguel, Ecuadoran science faculty member, February 19, 2004.

38. Conversation with Miguel, Ecuadoran science faculty member, February 19, 2004.

39. Conversation with Mariana Ferreira, Brazilian anthropologist who teaches in the United States, February 12, 2004; also see American Academy for the Advancement of Science, "AAAS Human Rights Action Network Case Number bro215_fer and bro215_top."

40. American Association for the Advancement of Science, "AAAS Human Rights Action Network Case Number br9802_gai."

41. Conversation with Miguel, Ecuadoran science faculty member, February 19, 2004.

42. The details of this story are explained in Soares, *Meu Casaco de General*.

43. Conversation with Carl, Canadian scientist who has conducted extensive research in Brazil since the 1970s, February 24, 2004.

44. Death squads are semisecret organizations that operated primarily under authoritarian regimes in many countries in Latin America to assassinate members of the political opposition. Death squads are typically informal organizations, although they have historically been composed of members of state security forces operating with tacit or active state approval while formally off-duty. Today, in Latin America some death squads continue to operate, but they are much less common than they were twenty years ago and they almost always operate without high-level government support.

45. On the civil war in Guatemala, see Schirmer, "Looting of Democratic Discourse by the Guatemalan Military," p. 86.

46. American Association for the Advancement of Science, "AAAS Human Rights Action Network Case Number GU0113.Gon"; American Association for the Advancement of Science, "AAAS Human Rights Action Network Case Number gu9702"; American Association for the Advancement of Science, "AAAS Human Rights Action Network Case Numbers gu9702 and gu937_cha."

47. Black, "Guatemala Rights Scientist Honoured."

48. Network for Education and Academic Rights, "Fear for Safety of Student Investigating Disappearances."

49. Conversation with Samuel, official with the Canadian Association of University Teachers, February 17, 2004.

50. American Association for the Advancement of Science, "AAAS Human Rights Action Network Case Number me9815_chi."

51. Conversation with Samuel, official with the Canadian Association of University Teachers, February 17, 2004.

52. Conversation with John, director of a nongovernmental organization working to help displaced academics, February 11, 2004.

53. American Association for the Advancement of Science, "AAAS Human Rights Action Network Case Number cu931; cu9804_bea"; American Association for the Advancement of Science, "AAAS Human Rights Action Network Case Number cu931; cu9804_bea; cu9813"; American Association for the Advancement of Science, "AAAS Human Rights Action Network Case Number cu931."

54. de Figueiredo-Cowen, "Latin American Universities, Academic Freedom, and Autonomy," pp. 482–483.

55. Personal correspondence with Miguel, Ecuadoran science faculty member, February 16, 2004.

56. Personal correspondence with Guillermo, Colombian academic living in the United States, February 18, 2004.

57. Argentina is an interesting case in this regard. Because public universities do not offer tenure as a result of the Córdoba Reforms, there seems to be a higher degree of equality between private universities and public universities. Unlike most other countries in the region (and Mexico is probably an exception), public and private universities seem to be on at least similar footing in Argentina. Questionnaire response from Rolando, Argentine social scientist working in the United States, November 19, 2003.

58. Conversation with Tomás, senior Brazilian academic conducting research in the United States, December 4, 2003.

59. Conversation with Miriam, Brazilian law professor and lawyer for the plaintiff in an academic freedom case, February 17, 2004.

60. Conversations with Miguel, Ecuadoran science faculty member, February 19, 2004.

61. Conversation with Debora Diniz, bioethicist and plaintiff in a case on academic freedom, February 10, 2004.

62. Conversation with Debora Diniz, bioethicist and plaintiff in a case on academic freedom, February 10, 2004; conversation with Miriam, Brazilian law professor and lawyer for the plaintiff in an academic freedom case, February 17, 2004.

63. Conversation with Debora Diniz, bioethicist and plaintiff in a case on academic freedom, February 10, 2004; conversation with Miriam, Brazilian law professor and lawyer for the plaintiff in an academic freedom case, February 17, 2004.

64. On this issue, see Sikkink, "The Emergence, Evolution, and Effectiveness of the Latin American Human Rights Network," pp. 70–71.

65. For an example and analysis of this type of problem, see Parker, "Victims and Volunteers," p. 53.

66. The Scholars at Risk Network and the Committee for Assisting Refugee Academics already do provide significant assistance to academics who need assistance, but, unfortunately, the efforts of these groups do not meet the great need to extended assistance in Latin America.

CHAPTER NINE

1. In the cases that O'Neil reviews, the professors did receive official reprimands for their remarks in class. I assume that there was a reasonable basis for the reprimands, given O'Neil's detailed knowledge of the cases.

2. It is perhaps also worth remarking that Downs's account of one of the cases that O'Neil deals with illustrates the difficulty of coming to judgments on administrative defenses of academic freedom. See their respective comments on the case of Professor Kenneth Hearlson.

3. Downs, this volume, Chapter 4.

4. Compare the accounts of O'Neil (this volume, Chapter 3) and Downs (this volume, Chapter 4) of treatment of speech in the Orange Coast (California) Community College case.

5. Tocqueville, *Democracy in America* (2000), p. 244.

6. Tocqueville, *Democracy in America* (2000), p. 244.

7. See Noelle-Neumann, *The Spiral of Silence*. This spiral is self-reinforcing, but of course not endlessly so. At some point the gap between publicly expressed and privately held beliefs becomes too wide to be sustained. Kuran, *Private Truths, Public Lies*, p. 19.

8. For an extended presentation, see Sunstein, *Why Societies Need Dissent*.

9. See O'Gorman, "Pluralistic Ignorance and White Estimates of White Support for Racial Segregation," and O'Gorman and Garry, "Pluralistic Ignorance."

10. Asch, *Social Psychology*.

11. Ross et al., "The Role of Attribution Processes in Conformity and Dissent"; Asch, *Social Psychology*.

12. See, for example, Berelson and Steiner, *Human Behavior*.

13. Huckfeldt et al., *Political Disagreement*.

14. Granovetter, "The Strength of Weak Ties," p. 215.

15. I owe this point, via one step of mediation, to Jack Citrin.

16. See Cialdini and Goldstein, "Social Influence."

17. The poll, taken in December 1996, was sponsored by the California Association of Scholars (CAS), an affiliate of the National Association of Scholars. Carried out by telephone, the response rate was 80 percent, remarkably strong these days, and the sample was representative of senate members distributed on all nine campuses and a range of the professoriat, from instructors to full professors.

18. Powers, "Review of *Reds*," p. 21.

19. Morgan, *Reds*, pp. 384–385.

20. Morgan, *Reds*, p. 407.

21. Glen Loury cites McCarthyism as a test case of his theory of self-censorship.

22. Stouffer, *Communism, Conformities, and Civil Liberties*, p. 59.

23. Polsby, "Towards an Explanation of McCarthyism," p. 264.

24. Polsby, "Towards an Explanation of McCarthyism," p. 262.

25. Loury, "Self-Censorship in Public Discourse."

26. Loury uses the terms *sender* and *receiver*, but to my ears, *speaker* and *listener* convey better his conception.

27. Loury, "Self-Censorship in Public Discourse," p. 436.

28. Loury, "Self-Censorship in Public Discourse," p. 437.

29. See Downs, *Restoring Free Speech and Liberty on Campus*.

30. Apart from the use of the word *practice*, I pass over an important element in Loury's theory. In his theory, establishment of a practice of punishment is necessary because then, but only then, will a speaker who offends communal values know he risks ostracism for running afoul of them. If he speaks, nonetheless, his listeners must infer that he does not share their community's values — or perhaps, what is not quite the same thing — that he is indifferent to being ostracized and cut out of the community. Loury's punishment premise captures the standard distinction between cheap talk and costly talk.

31. I owe this schema to my colleague Stephen Haber. His version of it is both deeper and more detailed; defects of my story line are not attributable to his.

32. Since writing this chapter, Downs has published a book on the problem of academic freedom in contemporary America, *Restoring Free Speech and Liberty on Campus*. On my reading, the force of his account has changed the burden of proof. It now rests with those who contend that there is not a problem. The book fascinates not least because it describes the passage of a supporter of speech codes to an opponent — with Downs as principled in support as in opposition.

CHAPTER TEN

1. Soley, *Leasing the Ivory Tower*, p. 145.

2. See Soley, *Leasing the Ivory Tower*, for numerous examples of these allegations.

3. Soley, *Leasing the Ivory Tower*, pp. 79–80.

4. Chin and Rao, "Pledging Allegiance to the Constitution."

5. 390 U.S. 36 (1968), summarily affirming the decision of the three judge court, 269 F. Supp. 339 (S.D. N.Y. 1967).

6. Ind.. Code Sec. 20-12-0.6-1(1).

7. Neb. Rev. Stat. Sec. 11-101.01 (2002).

8. See *Baggett v. Bullitt*, 377 U.S. 360 (1964).

9. The oath upheld in *Knight* required the individual to "solemnly swear (or

affirm) that I will support the Constitution of the United States of America and the constitution of the State of New York" (N.Y. Educ. Law Sec. 3002).

10. Bradley, "Contingent Faculty and the New Academic Labor System," p. 28.

11. Bradley, "Contingent Faculty and the New Academic Labor System," p. 28.

12. Nelson, "Can E.T. Phone Home?" pp. 31–32.

13. Nelson, "Can E.T. Phone Home?" pp. 31–32.

14. Nelson, "Can E.T. Phone Home?" p. 33.

15. Nelson, "Can E.T. Phone Home?" p. 32.

16. Nelson, "Can E.T. Phone Home?" p. 34.

17. Foucault, *Discipline and Punish*, pp. 195–228.

18. McCaughey, "Windows Without Curtains," p. 40.

19. McCaughey, "Windows Without Curtains," p. 40.

20. McCaughey, "Windows Without Curtains," p. 42.

21. 216 F.3d 401, 410 (4th Cir. 2000).

22. American Association of University Professors, "Academic Freedom and National Security in a Time of Crisis," p. 46.

23. American Association of University Professors, "Academic Freedom and National Security in a Time of Crisis," p. 46.

24. American Association of University Professors, "Academic Freedom and National Security in a Time of Crisis," p. 47.

25. Gates, "International Relations 101," p. A23.

26. Gates, "International Relations 101," p. A23.

27. Gates, "International Relations 101," p. A23.

28. American Association of University Professors, "Academic Freedom and National Security in a Time of Crisis," p. 49.

Bibliography

Adams, Christopher. "Call to Vet Scientists Who Work on Biological Agents." *Financial Times Limited* (London ed. 2), October 23, 2002, p. 6.

Addis Ababa University Alumni Network Discussion Forum. "Reverse Brain Drain Model for Ethiopia: The Thailand Model." January 2004. Available at http://trigonal.ncat.edu/AAU-Network

Allen, John L. "Tolerance Fuels Social Experiment: The Dutch Way." *National Catholic Reporter*, October 19, 2001, pp. 13–17.

American Academy for the Advancement of Science. "AAAS Human Rights Action Network Case Number br0215_fer and br0215_top." August 21, 2002. Available at http://shr.aaas.org/aaashran/alert.php?a_id=231

———. "AAAS Human Rights Action Network Case Number br9802_gai." January 26, 1998. Available at http://shr.aaas.org/aaashran/alert.php?a_id=82

———. "AAAS Human Rights Action Network Case Number cu931." March 24, 2003. Available at http://shr.aaas.org/aaashran/alert.php?a_id=250

———. "AAAS Human Rights Action Network Case Number cu931; cu9804_bea." October 5, 1998. Available at http://shr.aaas.org/aaashran/alert.php?a_id=107

———. "AAAS Human Rights Action Network Case Number cu931; cu9804_bea; cu9813." October 20, 1998, Available at http://shr.aaas.org/aaashran/alert.php?a_id=108

———. "AAAS Human Rights Action Network Case Number GU0113.Gon." October 25, 2001. Available at http://shr.aaas.org/aaashran/alert.php?a_id=197

———. "AAAS Human Rights Action Network Case Number gu9702." May 2, 1997. Available at http://shr.aaas.org/aaashran/alert.php?a_id=57

———. "AAAS Human Rights Action Network Case Numbers gu9702 and gu937_cha." April 6, 1997. Available at http://shr.aaas.org/aaashran/alert.php?a_id=232

———. "AAAS Human Rights Action Network Case Number me9815_chi." November 16, 1998. Available at http://shr.aaas.org/aaashran/alert.php?a_id=111

American Association of University Professors. "Academic Freedom and National Security in a Time of Crisis." *Academe* 89 (November-December 2003): 34–60.

———. "Academic Freedom and Tenure: University of South Florida." *Academe* 89 (May-June 2003): 59–73.

———. "On Freedom of Expression and Campus Speech Codes." November 1994. Available at http://www.aaup.org/statements/Redbook/speech%20codes.htm

———. "Report of Committee A, 2003–04." 2005. Available at http://www.aaup.org/Coma/coma.htm

American Center for Law and Justice. "Staff Counsel Letter to Kent Syverson." October 22, 2004. Available at http://www.uwec.edu/senate/APCIssues/ACLJLetter.htm

American Civil Liberties Union of Wisconsin. "ACLU and American Conservative Union Launch New Ads, Right-Left Partnership Calls for No Expansions of Patriot Act." September 28, 2004. Available at http://www.aclu-wi.org/wisconsin/safe_and_free/PatriotActextension.shtml

Amnesty International. "Cuba: Further Bans on Freedom of Expression." January 12, 2004. Available at http://web.amnesty.org/library/print/ENGAMR250032004

———. "PUBLIC AI Index: AFR 25/014/2001." Available at http://web.amnesty.org/library/Index/ENGAFR250142001?open&of=ENG-ETH

———. "Trade Unionists Subjected to Death Threats in the Department of Arauca." April 1, 2003. Available at http://web.amnesty.org/library/Index/ENGAMR230292003?open&of=ENG-394

Anderson, Don, and Richard Johnson. *University Autonomy in Twenty Countries*. Canberra, Australia: Department of Employment, Education, Training, and Youth Affairs, 1998.

Arnove, Robert F. "A Survey of Literature and Research on Latin America Universities." *Latin American Research Review* 3 (1967): 45–62.

Asch, Solomon E. *Social Psychology*. Englewood Cliffs, NJ: Prentice-Hall, 1962.

Auerbach, Alan J., Laurence J. Kotlikoff, and Willi Leibfritz, eds. *Generational Accounting Around the World*. Chicago: University of Chicago Press, 1999.

Badash, Lawrence. *Scientists and the Development of Nuclear Weapons: From Fission to the Limited Test Ban Treaty*. Atlantic Highlands, NJ: Humanities Press, 1995.

Baker, Peter, and Peter Slevin. "Bush Remarks on 'Intelligent Design' Theory Fuel Debate." *Washington Post*, August 3, 2005, p. A1.

Barschall, H. H., and J. R. Arrington. "Cost of Physics Journals: A Survey." *Bulletin of the American Physical Society* 33 (July 1988): 1437–1147.

Barka, Lalla Ben. "Statement." Presented at The Regional Conference on Brain Drain and Capacity Building in Africa, February 22, 2000. Available at http://www.uneca.org/eca_resources/speeches/2000_speeches/statement_by_lalla_ben_barka.htm

Basham, Patrick. *Public Policy Sources: The "Third Way."* Vancouver, Canada: Fraser Institute, 2003.

Beito, David T., Ralph E. Luker, and Robert David Johnson. "Consulting All Sides on 'Speech Codes.'" *Organization of Academic Historians Newsletter* 33 (May 2005): 11.

Bell, Peter D. "The Ford Foundation as a Transnational Actor." *International Organization* 25 (1971): 465–478.

Benjamin, Jules R. "The Machadato and Cuban Nationalism, 1928–1932." *Hispanic American Historical Review* 55 (1975): 66–91.

Berelson, Bernard, and Gary A. Steiner. *Human Behavior: An Inventory of Scientific Findings.* New York: Harcourt, Brace & World, 1964.

Bernstein, David E. *You Can't Say That.* Washington, DC: Cato Institute, 2003.

Beyerchen, Alan. *Scientists Under Hitler: Politics and the Physics Community in the Third Reich.* New Haven: Yale University Press, 1977.

Black, Richard. "Guatemala Rights Scientist Honoured." *BBC News World Edition*, February 15, 2004. Available at http://news.bcc.co.uk/go/em/fr/-/2/hi/science/nature/3489743.stm

Blakely, William Blakely. *American State Papers Bearing on Sunday Legislation*, rev. ed., Willard Allen Colcord (Ed.). Washington, DC: Religious Liberty Association, 1911.

Bollag, Burton. "Separatist Movement Seeks to Eliminate Any Who Criticize Its Views." *Chronicle of Higher Education*, February 16, 2001, pp. A51–A53.

Boyd, Clark. "A Task as Large as Africa Itself." *Christian Science Monitor*, March 4, 2003.

Bradley, Gwendolyn. "Contingent Faculty and the New Academic Labor System." *Academe* 90 (January-February 2004): 28.

"Brain Drain or Gain?" *South Africa News*, May-June 2003, p. 1.

Brainerd, Jim. "The Notion of Academic Freedom." *Astrophysics Spectator*, February 16, 2005. Available at http://www.astrophysicsspectator.com/commentary/commentary20050216.html

Browne, Kingsley R. "Title VII as Censorship: Hostile Environment and the First Amendment." *Ohio University Law Journal* 52 (1991): 481–550.

Bureau of Democracy, Human Rights, and Labor. "Country Reports on Human Rights Practices." 2003. Available at http://www.state.gov/g/drl/hr/c1470.htm

Burns, Jimmy. "Academics Warn Against Stricter Anti-Terror Vetting of Bioscience." *Financial Times Limited*, December 12, 2002, p. 4.

Byrne, J. Peter. "Academic Freedom: A 'Special Concern' of the First Amendment." *Yale Law Journal* 99 (1989): 251–339.

Cadwallader, Anne. "Halted N. Irish Election Dents Power-Sharing Process." *Christian Science Monitor*, May 29, 2003, pp. 13–14.

Canon, Bradley C., and Charles A. Johnson. *Judicial Policies: Implementation and Impact*, 2nd ed. Washington, DC: CQ Press, 1999.

Caplan, Craig, and Ellen Schrecker. *Regulating the Intellectuals*. New York: Praeger, 1983.

Carnegie Fund for the Advancement of Teaching. *Campus Life*. New York: Carnegie Fund, 1990.

Carter, Stephen L. "The Independent Counsel Mess." *Harvard Law Review* 102 (1988): 105–141.

Chaltain, Sam. "Does the First Amendment Have a Future?" *Social Education* 69 (April 2005): 126–130.

Chin, Gabriel, and Saira Rao. "Pledging Allegiance to the Constitution: The First Amendment and Loyalty Oaths for Faculty at Private Universities." *University of Pittsburgh Law Review* 64 (2003): 431–482.

Churchill, Ward. *On the Justice of Roosting Chickens: Reflections on the Consequences of U.S. Imperial Arrogance and Criminality*. Oakland, CA: AK Press, 2003.

Cialdini, Robert B., and Noah J. Goldstein. "Social Influence: Compliance and Conformity." *Annual Review in Psychology* 55 (2004):591–621.

Cole, David, and James X. Dempsey. *Terrorism and the Constitution: Sacrificing Civil Liberties in the Name of National Security*. New York: New Press, 2002.

Commission on Academic Freedom and Pre-College Education. *Liberty and Learning in the Schools: Higher Education's Concerns*. Washington, DC: American Association of University Professors, 1986.

Cowart, Billy F. "The Development of the Idea of University Autonomy." *History of Education Quarterly* 2 (1962): 259–264.

Cranford, Elizabeth, and Megan Rooney. "Speechless." *Chronicle of Higher Education*, June 6, 2003, p. A8.

Curtis, Michael Kent. *Free Speech, "The People's Darling Privilege": Struggles for Freedom of Expression in American History*. Durham, NC: Duke University Press, 2000.

Daly, Karen C. "Balancing Act: Teachers' Classroom Speech and the First Amendment." *Journal of Law and Education* 30 (2001): 1–30.

Davis, Diane E., and Viviane Brachet-Marquez. "Rethinking Democracy in Historical Perspective." *Comparative Studies in Society and History* 39 (1997): 86–119.

Dawson, Richard E., and Kenneth Prewitt. *Political Socialization: An Analytic Study*. Boston: Little, Brown, 1969.

de Figueiredo-Cowen, Maria. "Latin American Universities, Academic Freedom, and Autonomy: A Long-Term Myth?" *Comparative Education* 38 (2002): 471–484.

de Moraes, Eduardo R. Affonso. *História da Universidade Federal de Minas Gerais*, 2nd ed. Belo Horizonte, Brazil: Impresna da Universidade Federal de Minas Gerais, 1971.

Delgado, Richard. "Campus Antiracism Rules: Constitutional Narratives in Collision." *Northwestern Law Review* 85 (1991): 343–387.

———. "Words That Wound: A Tort Action for Racial Insults, Epithets, and Name-Calling." *Harvard Civil Rights–Civil Liberties Law Review* 17 (1982): 133–181.

Doughty, Howard A. "Academic Freedom: An Essentially Contested Concept." *College Quarterly* 2 (Spring 1996). Available at http://www.senecac.on.ca/quarterly/1995-vol02-num03-spring/doughty.html

Douglas-Scott, Sionaidh. "The Hatefulness of Protected Speech: A Comparison of the American and European Approaches." *William and Mary Bill of Rights Journal* 305 (1999): 305–346.

Downs, Donald A. "Human Rights/Civil Liberties." In *International Encyclopedia of Social and Behavioral Sciences*, Neil J. Smelser and Paul B. Bates (Eds.). Oxford: Pergamon/Elsevier, 2001.

———. *Restoring Free Speech and Liberty on Campus*. New York: Cambridge University Press, 2005.

DuBridge, Lee A. "The State, Industry, and the University." In *Mid-Century: The Social Implications of Scientific Progress*, John Ely Burchard (Ed.). Cambridge, MA: Technology Press of the Massachusetts Institute of Technology; and New York: Wiley, 1950.

Dworkin, Ronald. *Freedom's Law*. Cambridge, MA: Harvard University Press, 1996.

Eidelberg, Paul. *The Philosophy of the American Constitution: A Reinterpretation of the Intentions of the Founding Fathers*. New York: Free Press, 1968.

Elrod, Jennifer. "Academics, Public Employee Speech, and the Public University." *Buffalo Public Interest Law Journal* 22 (2003/2004): 1–2.

Emerson, Thomas I. *Toward a General Theory of the First Amendment*. New York: Random House, 1966.

Endicott, Stephen, and Edward Hagerman. *The United States and Biological Warfare: Secrets from the Early Cold War and Korea*. Indianapolis: Indiana University Press, 1999.

Environmental Protection Agency. "Internal Memo." April 29, 2003. Available at http://www.ucsusa.org/global_environment/rsi/page.cfm?pageID =1363

———. "Report on the Environment." June 23, 2003. Available at http://www.epa.gov/indicators/roe/index.htm

Epp, Charles R. *The Rights Revolution: Lawyers, Activists, and Supreme Courts in Comparative Perspective*. Chicago: University of Chicago Press, 1998.

FECODI. "Informe Sobre la Situación de los Derechos Humanos del Magisterio Colombiano." Bogotá: FECODI, October 6, 2003.

Feinberg, Joel. *Harm to Others*. New York: Oxford University Press, 1987.

Ferreira Paim, Antônio. *Liberadade Acadêmica e Opção Totalitário: Um Debate Memorável*. São Paulo, Brazil: Editora Artenova S.A., 1979.

Fish, Stanley. *There's No Such Thing as Free Speech, and It's a Good Thing Too*. New York: Oxford University Press, 1994.

Foucault, Michael. *Discipline and Punish: The Birth of the Prison*, Alan Sheridan (Trans.). New York: Vintage Books, 1979.

Foundation for Individual Rights in Education. "FIRE Declares War on Speech Codes." April 23, 2003. Available at http://www.thefire.org/index.php/article/40.html

———. "Issues." April 3, 2006. Available at http://www.thefire.org/index.php/article/4978.html

———. "Letter to UW-EC Chancellor Donald Mash." December 16, 2004. Available at http://www.thefire.org/index.php/article/5572.html

———. "Religious Liberty in Peril on Campus, National Surveys Reveal." November 10, 2003. Available at http://www.thefire.org/index.php/article/167.html

———. "University of Wisconsin-Eau Claire Wages Campaign Against Student Viewpoints," April 27, 2005. Available at http://www.thefire.org/index.php/article/5575.html

———. "Washington State University Bankrolls Vigilante Censorship: Student Play Fall Victim to Double Standard." July 18, 2005. Available at http://www.thefire.org/index.php/article/6106.html

———. "Writing Instructor Loses Job for Discussing Iraq War in Class." January 27, 2004. Available at http://thefire.org/index.php/article/165.html

Fox News. *The O'Reilly Factor*. March 31, 2003. Transcript 033103cb.256.

Franco, Jean. "South of Your Border." *Social Text* 9/10 (1984): 324–326.

Franklin, T. E., et al. "The State of the First Amendment in Wisconsin." UW-Stout Department of Psychology, 2004. Available at http://faculty.uwstout.edu/shiellt/freespeech1/survey/index.html

French, David A. *FIRE's Guide to Religious Liberty on Campus*. Philadelphia: Foundation for Individual Rights in Education, 2002.

Gale, Mary Ellen. "Reimagining the First Amendment: Racist Speech and Equal Liberty." *St. John's Law Review* 65 (1991):119–185.

Gaouette, Nicole. "Senate Republicans Announce Deal for Renewal of Patriot Act." *Los Angeles Times*, February 10, 2006, p. A7.

Gates, Robert. "International Relations 101." *New York Times*, March 31, 2004, p. A23.

Gazlay, Kristen. "Bombings Target London Minorities." *Associated Press*, May 5, 1999.

Geary, James. "Who's Bombing London? Terrorist Explosions Target Minority Communities." *Time*, May 10, 1999, pp. 37–39.

Glenn, David. "The War on Campus." *The Nation*, November 15, 2001. Available at http://www.thenation.com/doc/20011203/glenn

Golden, Daniel. "Colleges Object to New Wording in Ford Grants." *Wall Street Journal*, May 4, 2004, p. B1.

Golding, Martin P. *Free Speech on Campus*. Lanham, MD: Rowman and Littlefield, 2000.

Goodman, Margaret Ann. "The Political Role of the University in Latin America." *Comparative Politics* 5 (1973): 279–292.

Gould, Jon B. "The Precedent That Wasn't: College Hate Speech Codes and the Two Faces of Legal Compliance." *Law and Society Review* 35 (2001): 345–392.

Graff, Gerald. "To Debate or Not to Debate Intelligent Design?" *Inside Higher Ed Views.* September 28, 2005. Available at http://insidehighered.com/views/2005/09/28/graff

Granovetter, Mark. "The Strength of Weak Ties: A Network Theory Revisited." *Sociological Theory* 1 (1983): 201–233.

Gray, Kathy Lynn. "Bill Could Limit Open Debate at Colleges." *Columbus Dispatch*, January 27, 2005, p. 1C.

Greco, Pietro. "Political Censorship of Science." *International Journal of Science Communication* 6 (2003): 1–3.

Greenawalt, Kent. *Fighting Words.* Princeton, NJ: Princeton University Press, 1995.

Greenwell, Megan. "Bollinger: No Plan to Reprimand De Genova." *Columbia Daily Spectator*, April 10, 2003, p. 1.

Grey, Thomas C. "Civil Rights vs. Civil Liberties: The Case of Discriminatory Verbal Harassment." *Social Philosophy and Policy* 8 (1991): 81–107.

———. "Discriminatory Harassment and Free Speech." *Harvard Journal of Law and Public Policy* 14 (1991): 157–164.

Haiman, Franklyn. *Speech Acts and the First Amendment.* Carbondale: Southern Illinois University Press, 1993.

Hajdin, Mane. *The Law of Sexual Harassment: A Critique.* Selinsgrove, PA: Susquehanna University Press, 2002.

Hamilton, Neil. *Zealotry and Academic Freedom: A Legal and Historical Perspective.* New Brunswick, NJ: Transaction Books, 1995.

Hansen, W. Lee (Ed.). *Academic Freedom on Trial: 100 Years of Sifting and Winnowing at the University of Wisconsin-Madison.* Madison: Office of University Publications, University of Wisconsin, 1998.

Harris, Sheldon. *Factories of Death: Japanese Biological Warfare 1932–1945 and the American Cover-Up.* New York: Routledge, 2002.

Harrub, Brad, and Bert Thompson. "The Illusion of Academic Freedom." 2003. Available at http://www.apologeticspress.org/articles/51

Haynes, Charles C. "Darwin Under Fire (Again): Intelligent Design vs. Evolution." *First Amendment Topics*, December 5, 2004. Available at http://www.fac.org/commentary.aspx?id=14476&SearchString=haynes_darwin

Heilbron, John L. *The Dilemmas of an Upright Man: Max Planck as a Spokesman for German Science.* Berkeley: University of California Press, 1986.

Hentoff, Nat. *Free Speech for Me, But Not for Thee: How the American Left and Right Relentlessly Censor Each Other.* New York: Harper Collins, 1992.

Herfurth, Theodore. "Sifting and Winnowing: A Chapter in the History of Academic Freedom at the University of Wisconsin." In *Academic Freedom on Trial*, W. Lee Hansen (Ed.). Madison: University of Wisconsin Press, 1998.

Herken, Gregg. *Brotherhood of the Bomb: The Tangled Lives and Loyalties of Robert Oppenheimer, Ernest Lawrence, and Edward Teller.* New York: Henry Holt, 2002.

Higher Education Authority. "Financial Management of Irish Institutions of Higher Education." Dublin, Ireland: Higher Education Authority, 2003. Available at http://www.hea.ie/3Final.doc

Hofstadter, Richard, and Walter P. Metzger. *The Development of Academic Freedom in the United States*. New York: Columbia University Press, 1955.

Hollinger, David. *Science, Jews, and Secular Culture: Studies in Mid-Twentieth Century American Intellectual History*. Princeton, NJ: Princeton University Press, 1996.

Huckfeldt, Robert, Paul E. Johnson, and John Sprague. *Political Disagreement: The Survival of Diverse Opinions Within Communication Networks*. New York: Cambridge University Press, 2004.

Human Rights Watch. "Academic Freedom." *Human Rights Watch Report*. New York: Human Rights Watch, 2002.

———. "Scared at School: Sexual Violence Against Girls in South African Schools." New York: Human Rights Watch, March 2001.

Huneeus, Carlos. *La Reforma en la Universidad de Chile*. Santiago, Chile: Sala Gráfica de CPU, 1973.

Hyman, Herbert Hiram. *Political Socialization: A Study in the Psychology of Political Behavior*. Glencoe, IL: Free Press, 1959.

Inglehart, Ronald. *Culture Shift*. Princeton, NJ: Princeton University Press, 1990.

———. *Human Values and Social Change: Findings from the Values Surveys*. Boston: Brill, 2003.

———. *Modernization and Postmodernization: Cultural, Economic, and Political Change in 43 Societies*. Princeton, NJ: Princeton University Press, 1997.

Jaksic, Ivan. "Philosophy and University Reform at the University of Chile: 1842–1973." *Latin American Research Review* 19 (1984): 57–86.

Jayson, Sharon. "UT System Revises Employee Policy." *Austin-American Statesman*, November 27, 2002, p. B6.

Jenkinson, Edward B. "Child Abuse in the Hate Factory." In *Academic Freedom to Teach and to Learn: Every Teacher's Issue* (pp. 60–76), Anna S. Ochoa (Ed.). Washington, DC: National Educational Association, 1990.

Jennings, M. Kent. "Pre-Adult Orientations to Multiple Systems of Government." *Midwest Journal of Political Science* 11 (1967): 291–317.

Jensen, Robert. "Ward Churchill Has Rights, and He's Right." February 14, 2005. Available at http://www.commondreams.org/views05/0214-20.htm

Kapuya, Tapera. "I Will Face the Gun to Fight for Academic Freedom." June 6, 2003. Available at http://www.nearinternational.org/alerts/zimbabwe16200306060000en.php

Katz, Kathryn. "The First Amendment's Protection of Expressive Activity in the University Classroom: A Constitutional Myth," *UC-Davis Law Review* 16 (1983): 857–926.

Keck, Margaret, and Kathryn Sikkink. *Activists Beyond Borders: Advocacy Networks in International Politics*. Ithaca, NY: Cornell University Press, 1998.

Kelly, John. "Lesson One: Privatising Our Universities." *Irish Independent*, January 5, 2004. Available from Lexis-Nexis.

Kennedy, Donald. *Academic Duty*. Cambridge, MA: Harvard University Press, 1997.

Klaiber, Jeffrey L. "Popular Universities and the Origins of Aprismo, 1921–1924." *Hispanic American Historical Review* 55 (1975): 693–715.

Kors, Alan Charles, and Harvey A. Silverglate. *The Shadow University: The Betrayal of Liberty on America's Campuses*. New York: Free Press, 1998.

Kuran, Timur. *Private Truths, Public Lies: The Social Consequences of Preference Falsification*. Cambridge, MA: Harvard University Press, 1995.

Krotoszynski, Ronald J., Jr. "The Chrysanthemum, the Sword, and the First Amendment: Disentangling Culture, Community, and Freedom of Expression." *Wisconsin Law Review* 905 (1998): 905–992.

Lahav, Pnina. "Holmes and Brandeis: Libertarian and Republican Justifications for Free Speech." *Journal of Law and Politics* 4 (1987): 451–482.

La Haye, Tim. *The Battle for the Public School*. Old Tappan, NJ: Fleming H. Revell, 1983.

Lange, Ellen L. "Racist Speech on Campus: A Title VII Solution to a First Amendment Problem." *Southern California Law Review* 64 (1990): 105–134.

Lawrence, Charles R. "If He Hollers Let Him Go: Regulating Racist Speech on Campus." *Duke Law Journal* (June 1990): 431–482.

Lee, Wen Ho, and Helen Zia. *My Country Versus Me: The First Hand Account by the Los Alamos Scientist Who Was Falsely Accused of Being a Spy*. New York: Hyperion, 2003.

Leo, John. "Campus Censors in Retreat." *U.S. News and World Report*, February 16, 2004, p. 64.

Leslie, Stuart. *The Cold War and American Science: The Military-Industrial-Academic Complex at MIT and Stanford*. New York: Columbia University Press, 1993.

Levy, Daniel. "Chilean Universities Under the Junta: Regime and Policy." *Latin American Research Review* 21 (1986): 95–128.

———. "University Autonomy in Mexico: Implications for Regime Authoritarianism." *Latin American Research Review* 14 (1979): 129–152.

Lewis, Anthony. "Kastenmeier Lecture: Civil Liberties in a Time of Terror." *Wisconsin Law Review* 31 (2003): 257–272.

Lichtblau, Eric. "House Votes for a Permanent Patriot Act." *New York Times*, July 22, 2005, p. A11.

Lipstadt, Deborah. *Denying the Holocaust: The Growing Assault on Truth and Memory*. New York: Free Press, 1993.

———. *History on Trial: My Day in Court with David Irving*. New York: Ecco, 2005.

Littlefield, Christina. "Effort to Punish UNLV Professor Gains Exposure." *Las Vegas Sun*, February 8, 2005. Available at http://www.lasvegassun.com/sunbin/stories/lved/2005/feb/08/518257103.html

Loury, Glen C. "Self-Censorship in Public Discourse." *Rationality and Society* 6 (1994): 428–461.

Lowi, Theodore J. *The End of Liberalism: The Second Republic of the United States*, 2nd ed. New York: Norton, 1979.

MacIver, Robert M. *Academic Freedom in Our Time*. New York: Gordian Press, 1967 [1955].

Macmillan, Hugh. "NEAR Research Paper for UNESCO." Available upon request from the Network for Education and Academic Rights (NEAR).

Madison, James. "Federalist No. 51." In *The Federalist Papers*, by James Madison, Alexander Hamilton, and John Jay; Clinton Rossiter (Ed.). New York: Penguin, 1961.

Mann, Michael, Caspar Amman, Ray Bradley, Keith Briffa, Philip Jones, Tim Osborn, Tom Crowley, Malcom Hughes, Michael Oppenheimer, Jonathan Overpeck, Scott Rutherford, Kevin Trenberth, and Tom Wigley. "On Past Temperatures and Anomalous Late 20th Century Warmth." *EOS* 84 (2003): 256–258.

Marcuse, Herbert. "Repressive Tolerance." In *A Critique of Pure Tolerance* (pp. 95–137), Robert P. Wolff, Barrington Moore Jr., and Herbert Marcuse (Eds.). Boston: Beacon Press, 1969.

Martin, Karyl Roberts. "Demoted to High School: Are College Student Speech Rights the Same as Those of High School Students?" *Boston College Law Review* 45 (2003): 173–204.

Matsuda, Mari. "Public Response to Racist Speech: Considering the Victim's Story," *Michigan Law Review* 87 (1989): 2320–2381.

Matsuura, Koïchiro. "The Unfulfilled Promise." *Al-Ahran Weekly Online*, September 26–October 2, 2002. Available at http://weekly.ahram.org.eg/2002/605/op11.htm

Mattijssen, Astrid A. M., and Charlene L. Smith. "Dutch Treats: The Lessons the U.S. Can Learn from How the Netherlands Protects Lesbians and Gays." *American University Journal of Gender and the Law* 6 (1996): 303–333.

McCann, Michael. *Rights at Work: Pay Equity Reform and the Politics of Legal Mobilization*. Chicago: University of Chicago Press, 1994.

McCaughey, Martha. "Windows Without Curtains: Computer Privacy and Academic Freedom." *Academe* 89 (September-October 2003): 39–42.

Meiklejohn, Alexander. *Political Freedom: The Constitutional Powers of the People*. New York: Harper & Row, 1960.

Melden, A. I. *Rights and Persons*. Berkeley: University of California Press, 1977.

Merret, Christopher, and Roger Gravil. "Comparing Human Rights: South Africa and Argentina, 1976–1989." *Comparative Studies in Society and History* 33 (1991): 255–287.

Mill, John Stuart. *On Liberty*. London: J. W. Parker, 1859.

Miller, John Dudley. "Butler Gets Two Years in Prison." *The Scientist*, March 11, 2004. Available at http://www.biomedcentral.com/news/20040311/02

———. "Smallpox Expert Decries Treatment of Two Scientists." *The Scientist*, September 5, 2003. Available at http://www.biomedcentral.com/news/20030905/04

Morgan, Ted. *Reds: McCarthyism in Twentieth Century America*. New York: Random House, 2003.

Moshman, David. "Intellectual Freedom for Intellectual Development." *Liberal Education* 89 (2003). Available at http://www.aacu.org/liberaleducation/le-su03/le-su3feature2.cfm

Murphy, William P. "Academic Freedom: An Emerging Constitutional Right." *Law and Contemporary Problems* 28 (1963): 447–486.

National Public Radio. "All Things Considered." May 6, 2003.

Nelkin, Dorothy. *The Military and the University: Moral Politics at MIT.* Ithaca, NY: Cornell University Press, 1972.

Nelson, Cary. "Can E.T. Phone Home? The Brave New World of University Surveillance." *Academe* 89 (September-October 2003): 30–36.

Nelson, Jack. "The Significance of and Rationale for Academic Freedom." In *Academic Freedom to Teach and to Learn: Every Teacher's Issue* (pp. 21–30), Anna S. Ochoa (Ed.). Washington, DC: National Educational Association, 1990.

Network for Education and Academic Rights. "Biology Professor Sentenced for 'Subversive' Essays." December 8, 2003. Available at http://www .nearinternational.org/alerts/china13200312080000000en.php

———. "Egypt Tortures Students." April 25, 2003. Available at http://www .nearinternational.org/alerts/egypt1220030425en.php

———. "Ethnical Mass Arrest of Students Condemned." March 3, 2004. Available at http://www.nearinternational.org/alerts/ethiopia7200403030000en .php

———. "Fear for Safety of Student Investigating Disappearances." November 5, 2002. Available at http://www.nearinternational.org/alerts/ argentina120021105en.html

———. "Former President of University Released." August 20, 2003. Available at http://www.nearinternational.org/alerts/ethiopia6200308200000en.php

"New Group to Monitor Academic Freedom." *Academe* 88 (January-February 2002): 6–7.

Newton, Ronald C. "Students and the Political System of the University of Buenos Aires." *Journal of Inter-American Studies* 8 (1966): 633–656.

Nicholson, Kieran. "At CU, Arab Activist Urges Free Palestine." *Denver Post,* September 15, 2002, p. B5.

Nidiry, John P. "CUNY Trustees: Let Free Speech Flourish." *Newsday,* October 19, 2001, p. A50.

Noelle-Neumann, Elisabeth. *The Spiral of Silence: Public Opinion, Our Social Skin,* 2nd ed. Chicago: University of Chicago Press, 1993.

O'Connor, Anne-Marie. "You're Being Watched." *Los Angeles Times,* May 26, 2004, pp. E1 and E8.

O'Donnell, Guillermo, and Philippe C. Schmitter. *Transitions from Authoritarian Rule: Tentative Conclusions About Uncertain Democracies.* Baltimore: Johns Hopkins University Press, 1986.

O'Gorman, Hubert J. "Pluralistic Ignorance and White Estimates of White Support for Racial Segregation," *Public Opinion Quarterly* 39 (1975): 313–330.

O'Gorman, Hubert J., and Stephen L. Garry. "Pluralistic Ignorance: A Replication and Extension." *Public Opinion Quarterly* 40 (1976–1977): 449–458.

O'Neil, Robert M. "Academic Freedom and National Security in Times of Crisis." *Academe* 89 (May-June 2003): 21–25.

———. "First Amendment Rights When Discourse Offends or Demeans." *Chronicle of Higher Education,* September 19, 1997, pp. B6–B7.

Palombini, Augusto. "Stories of Italian Researchers Fled Abroad." Paper presented at the Brains on the Run Conference. Cambridge, U.K., March 2, 2002.

Parker, Ian. "Victims and Volunteers." *New Yorker*, January 26, 2004, pp. 50–61.

Paulsen, Ken. "Keeping Government Out of Religion—and Vice Versa." February 15, 2002. Available at http://morrock.com/speech.htm

Pavela, Gary. "A Balancing Act: Competing Claims for Academic Freedom." *Academe* 87 (November-December 2001): 25–30.

Pelikan, Jaroslav. *The Idea of the University: A Reexamination*. New Haven: Yale University Press, 1992.

Pereira, Anthony W. "An Ugly Democracy? State Violence and the Rule of Law in Postauthoritarian Brazil." In *Democratic Brazil: Actors, Institutions, and Processes* (pp. 217–235), Peter R. Kingstone and Timothy J. Power (Eds.). Pittsburgh, PA: University of Pittsburgh Press, 2000.

Peters, E. Kirsten. "Battle over Students Rights Comes to Head; College of Education Backing Off Under FIRE." *Moscow-Pullman Daily News*, October 11, 2005. Available at http://www.educationnews.org/battle-over -students-rights-come.htm

Pimenta, Aluísio. *Universidade: Destruição de uma Experiénciao Democrática*. Petropolis, Brazil: Editora Vozes, 1985.

Pincoffs, Edmund L. "Introduction." In *The Concept of Academic Freedom* (pp. vii–xiv), Edmund L. Pincoffs (Ed.). Austin: University of Texas Press, 1972.

Pinker, Steven. "Sex Ed." *New Republic*, February 14, 2005, p. 15.

Poch, Robert K. "Academic Freedom in American Higher Education: Rights, Responsibilities, and Limitations." 1994. Available at http://www.ericdigests .org/1994/academic.htm

Polsby, Nelson W. "Towards an Explanation of McCarthyism." *Political Studies* 8 (1960): 250–271.

Powers, Thomas. "Review of *Reds*." *New York Review of Books*, February 12, 2004. Available at http://www.nybooks.com/contents/20040212

Price, Joyce Howard. "Jesuit College Bars Pro-Life Group for 'Bias.'" *Washington Times*, December 23, 2003, p. A9.

Primus, Richard A. *The American Language of Rights*. New York: Cambridge University Press, 1999.

Proctor, Robert. *Cancer Wars: How Politics Shapes What We Know and Don't Know About Cancer*. New York: Basic Books, 1995.

———. *The Nazi War on Cancer*. Princeton, NJ: Princeton University Press, 1999.

———. *Racial Hygiene: Medicine Under the Nazis*. Cambridge, MA: Harvard University Press, 1988.

Rabban, David M. *Free Speech in Its Forgotten Years*. New York: Cambridge University Press, 1997.

Radosh, Ronald, and Joyce Milton. *The Rosenberg File*. New Haven, CT: Yale University Press, 1997.

Randall, Richard S. *Freedom and Taboo: Pornography and the Politics of the Divided Self*. Berkeley: University of California Press, 1989.

Rauch, Jonathan. "A College Newspaper Messes Up, and So Might You." *National Journal*, March 24, 2001, p. 86.

————. *Kindly Inquisitors: The New Attacks on Free Thought.* Chicago: University of Chicago Press, 1993.

Rawls, John. *A Theory of Justice.* Cambridge, MA: Harvard University Press, 1971.

Redlawsk, David P. "'We Don't Need No Thought Control': The Controversy over Multiculturalism at Duke." In *Hate Speech on Campus: Cases, Case Studies, and Commentary* (pp. 213–252), Milton Heumann and Thomas W. Church (Eds.). Boston: Northeastern University Press, 1997.

Regal, Philip J. "Bioterror: Universities, Corporations, Governments, and Ethics." Essay prepared for the University of Minnesota College of Biological Sciences, January 2, 2002.

Reid, T. R. "Professor Under Fire for 9/11 Comments." *Washington Post*, February 5, 2005, p. C1.

Revkin, Andrew C., and Katherine Q. Seelye. "Report by EPA Leaves Out Data on Climate Change." *New York Times*, June 19, 2003, p. A1.

Robbins, Lionel. "Of Academic Freedom." 1966. Available at http://www.proc.britac.ac.uk/tfiles/397450A/52p045-001.pdf

Robinson, Claire. "Ignacio Chapela: Biotech Critic Denied Tenure." *Science in Society*, March 8, 2004, p. 21.

Rodriguez Grez, Pablo. *Contrareforma Universitária.* Santiago, Chile: La Universidad de Hoy y de Mañana, 1975.

Rosen, Mike. "CU Is Worth Fighting For." *Rocky Mountain News*, March 4, 2005, p. 43A.

Rosenberg, Gerald. *The Hollow Hope: Can Courts Bring About Social Change?* Chicago: University of Chicago Press, 1991.

Rosenberg, Tina. *Children of Cain: Violence and the Violent in Latin America.* New York: Penguin, 1991.

Ross, Lee, Gunter Bierbrauer, and Susan Hoffman. "The Role of Attribution Processes in Conformity and Dissent." *American Psychologist* 31 (1976): 148–157.

Sacerdoti, Giorgio. "The European Charter of Fundamental Rights: From a Nation-State Europe to a Citizens' Europe." *Columbia Journal of European Law* 8 (2002): 37–52.

Sall, Ebrima (Ed.). *Women in Academia: Gender and Academic Freedom in Africa.* Dakar, Senegal: Council for the Development of Social Science Research in Africa, 2000.

Schirmer, Jennifer. "Looting of Democratic Discourse by the Guatemalan Military: Implications for Human Rights." In *Constructing Democracy: Human Rights, Citizenship, and Society in Latin America* (pp. 85–100), Elizabeth Jelin and Eric Hershberg (Eds.). Boulder, CO: Westview Press, 1996.

Schlabach, Theron F. "An Aristocrat on Trial: The Case of Richard T. Ely." In *Academic Freedom on Trial* (pp. 37–57), W. Lee Hansen (Ed.). Madison: University of Wisconsin Press, 1998.

Schmitt, Richard. "Academic Freedom: The Future of a Confusion." In *The Concept of Academic Freedom* (pp. 111–124), Edmund Pincoffs (Ed.). Austin: University of Texas Press, 1972.

Schmitter, Phillipe. "The Persecution of Political and Social Scientists in Brazil." *PS* 3 (1970): 124–128.

Schneider, Alison. "To Many Adjunct Professors, Academic Freedom Is a Myth." *Chronicle of Higher Education*, December 12, 1999. Available at http://chronicle.com/colloquy/99/adjunct/background.htm

Schrecker, Ellen. *No Ivory Tower: McCarthyism and the Universities*. New York: Oxford University Press, 1986.

Schurz, Carl. *Speeches, Correspondence, and Political Papers of Carl Schurz*, v. 1, Frederic Bancroft (Ed.). New York: Putnam, 1913.

Schweber, Silvan S. *In the Shadow of the Bomb: Bethe, Oppenheimer, and the Moral Responsibility of the Scientist*. Princeton, NJ: Princeton University Press, 2000.

Searle, John. "Two Concepts of Academic Freedom," in *The Concept of Academic Freedom* (pp. 86–96), Edmund L. Pincoffs (Ed.). Austin: University of Texas Press, 1972.

Shapiro, John T. "The Call for Campus Conduct Policies: Censorship or Constitutionally Permissible Limitations on Speech?" *Minnesota Law Review* 75 (1990): 201–238.

Shiell, Timothy C. *Campus Hate Speech on Trial*. Lawrence: University of Kansas Press, 1998.

Siegel, Jim. "Ohio's Public Universities Keep Politics out of Class." *Columbus Dispatch*, September 15, 2005, p. C4.

Sikkink, Kathryn. "The Emergence, Evolution, and Effectiveness of the Latin American Human Rights Network." In *Constructing Democracy: Human Rights, Citizenship, and Society in Latin America* (pp. 59–84), Elizabeth Jelin and Eric Hershberg (Eds.). Boulder, CO: Westview Press, 1996.

Simmons, Kelly. "Students Fight Alleged Political Prejudice." *Atlanta Journal-Constitution*, March 24, 2004, p. 1B.

Smolla, Rodney. *Free Speech in an Open Society*. New York: Knopf, 1992.

Soares, Luis Eduardo. *Meu Casaco de General: Quinhentos Dias no Front da Segurança Pública no Rio de Janeiro*. São Paulo, Brazil: Compania das Letras, 2001.

Soley, Lawrence C. *Leasing the Ivory Tower: The Corporate Takeover of Academia*. Boston: South End Press, 1995.

Soon, Willie, and Sallie Baliunas. "Proxy Climatic and Environmental Changes of the Past 1,000 Years." *Climate Research* 23 (2003): 89–110.

Soyfer, Valery N. *Lysenko and the Tragedy of Russian Science*. New Brunswick, NJ: Rutgers University Press, 1994.

Standler, Ronald B. "Academic Freedom in the USA." 2000 [1999]. Available at http://www.rbs2.com/afree.htm

Staten, Clarke. "Carlos Captured; Revolutionary Terrorist." *Emergency Net News Service*, October 10, 1994. Available at http://www.emergency.com/carlos-j.htm

Stober, Dan, and Ian Hoffman. *A Convenient Spy: Wen Ho Lee and the Politics of Nuclear Espionage*. New York: Simon and Schuster, 2002.

Stone, Geoffrey. "Academic Freedom and Responsibility." *University of Chicago Record*, October 12, 1995, pp. 7–10.

Stouffer, Samuel A. *Communism, Conformity, and Civil Liberties: A Cross-Section of the Nation Speaks Its Mind*. Garden City, NY: Doubleday, 1955.

Suchlicki, Jaime. "Sources of Student Violence in Latin America: An Analysis of the Literature." *Latin American Research Review* 7 (1972): 31–46.

Sunstein, Cass R. *Democracy and the Problem of Free Speech*. New York: Free Press, 1993.

———. *Why Societies Need Dissent*. Cambridge, MA: Harvard University Press, 2003.

Suroor, Hasan. "Indian Scholars on U.K.'s Vetting List." *Financial Times Limited*, July 11, 2003, pp. 3–5.

Tamale, Sylvia, and Joe Oloka-Onyango. "'Bitches' at the Academy: Gender and Academic Freedom in Africa." In *Women in Academia* (pp. 1–23), Ebrima Sall (Ed.). East Lansing: Michigan State University Press, 2000.

Tobin, Susannah Barton. "Divining *Hazelwood*: The Need for a Viewpoint Neutrality Requirement in School Speech Cases." *Harvard Civil Rights–Civil Liberties Law Review* 39 (2004): 217–265.

Tocqueville, Alexis de. *Democracy in America*. New York: Schocken Books, 1961.

Tocqueville, Alexis de. *Democracy in America*, Harvey C. Mansfield and Delba Winthrop (Trans., Eds.). Chicago: University of Chicago Press, 2000.

U.K. Government Foreign and Commonwealth Office. "Colombia." Available at http://www.fco.gov.uk under "Country Profiles."

Unger, Roberto. *Law in Modern Society*. New York: Free Press, 1977.

Union of Concerned Scientists. "Scientific Integrity in Policy Making: Investigation of the Bush Administration's Abuse of Science." 2004. Available at http://www.ucsusa.org/scientific_integrity/interference/reports-scientific-integrity-in-policy-making.html

United Nations Ad Hoc Committee on International Convention Against Reproductive Cloning of Human Beings. "Meeting Minutes." March 2003. Available at http://www.un.org/law/cloning

United Nations Economic Commission for Africa. "Report of the Regional Conference on Brain Drain and Capacity Building in Africa." Regional Conference on Brain Drain and Capacity Building in Africa, February 22–24, 2000, Addis Ababa, Ethiopia.

U.S. Agency for International Development. *Foreign Aid in the National Interest: Promoting Freedom, Security, and Opportunity*. Washington, DC: U.S. Agency for International Development, 2002.

USF/UFF. "Why Freedom for Academics?" Available at http://w3.usf.edu/~uff/AlArian/IssuesAcadFree.html

Van Aken, Mark J. "University Reform Before Cordoba." *Hispanic American Historical Review* 51 (1971): 447–462.

Van Alstyne, William W. *Freedom and Tenure in the Academy*. Durham, NC: Duke University Press, 1993.

———. "The Specific Theory of Academic Freedom and the General Theory of Civil Liberty." In *The Concept of Academic Freedom* (pp. 59–85), Edmund L. Pincoffs (Ed.). Austin: University of Texas Press, 1975.

Villa, Dana. *Socratic Citizenship*. Princeton, NJ: Princeton University Press, 2001.

Walker, Samuel. *Hate Speech: The History of an American Controversy*. Lincoln: University of Nebraska Press, 1994.

Wallach Scott, Joan. "Higher Education and Middle Eastern Studies Following September 11, 2001." *Academe* 88 (November-December 2002): 50–54.

Walsh, Sharon. "The Drake Affair." *Chronicle of Higher Education*, March 5, 2004, p. A8.

Walter, Richard J. "The Intellectual Background of the 1918 University Reform in Argentina." *Hispanic American Historical Review* 49 (1969): 233–253.

Wanderly Reis, Fabio. "The State, the Market, and Democratic Citizenship." In *Constructing Democracy: Human Rights, Citizenship, and Society in Latin America* (pp. 121–140), Elizabeth Jelin and Eric Hershberg (Eds.). Boulder, CO: Westview Press, 1996.

Wang, Jessica. *American Science in an Age of Anxiety: Scientists, Anti-Communism, and the Cold War*. Chapel Hill: University of North Carolina Press, 1999.

Weinberg, Alvin. *The First Nuclear Era: The Life and Times of a Technological Fixer*. Woodbury, NY: American Institute of Physics, 1994.

Weinstein, James. *Hate Speech, Pornography, and the Radical Attack on Free Speech Doctrine*. Boulder, CO: Westview Press, 1999.

Wernicke, Vanessa A. "Teachers' Speech Rights in the Classroom: An Analysis of *Cockrel v. Shelby County School District*." *University of Cincinnati Law Review* 71 (2003): 1471–1494.

"What Exactly Is the Bible?" *Stoutonia*, March 25, 2004, p. 1.

Will, George. "Academic Liberal's Brand of Censorship." *San Francisco Chronicle*, November 7, 1989, p. A22.

———. "In Praise of Censure," *Time*, July 31, 1989, pp. 71–72.

Williams, Jason. "Student: Attack Praised." *Daily Aztec*, October 17, 2001. Available at http://www.dailyaztec.com/Archive/Fall-2001/10-17-01/city/city01 .html

Wilson, John. *The Myth of Political Correctness: The Conservative Attack on Higher Education*. Durham, NC: Duke University Press, 1995.

Wilson, Robin, and Scott Smallwood. "One Professor Cleared, Another Disciplined over September 11 Remarks." *Chronicle of Higher Education*, January 11, 2003, p. A12.

"World Watch." *Time*, June 14, 1999, pp. 17–20.

"Writer and Academic Lesley McCulloch Detained." *Network for Education and Academic Rights*, September 23, 2002. Available at http://www .nearinternational.org/alerts/7e3c2f5f3ac4e6f3efc67be8ea4640d63636.php

Yardley, Jonathan. "Politically Corrected." *Washington Post*, March 5, 2001, p. C2.

Young, Gary. "Free Speech Dilemmas: Free Speech 'Zones' and 'Codes' Go from Campus to Court." *National Law Journal* (January 12, 2004). Available at http://www.thefire.org/index.php/article/5183.html

Zinsmeister, Karl. "The Shame of America's One-Party Campuses." *American Enterprise Magazine* 13(6) (September 18–25, 2002): 20.

Contributors

John Akker, *Executive Director of the Network for Education and Academic Rights (NEAR).* NEAR, a London-based UNESCO-sponsored non-governmental organization, is a worldwide watchdog group with the mission of facilitating academic freedom.

Enrique Desmond Arias, *Assistant Professor of Government, John Jay College of Criminal Justice.* Professor Arias received a B.A. from the Johns Hopkins University and a Ph.D. from the University of Wisconsin at Madison. His research focuses on the structure of criminal organizations in Brazilian shantytowns and the implications of ongoing social violence for democracy. Professor Arias teaches classes on comparative political science and comparative criminal justice.

Antonio Brown, *Assistant Professor of Political Science, Loyola Marymount University.* Professor Brown's teaching and research focus on quantitative and qualitative studies of political culture and national identity in the United States and Western Europe.

Donald A. Downs, *Hawkins Professor of Political Science, Professor of Law, and Professor of Journalism, University of Wisconsin, Madison.* Professor Downs's books include *The New Politics of Pornography* (University of Chicago Press), *More Than Victims: Battered Women, the Syndrome Society, and the Law* (University of Chicago Press), and *Nazis in Skokie: Freedom, Community, and the First Amendment* (University of Notre Dame Press). His books have won the Corwin, Gladys M.

Kammerer, and Anisfield-Wolf book awards. He has written widely on free speech issues, including issues of academic freedom.

Evan Gerstmann, *Associate Professor and Chair of the Political Science Department, Loyola Marymount University*. Professor Gerstmann is the author of *The Constitutional Underclass: Gays, Lesbians, and the Failure of Class-Based Equal Protection* (University of Chicago Press) and *Same-Sex Marriage and the Constitution* (Cambridge University Press). He has also published in the *Election Law Journal* and *PS* and has written several book chapters, including a chapter on executive immunity with Christopher Shortell in *The Presidency and the Law: The Clinton Legacy* (University of Kansas Press).

M. Susan Lindee, *Professor of History and Sociology of Science, University of Pennsylvania*. Professor Lindee's books include *The DNA Mystique: The Gene as a Cultural Icon* (W. H. Freeman) and *Suffering Made Real: American Science and the Survivors at Hiroshima* (University of Chicago Press). Among her interests are issues of censorship of scientific research.

Robert M. O'Neil, *Professor of Law, University Professor, and Director of the Thomas Jefferson Center for the Protection of Free Expression, University of Virginia*. A former president of the University of Virginia, Professor O'Neil's has written several books, including *The First Amendment and Civil Liability* (Indiana University Press) and *Free Speech in the College Community* (Indiana University Press). Professor O'Neil is the president of the Virginia Council for Open Government, chairman of the Council for America's First Freedom, director of the Commonwealth Fund and the James River Corporation, and chair of the American Association of University Professors Committee on Academic Freedom and Tenure.

David M. Rabban, *Centennial Chair in Law, University of Texas Law School*. Professor Rabban is a former general counsel to the American Association of University Professors and is the author of *Free Speech in Its Forgotten Years, 1870–1920* (Cambridge University Press), which received the Forkosch Prize from the *Journal of the History of Ideas* for "the best book in intellectual history published in 1997." His articles have appeared in the *Yale Law Journal*, the *Stanford Law Review*, the *University of Chicago Law Review*, and elsewhere.

Timothy C. Shiell, *Professor of Philosophy, University of Wisconsin, Stout.* Professor Shiell is a former Maybelle Ranney Price Professor (1998–99) and Reinhold and Borghild Dahlgren Professor (2003–2005). He has written several books, including *Campus Hate Speech on Trial* (University Press of Kansas) and *Legal Philosophy: Selected Readings* (Wadsworth). He is currently working on Wisconsin's Free Speech Legacy, a multimedia resource for teachers, students, and citizens.

Paul M. Sniderman, *Professor and Chair of the Political Science Department, Stanford University.* Professor Sniderman has been the winner of many top awards, including the E. E. Schattschneider Award, the Mellon Fellowship, the Guggenheim Fellowship, and the Woodrow Wilson Foundation Prize of the American Political Science Association for best book published in political science, considering all fields. Books that he has written or co-written include *The Scar of Race* (Harvard University Press), *The Clash of Rights: Liberty, Equality, and Legitimacy in Pluralist Democracies* (Yale University Press), *Reaching Beyond Race* (Harvard University Press), and *The Outsider: Prejudice and Politics in Italy* (Princeton University Press).

Matthew J. Streb, *Assistant Professor of Political Science, Northern Illinois University.* Professor Streb is the author, co-author, editor, or co-editor of five books, including *The New Electoral Politics of Race* (University of Alabama Press) and *Polls and Politics* (SUNY Press). He has published more than a dozen articles and book chapters, including publications in *Political Research Quarterly*, *Public Opinion Quarterly*, *Social Science Quarterly*, and *Election Law Journal*.